Saving the School

Saving the School

The True Story of a Principal,
a Teacher, a Coach, a Bunch of Kids,
and a Year in the Crosshairs
of Education Reform

MICHAEL BRICK

THE PENGUIN PRESS

NEW YORK

2012

THE PENGUIN PRESS
Published by the Penguin Group
Penguin Group (USA) Inc., 375 Hudson Street, New York, New York 10014, U.S.A. •
Penguin Group (Canada), 90 Eglinton Avenue East, Suite 700, Toronto, Ontario, Canada
M4P 2Y3 (a division of Pearson Penguin Canada Inc.) • Penguin Books Ltd, 80 Strand,
London WC2R 0RL, England • Penguin Ireland, 25 St. Stephen's Green, Dublin 2,
Ireland (a division of Penguin Books Ltd) • Penguin Books Australia Ltd, 250 Camberwell
Road, Camberwell, Victoria 3124, Australia (a division of Pearson Australia Group
Pty Ltd) • Penguin Books India Pvt Ltd, 11 Community Centre, Panchsheel Park,
New Delhi – 110 017, India • Penguin Group (NZ), 67 Apollo Drive, Rosedale, Auckland
0632, New Zealand (a division of Pearson New Zealand Ltd) • Penguin Books (South
Africa) (Pty) Ltd, 24 Sturdee Avenue, Rosebank, Johannesburg 2196, South Africa

Penguin Books Ltd, Registered Offices:
80 Strand, London WC2R 0RL, England

First published in 2012 by The Penguin Press,
a member of Penguin Group (USA) Inc.

"D-day-vuss!" by Jermiah Wooley. Used by permission of Jermiah Wooley.
Excerpt from Isaiah from *The Holy Bible, New International Version*. Copyright © 1973,
1978, 1984, 2011 by Biblica, Inc. Used by permission. All rights reserved.
Excerpts from "Shine Right Now" and "Glory Honor Praise" by SaulPaul.
Used by permission of SaulPaul.
Test question from Texas Education Agency. Copyright © Texas Education Agency, 2010.
Used by permission of Texas Education Agency.
Excerpt from "Respect," words and music by Otis Redding. Copyright © 1965 Irving
Music, Inc. Copyright renewed. All rights reserved. Used by permission of Hal Leonard
Corporation.

LIBRARY OF CONGRESS CATALOGING-IN-PUBLICATION DATA
Brick, Michael,——.
Saving the school : the true story of a principal, a teacher, a coach, a bunch of kids, and a
year in the crosshairs of education reform / Michael Brick.
p. cm.
ISBN 978-1-59420-344-2 (hardback)
1. John H. Reagan High School (Austin, Tex.) 2. School improvement programs—Texas—
Austin. 3. Garza, Anabel. I. Title.
LD7501.A8735B75 2012
373.22'40976431—dc23   2011050569

Printed in the United States of America
1   3   5   7   9   10   8   6   4   2

DESIGNED BY AMANDA DEWEY

ALWAYS LEARNING   PEARSON

For Stacy

Claro que sí

I see hundreds of men come by on the road an' on the ranches
with their bindles on their back an' that same damn thing in
their heads. Hundreds of them. They come, an' they quit an' go
on; an' every damn one of 'em's got a little piece of land in his
head. An' never a God damn one of 'em ever gets it. Just like
heaven. Ever'body wants a little piece of lan'.

—John Steinbeck

Mr. Rabbit, Mr. Rabbit
Your coat is mighty gray
Yes, bless God it was made that way
Every little soul must shine, shine
Every little soul must shine

—Traditional American folk song

There's a heartbeat in the school. There's a heartbeat,
and it's not too late to save.

—Anabel Garza

Saving the School

One

Anabel Garza made a visor of her right palm and squinted across the parking lot. The light-headed feeling had not yet come on and neither had the daylong headaches, the sluggishness and the photosensitivity. By October she would check her blood pressure and see the toll all this was taking and go to the doctor and join a boot camp gym and start swallowing supplements. Iron deficient at forty-seven: Didn't that happen to teenage girls? Anabel was full-figured; nothing to be ashamed of after two kids on a five-foot frame. She had raven hair, a husky voice, and skin almost light enough to pass for white. She did not eat much but when she ate she ate sweets, the good fried sopaipillas dusted with confectioners' sugar and plated with single-serving plastic containers of honey at the La Palapa cantina across from the high school, or the miniature Kit Kats and peanut butter cups she served in her office to keep the students alert during the Friday morning meetings where they talked about saving the school.

Saving the school was the way everybody else described her job. She described it as "educator, police officer, nurse, psychiatrist, counselor, custodian, translator, gang unit, parking lot attendant, gardener, and firefighter." It paid $107,000 a year as long as it lasted. It came with a forty-dollar cell phone allowance, so there was that. Some days she told people saving the school might be a fool's errand, a setup even. Six other principals had come and gone in as many years and she was never exactly the darling of the district administration and maybe that was the point: You wanted to be a principal, Anabel? Well, here you go, *mamacita*, Reagan High. Those kids were a write-off, with the standardized test scores to prove it. The senior class was less than half the size of the freshman class. Among those who did graduate, 17 percent were classified as college-ready. The football team was a punching bag. The girls were good at getting pregnant.

Anabel took the job in July 2008. Her first task was triage. The Texas Education Agency had long since labeled Reagan "academically unacceptable," so every summer the district would send home letters reminding parents of their right to transfer out. Enrollment was down to half capacity. She started by firing ten teachers, including one who produced a yardstick to lament the distance from the parking lot to her classroom door. As union leaders pushed back and ministers summoned her to Greater Calvary, Anabel raised the rate of students passing all subjects on the standardized tests by seven percentage points, but nobody threw a party. That only brought the rate up to 34 percent. The worst single-subject passing rates were in math, 38 percent, and science, 42 percent. The state was calling for 60 percent in math and 55 percent in science to be considered acceptable. The education commissioner could shut a school down after three years of failing scores. For Reagan, this made four.

In July 2009, Commissioner Robert Scott sent a clear message:

Anabel had one more year to finish the job, or else. To underscore the point, he ordered the district to close the main feeder into Reagan High, Pearce Middle School, which had missed the state standards for five consecutive years. The governor who had appointed him, Rick Perry, was setting the groundwork for a presidential bid, with a job-creation platform bound to draw new scrutiny of the state's education statistics. Firing the students wasn't an option for a public school, so Anabel would have to make the numbers with kids who were too proud or lazy or sentimental or ignorant or employed or poor or some combination of the above to take a ride across the highway to the west side of the city where the schools weren't so— what was the word the newspaper used?—"high-need."

Today's front page carried a feature on the new look of Albert Sidney Johnston High School, an Eastside institution the state had closed the previous year. Forced to "repurpose" the building, the Austin Independent School District had broken up the staff, shedding teachers with master's degrees and decades of service. Of the eighty-seven teachers, twenty-nine lost their jobs, twenty-two got transferred to other schools, and half a dozen others were made full-time substitutes. A year later, the passing rate on standardized tests remained well below the cutoff, at 36 percent. So a unit of the school district called the Office of Redesign was spending $6.5 million to turn Johnston into a pair of magnet academies called Eastside Memorial Green Tech High School and Eastside Memorial Global Tech High School, collectively the Eastside Memorial High Schools at the Johnston Campus.

Johnston's fate sounded gloomy and soulless enough, but there were worse rumors about what would happen if Anabel didn't make the numbers at Reagan. Some people said the school would turn into a detention center, just what the Eastside needed, a little day jail for all the delinquents and gangstas from all over the city. Some people said the district wanted the space for offices to relieve the rent burden downtown. And some people said a private company with a charter would come in and fire all the teachers and create some sort of test-score factory, handpicking the most promising students and shutting out kids from the neighborhood, which sounded paranoid but was actually the most likely scenario.

All over the country, from New York to Seattle to Baltimore to Denver, education reformers were closing schools, firing teachers, and pulling kids out of familiar surroundings. It was nothing personal. It was all about numbers. Numbers had reduced crime in New York City, numbers had won the World Series, and now numbers were supposed to decide the fate of entire generations.

This school closure movement was a long time coming. Ever since the Soviets put the first satellite into orbit, Americans had been trying to fix public education. In 1983, a presidential commission found a worrisome number of high school students functionally illiterate, baffled by multistep mathematical problems, and losing ground to foreigners on achievement tests. The commission report, *A Nation at Risk,* convinced lawmakers across the country to set up reward and punishment systems drawn from the corporate realm. They ranked schools by standardized test scores. They publicized the rankings.

The pressure to cheat, to cut corners and cook the test results, was no surprise to anyone familiar with the way things worked on Wall Street. Even in the best of circumstances, conscientious educators soon cut funding for critical thinking, the arts, recreational sports, and anything else that might be hard to quantify. At the top-scoring schools, administrators got promotions, teachers got bonus pay, and kids got scholarships. At the low-scoring schools, everybody got a public shaming. Principals lost their jobs. Teachers grew cynical, strengthened their unions, and dug in against any suggestion of more change. And kids either dropped out or learned to play along, taking an early lesson in life's small gamesmanship.

Instead of raising standards all around, the ranking systems shifted the whole urban landscape. Educators weren't the only ones playing the game. Politicians campaigned on the results. Real estate brokers emphasized the rankings in their brochures. Home values rose and fell across entire neighborhoods. Some people moved; others got stuck. Slums, hardly a new phenomenon, developed boundaries to match school feeder patterns. The selling out of public education wasn't a matter of corruption, just economics, winners and losers.

By the turn of the century, politicians on both sides were promising action. President George W. Bush, a Republican elected partly on the strength of a "Texas Miracle" performed during his time as governor, elevated the superintendent of the Houston school district to the post of education secretary. Joining forces with the liberal lion of the U.S. Senate, Edward M. Kennedy of Massachusetts, he passed a reform act known as No Child Left Behind, based on standardized testing programs in Texas. In 2002, the U.S. Department of Education classified eighty-six hundred of the nation's ninety-five thousand public schools as "identified for improvement."

Under the banner of accountability, the law formalized the reward and punishment systems. To aspiring visionaries and their philanthropically inclined benefactors, it presented a singular opportunity. The schools on the list started losing ambitious educators to new charter organizations with private money, miracle promises, and curriculums based on corporate values.

When the charter groups finished drafting their chosen students, sometimes by lottery and often simply by the highest test scores, the kids left behind became a target for the next wave of reformers, the get-tough crowd. Starting in 2001, Chicago closed forty-four public schools. In New York City, Mayor Michael R. Bloomberg, a former financial data executive, took control of the board of education and closed ninety-one schools. In California, when orders came down to close Sacramento High, the second-oldest public high school west of the Mississippi, one teacher compared it to divorce at Christmas.

But the reformers were just getting started. In 2009, President Barack Obama appointed a star of the movement, Arne Duncan, to serve as federal education secretary. Duncan, a former pro basketball player, came from a realm of winners and losers measured by scores. His orders had closed all those schools in Chicago, and though he had little more to show for it than disruption, he was planning to expand the use of rankings to individual teachers. His first step on the national stage was pitting states against each other. With more than $4 billion in economic stimulus funds at his command, he started a contest to pass laws advancing his numerical accountability agenda. Race to the Top, his education funding program was called.

In Texas, where closer scrutiny showed that officials had manipulated the data supporting the education reform movement in the first place, Governor Perry was in no hurry to join the contest. His reasons involved the as-yet-unofficial anti-Washington platform of his as-yet-unofficial presidential campaign, but he couldn't stop the U.S. Department of Education from putting 352 Texas schools on its 2009 watch list (including a good many charter schools that couldn't keep up with the ever-changing standards of the federal law). For eleven schools, including Reagan High, the state commissioner and his separate accountability system posed a more immediate threat: complete shutdown. Forget about your gathering place, your common ground, your source of shared history, your symbol of continuity, your alma mater. Anybody who had a problem with it was told to look at the numbers.

Anabel had looked at the numbers. As she squinted across the parking lot, she was trying to look calm. If she quit now she would betray the kids, but what if the kids betrayed her? What if one or two or ten kids decided the first day of school at the school everybody said was going to get shut down would be a good time to start something, make it look like a race thing, or maybe it actually would be a race thing, a full-blown riot in the parking lot? The new superintendent was arriving for an inspection. Anabel stood there in her black pantsuit and the pearls from her mother, thinking: "We just need a little miracle on this one, and then it needs to become routine, so God can go use His miracles elsewhere."

High school had saved her life. Not this high school, but a regular American public high school thirty years ago in the border town of Brownsville. Anabel was a pretty girl, but not as pretty as her mother, and she grew up sensing an unspoken competition. She felt restless, wanting for affection, out of place in the family. Some people called her headstrong. Some people had other words for it.

Brownsville was slow and tired then and still is. The climate was subtropical. Only half the adults had high school diplomas. Even the gangs were old and unambitious. La Muralla controlled the levee and the Ramireños stayed across the railroad tracks. Sometimes the Murallas demanded protection money and Anabel's father always paid. One time a burglar made off with some pants. Pants! Anabel's father saw the young man the next day in the street, wearing the pants, and said, "He needed them more than me."

Her father took the long view. He was building a life better than

La Muralla. He bought a two-bedroom, pink brick fixer-upper with white trim and aquamarine ceramic tile where caliche dust gathered from the road. He hung a wedding picture on the wall. He made repairs. He planned an addition. He taught his three girls to sand plywood. They wore Shirley Temple curls and shiny black *zapatos de charol* and shared a single bedroom with two twin beds and a mattress on the floor. They took turns on the beds and knew by the sanding of the plywood that they would not always. When Anabel grew asthmatic and sickly, her parents acquired Chihuahuas, praying for the transference of her ailments.

In the house there were no hugs, there were no probing questions. There were expectations. You worked hard. You made good grades. The shelves were stocked with encyclopedias and dictionaries, the classics, Dickens. "There are the books," Anabel's little sister would remember. "Read them."

At Homer Hanna High School Anabel earned her place on the cheerleading squad, the choir, Ballet Folklorico, and the Pan-American Student Forum. She could balance a glass of water on her head and dance a huapango and not spill a drop, but she never felt pretty enough or smart enough. The Rio Grande Valley was humid and the frizz wouldn't come out of her hair ever. Sophomore year a boy paid her attention and she thought: "This is what songs are made of. This is forever."

They dated for two years. She quit the cheerleading squad. She did his homework. On the radio Eddie Money was singing baby hold on to me, whatever will be will be. Summer before her senior year Anabel went into the bathroom and peed on a stick and came out with a different life.

When she told him about the baby her boyfriend said he didn't have any money. Pretty soon they broke up. He started dating a blond girl, Anabel's sister's best friend, a girl he'd met at Anabel's house.

Anabel tried to think of a reason to live. Suicide was a sin, so she imagined somehow just falling down and dying. Her cousin called her a slut to her face in her own house. She stopped eating. Instead of gaining weight she lost some. It was a hundred degrees, so bulky clothes were out of the question, and still nobody asked what was wrong. She looked bad, vacant and withdrawn.

At school she walked the halls alone, a sunken-cheeked apparition of the fall from cheerleader to pregnant. She stood next to her locker and watched the teenage traffic. Sometimes her sister, three years younger, took her arm and walked her down the hall.

In English they were reading *Gatsby*. Anabel looked at the words as if they were written in some foreign language. The teacher, Mr. Ericson, was the kind people describe as bringing books to life. He carried himself with the calming manner of an aged cowboy. He made you think the world was big and you belonged in it. One day he pulled Anabel aside. The other students filed out. Anabel stood there with red-rimmed eyes and a T-shirt that didn't fit anymore and corduroy pants with the hems raised for fashion.

"There's something not right about you. There's something going on with you. You're not your old self," Mr. Ericson told her. Anabel stood and listened.

"You can always come here. You can always tell me, if you need to," Mr. Ericson said. Anabel turned and walked down the hall.

The front table in the cafeteria was where the gay kids sat. Anabel recognized some of them from the Pan-American Student Forum. She didn't belong there anymore, or anywhere. Not all the gay kids were actually gay, or sure of it at that age, but they fell outside the high school hierarchy together. High school made that kind of improvisation possible. High school demanded it. And an American high school could almost always find a friend for the friendless.

Anabel found her new friends at the front table. They were all broken toys, she thought. There was a freshman boy whose mother had died of cancer. There was a girl who dressed provocatively, later to become a porn actress. There was a kid named James, who had a car.

The gay kids took Anabel to see a Miss September contest at a community center. They met a drag queen named Ernest, who performed as a woman called Llana. Anabel sat in the corner and felt lost, but not alone. The freshman boy proposed marriage. He was lost too.

At Homecoming Anabel performed with the dance squad, several weeks pregnant and thirty pounds underweight. Her uniform sagged off her chest and flapped to each pirouette. Her old boyfriend was there, deejaying the dance, escorting the blond girl. "My Sharona," "Heart of Glass," "I Will Survive": Anabel danced with the freshman boy. Her old boyfriend stepped in, then out again.

After the dance some kids went to eat. Anabel sat with the freshman boy. After dinner she stood up and her chair was stained with blood and her peach taffeta gown was stained too. The freshman boy took her hand and walked her out and she could hear the kids whispering jokes and worse. The freshman boy washed her gown and took her home.

The next morning Anabel's father woke her up for church. All that day the gay kids plotted a way to get her to a hospital. The oldest person they knew, Ernest, the drag queen, agreed to pretend to be her mom.

Anabel rode a city bus to the free clinic. Ernest was waiting out front, dressed as Llana. He looked a lot like Donna Summer. The clinic didn't ask questions. The nurse had some trouble finding a pulse but none diagnosing a miscarriage.

Anabel went back to school. She graduated on time. She got back together with her old boyfriend, but not for love. She stayed another year in Brownsville, working at Kmart and studying at Texas Southmost College. Her days were long. She enrolled in four classes for the fall, then eight for the spring and two more for the summer. She earned basic credits in history and math and composition. She joined the choir. She studied tennis and dance and psychology. She wrote for the school paper. She dreamed of traveling the world for *National Geographic*. It felt good to be dreaming.

Her boyfriend found work at a printing company. One day he put a poster-size picture of Anabel on his bedroom wall. Anabel knew she had him then: He loved her, he needed her, all the stuff songs are made of. She applied to the University of Texas at Austin, three hundred miles away. She packed her bags and broke up with him. Then she got into the car and drove. She prayed to God not to make her hateful and hurtful for good, but she needed to hurt that boy that day.

Now she was watching for the dropouts. Fifteen of them, spotted over the weekend by a truant officer at Highland Mall, had made a reluctant pledge to come back for the first day of school. The parking lot was getting crowded with F-150s and junkers and crazy things with neon lights and tinted windows and wrong-way doors jacked up on hydraulics. More kids were arriving on foot, hundreds more in a half-waking march through the late August swelter, under the highway overpass, through the Exxon station, and past the La Palapa cantina, the boys in baggy shorts and the girls in tight jeans, some with tattoos and some with superhero backpacks, a kid with a metalhead goatee, another rapping under his breath about what all the real niggas do, some pushing strollers, some sending text messages, and some looking scared to death. Anabel was still squinting across the parking lot when her cell phone rang.

"Yeah, I'm nervous," she told her caller. "When you care, you're nervous. And we're going to care around here."

Caring was all well and good, but there were other reasons to be nervous. The new superintendent was one. Dr. Meria J. Carstarphen, a slight, severe-looking Harvard graduate with her hair up in a tight bun, was a veteran of the reform movement. She had worked as the chief accountability officer for the school district in Washington, D.C. She had run the district in St. Paul, Minnesota, where she closed down elementary schools that were losing students for the same reason as Reagan. She had told a newspaper reporter there, "If we don't want to close schools, somebody give me a different direction." Her public statements had focused on a vision for bringing students up to grade level, meaning on standardized tests. She had floated ideas about consolidating campuses. Just a week ago, she had called all twelve thousand teachers and administrators together at the county expo center, where she paced the stage with a headset microphone and said, "This district must be ready for change. And I believe you have the right leader, right here right now, with the right staff, right here right now, to get the job done." Now she was leading a clutch of assistants, two public relations officers, and a newspaper photographer toward the front sidewalk, where Anabel was still scanning the parking lot.

Right on time, the dropouts last seen at Highland Mall pulled up with the sound system booming, the boys showing their boxer shorts, and the girls showing at least two kinds of cleavage around the fringes of their stretch-fabric minidresses. The superintendent spotted them right away. Anabel braced for a lecture.

"That," the superintendent told her, "was inappropriate for school."

Anabel almost said: "When you come in with eyes for what it should look like rather than appreciating what's been done . . ."

She let the thought die in her mind. Then she almost said: "The kids have to come before you can tell them what they can't do . . ."

She extinguished that thought too. Instead, she said: "We'll take care of it."

Anabel smiled a good little trouper smile. There was so much more to show the superintendent. Reformers were businesspeople, right? They looked at the school like a production line, scrutinizing what came out. The product was supposed to be young men and women who could read and write, who could solve problems and perform tasks, who could qualify for higher education, support themselves, make a contribution. Everybody wanted that, parents and teachers, politicians and administrators all the same. But a generation of reform had stolen the pride of the whole neighborhood. People heard the school was a failure and didn't come. Some transferred. Some got jobs, legal or otherwise. Kids who fell behind just stayed behind, didn't catch up in summer school the way they once had.

In her first year on the job, Anabel had shown she could play the numbers game. Reagan was failing better. By the shifting algorithms applied to "academically unacceptable" schools, the latest test results came within striking distance of the "required improvement." Now she had one more year to hit that moving target in math and science, one more year to reduce the dropout rate. It made for a good rallying cry, but she knew even making the numbers wouldn't really save the school. Provisions in the state and federal laws were set to keep raising the standards every year. And every year a new batch of kids would arrive in need of frenzied tutoring. Her patient was almost stable; now came the real work. Anabel wanted a neighborhood public school, open to all, with dances and crowded bleachers, band performances and yearbooks, Pan-American clubs and teachers who brought books alive. She wanted to restore Reagan to its founding ideal, its solar pride, its place at the center of something defined only by itself. She wanted to reach out into the middle schools, into the neighborhoods, into homes and families to make people believe in the school again so maybe the cycle would end. She wanted love and expectations.

A few minutes later the superintendent was gone, sent off with a warm cup of coffee from a parent-teacher-student association volunteer in a blue T-shirt that said "I am standing up for Reagan High School."

Anabel's smile wilted. She walked into the office.

"The superintendent visited this morning, but she focused on the dress code," she told her staff, noting the untimely arrival of the dropouts rounded up at the mall. "They showed up at the door in all their bling and getup that they've probably been planning for weeks. The problem is that if you tell them 'Go home' now, they aren't going to come back."

Then she went to the intercom and her voice echoed down the hall.

Raiders, pardon the interruption, she said. *Classrooms look wonderful, everyone looks wonderful. Looks like we're starting the year on the right foot.*

Two

Anabel put the microphone down. Her office looked like a sublet. Other than pictures of her own children, she had managed to hang little more than an outdated portrait of the city skyline taken before all the new condo towers went up, a whiteboard to be used in planning nine hundred student schedules after one of the assistant principals tried to do it on a computer and of course that hadn't worked out because Anabel didn't trust computers much, and a sign that said "Sometimes you just have to take the leap and build your wings on the way down."

There hadn't been much time to decorate. The lobby's trophy case looked like a time capsule. Newer photos showed charity scholarship winners flashing wads of play cash. A sign written with a felt marker proclaimed: Raiders Raid Knowledge. A week ago, with the superintendent's visit looming, Anabel had finally taken one of the guidance counselors aside and asked, "Carstarphen will be here Monday. What do you need to make this presentable?"

"Money."

So Anabel went digging in her purse to pay for a trip to IKEA and then walked across the courtyard picking up trash, muttering, "The other principals are not doing this right now."

The other principals also didn't have their younger sisters moving in to take care of their ten-year-old daughters so they could spend more time at the high school, but Anabel did. Most nights she was out past dark, negotiating with missionaries to open a social services center on campus, trying to fill a job called school improvement facilitator, and making mental lists of who was missing books, who was missing desks, and who was just missing.

"So, what's the drama?" Anabel said, opening a last-minute staff meeting.

"Can I give you the short version?" an assistant principal said, scanning a detailed e-mail concerning a science teacher's informal largess and the jealousy it had inspired. "Ms. Kaiser gave her beat-up cafeteria tables to Ms. Bauer."

Somebody suggested confiscating all the furniture from the science wing. That'd show 'em. Anabel laughed her head-back laugh.

"Learning happens in many different ways," she said. "I'm just saying."

But even something this silly could get out of hand and she knew it; the way resources were stretched, the pressure everybody was under. The science teachers especially: That was where scores most needed to come up. Anabel looked to the ceiling. After fifteen years as an administrator, she knew Ms. Kaiser's kind. Ms. Kaiser was young. Ms. Kaiser had time and energy to spare and apparently tables too. Anabel had been like Ms. Kaiser once. In another life, it seemed.

"Can you tell Carmen to lasso those teachers up?" she said. "I told them, 'Do not move furniture.'"

Then she hurried the talk along to bell schedules and bus schedules. Some ordinary drama made for a pleasant distraction, and after that there was still the matter of the squirrel eating through IT cables to address. After the meeting Anabel made her rounds. She came across a teacher agonizing over whether to shut down his fish tank on account of the citywide drought restrictions.

"No," Anabel told him, peering into the bubbling aquarium. "There's a living thing in there."

Sometimes it seemed as if her whole first year at Reagan had gone by this way, in a blur. She'd arrived as an interloper late in the summer of 2008, unwanted and expected to fail. The reasons were as plain as the landscape outside her window.

The school stood at a crossroads. From her office, Anabel gazed out at delivery trucks rumbling into the west side of the city, a place of music festivals and liberal politics, a wealthy university and a booming technology industry, film stars and famous athletes, a long-standing domain of the white and moneyed where radio deejays played just enough Bob Marley to keep up appearances. Off to the right she watched sport utility vehicles climbing north into the new exurban landscape, a place of bulk groceries and radar speed monitoring, arena churches with ample parking and outsize replicas of downtown restaurants, carpeted houses available in three different floor plans priced reasonably for the square footage and set back a suitable distance from the boondock remnants of rifle ranges and catfish fries, a place that was drawing some of the black families away. And around the perimeter she saw the *carnicerías,* infant-care centers, and purveyors of usurious lending that beckoned to the strivers and the squatters, the hustlers and the *perdidos,* all the faces brown as her own following the great migration into the aged housing stock of the first suburbs. So many had gone and so many had taken their place, and still here was the school, at the northeastern corner of a heady intersection.

Here was the school, with the suggestion of bygone glories protruding from its weatherworn facade. Numbers emblazoned in calligraphic blue memorialized consecutive state football championships, evoking an era of honors for the drill team, the track team, the choir, and the oratorical darling of the Optimist Club. Coaches from the University of Texas had once come to visit and stars of the Dallas Cowboys too. Boosters had waved signs all over town. President Richard M. Nixon had paid respects. Baskin-Robbins, The Apothecary Shop, and Midway Grocery & Bar-B-Q had all hastened to associate themselves with the Big Blue, the storied Raiders of Reagan High School in East Austin, Texas.

A generation later, here was the school, diminished, chaotic, a ship for Anabel to go down with, a relic of the great American century, a bold experiment in education and social progress built on the long-since-spent goodwill of a rising time.

Or perhaps: Here was the once and future center of Reagan Country, the otherwise nonexistent nexus of two suburban neighborhoods, St. John's and University Hills, one named for desperate faith and the other for calculated prosperity.

Along the dirty banks of Buttermilk Creek, the Reconstruction preachers of the St. John Regular Baptist Association set out to save a quarter of the state's 250,000 black souls, leaving the rest to the Guadalupe, Lincoln, and Mt. Zion associations. Soul saving was muddy, mule-drawn, and thankless work, but by the turn of the twentieth century, Rev. L. L. Campbell was ready to deploy St. John's accumulated tithings to advance education. On a three-hundred-acre parcel five miles northeast of the state Capitol, Campbell opened the St. John's Industrial Home for Negro Orphans, which promptly burned to the ground under unresolved though probably not-so-mysterious circumstances. The school reopened in 1912 for hundreds of children to study mathematics, English, history, chemistry, and agriculture, as well as subjects called Domestic Science and Manual Training.

None of it lasted long. When St. John's finances crumbled in the Great Depression, the Reverend A. K. Black started selling small parcels of earth along the creek to onetime sharecroppers for fifty dollars apiece. The orphanage closed for good in 1942. The city annexed the land in 1951, only to leave the streets unpaved, the creek flood-prone, and the garbage uncollected. More than a decade later, a Community Renewal Program survey counted 286 families, all Negro, with a median annual income of $1,854 in rural conditions steps away from the site of a new highway. In the early 1960s, there was no mistaking Interregional Highway 35 for anything but a heavily trafficked four-lane barricade to seal the old divisions of west from east.

But on the northern outskirts, much remained unsettled. After a century of middling efforts, the city was evolving into a real Texas boomtown, with a cast of computing visionaries to rival the madcap bankers of Dallas and the casino oilmen of Houston. The University of Texas was expanding at a rate of two thousand students a year, producing companies with names like Austron and Textran. President Lyndon B. Johnson, once the local congressman, was sending home resources in the form of new federal offices. The state government was trebling its capital workforce. And International Business Machines was planning to open a plant on the north side of town, with Texas Instruments and Motorola not far behind.

The promise of the suburbs was the promise of midcentury

America, open to any city blessed with enough self-regard to chase the tourist trade, enough ambition to fancy itself the next Silicon Someplace, and enough character to inspire a provincial backlash. Why not here, in the enlightened lakeside home of the first major southern university to admit black undergraduates, a place where progress came slowly but peaceably? The riots and bombings and murders of Selma and Newark and Watts never scarred Austin. The city was one of the most pleasant places to live in the whole country, by the estimation of *U.S. News & World Report*.

So out they went, north up the new interstate, sharp right through the St. John's encampment, and into the fields, carloads of real estate speculators looking out over the loam flatlands east of the Balcones Escarpment at acres of dying cotton where the market for middle-class subdivisions seemed to trump the old racial geography. This far north maybe the rules were different, maybe the rules would change with the times. Maybe there weren't any rules (as long as there was money). A developer called Walter Carrington put single-family starter homes on the market for fifteen thousand dollars. University Hills: On a clear day, the view from the high dive at the Olympic-size swimming pool opened on a panorama of live oaks and pecans, stretching toward the rooftops of new apartment buildings, the owl-eyed tower of the university's main building, and the distant Goddess of Liberty hoisting her lone star atop the pink granite dome of the Capitol.

The city was growing. This was the new place. But the full ambition of the suburbs was a promise extended from one generation to the next. To make it come true, Mayor Lester Palmer acquired a parcel of land on a slight rise between St. John's and University Hills, hired the locally prominent firm of Page, Southerland and Page, and ordered something suitably impressive for parents of the space age. Louis Page took the school board members to Abilene for a look at the AC they'd installed up there, and when he told how the kids would still be able to breathe after it shut off in the wintertime the board members came home and voted unanimously, as reported at the top of the front page of the *Austin American:* "Northeast High School to Be Air-Conditioned." After that Page designed a cross between the Paris Arcades and the National Palace of Mexico, an educational salon organized around outdoor courtyards with doorless classrooms, lockers al fresco, and a high-ceilinged "cafetorium." Construction bids came in a little below his $2.2 million estimate ("Vinyl asbestos flooring gives all the properties of vinyl at low cost"), and the school board approved $146,756 for desks, lecterns, blackboards, and so on.

"Besides being Austin's first all air-conditioned school building, Reagan will be the first school to have 'teacher centers,'" the *American* reported. "Instead of each teacher having her own room and jealously guarding it, she will have a desk, conference table and filing cabinet with other teachers in a 'teacher center.'"

John H. Reagan High School—named for a onetime Confederate official known as the Old Roman of Texas politics, champion of state constitutional provisions dedicating public lands to endow public schools—arrived as the showpiece of a not-so-sleepy government town. In keeping with the progressive spirit (and in minimal compliance with *Brown v. Board of Education*), the school board drew boundaries to include students from University Hills and St. John's alike. In February 1965, an education editor for the *Austin Statesman* drafted a feature on the excitement surrounding the first principal, J. Davis Hill: "Although it is still seven months before the Reagan student body will move into the new school, a school spirit is being planned and will soon 'jell,'" she wrote. "Course choice slips will be handed out to future Reagan students and they will pre-register for next fall's work. Within a few weeks Hill will hold student meetings for the selection of school colors, the name of the athletic teams, the name of the marching unit, the school song, the design of the band and marching unit costumes, and all the thousand and one incidentals that make up the character and personality of a school."

In time the city, the state, and eventually the whole country would know their choices: Columbia blue and white, the Raiders, and "Not Without Honor," proud symbols to set a foundation for all those thousand and one incidentals. But first the neighborhood converged on the school, getting things ready. There were six thousand new books to stack, and the newspaper dutifully reported that "mothers who have been helping out regularly include Mesdames Fred Gentry, Jim Frazier, Jack Wilkinson, Kent Rider and Nayland Baxter," noting that "the ladies who help in the library have time for coffee and conversation."

Principal Hill convened a forum called A Preview of Things to Come, and the new school opened in 1965 to fifteen hundred teenagers, the largest enrollment in the district. Over the next few years the student body would swell to more than two thousand students, learning the arts and sciences, homemaking and business training, industrial vocations and athletics, all in the air-conditioned comfort of fifty-one classrooms connected by covered walkways to new ball fields, separate boys' and girls' gymnasiums, and a library filled with volumes ranging from *The Teenage Diet Book* to *The Poems of John Keats*. Right away, *Nation's Schools* magazine pronounced Reagan school of the year.

"As the doors of John H. Reagan were opened in 1965, another stage of history was revealed," the editors of the first yearbook wrote. "As new clubs formed, as football season progressed, and as classes made headway, the student body began to feel united. Upon this unity, the Reagan Raiders built a school of spirit and tradition— a school 'Not Without Honor.'"

Principal Hill outlined even grander ambitions in a message to students:

Over 1,550 of us have come together at Reagan for one main purpose—EDUCATION. At least we hope that is the main purpose. We come from many Austin junior and senior high schools, parochial schools and from towns large and small from across the nation. We even have foreign countries represented. We represent many races and many religious beliefs. This is America and this is what makes America great. We should be thankful.

All of us who are among the 1,550 have responsibilities to ourselves, to our parents, to our school and to our community. We have a responsibility to ourselves to do our best and get as much out of our educational opportunity as we can so that we may compete favorably in this rugged world. We have a responsibility to our parents not to disappoint them and to make their sacrifices not be in vain. We have a responsibility to our school to help make it the best school possible—a school that has a good image in the community. We also have the responsibility to set school traditions of which all future students at Reagan can be proud. We have a responsibility to our country to learn as individuals how to solve the many and complex problems which confront our nation today, and to help make America a bulwark of democracy in the years to follow.

Here, then, was the new school, the pride of the city. Here was the pastor from Memorial Methodist giving an invocation. Here was Reinhold Hunger, the band director, composing a theme. Here were the ladies from the Albert Sidney Johnston chapter of the United Daughters of the Confederacy presenting an oil portrait to hang in the foyer. Here was Bunky Klein, the student council president, hoisting a cone at the ice cream social. Here was Gene Swenson, the senior with a knack for the stock market, opening his own pet store before graduation. Here were the Madrigal Singers performing at the Montreal Expo, here was Mayor Travis LaRue raising money to send the chorale group on a European tour, and here was a young soprano relating her impressions of the Continent in the pages of the local paper. Here was Coach Travis Raven reading poetry in the locker room, here was Hap Feuerbacher charging some luckless quarterback, here was a citywide pep rally at Nelson Field, and here was the shoe polish on windshields spelling Go Big Blue.

When the Reagan football team—three-touchdown underdogs in the betting line for the 1967 state championship—managed to stop the future All-America quarterback (and Oklahoma lieutenant governor) Jack Mildren at the goal line to beat Abilene Cooper by a score of 20–19, a victory banquet speaker told the triumphant Raiders, "When you ain't supposed to win and win, that's what I like." And when the Raiders beat Odessa Permian to claim a second consecutive state championship four days before Christmas 1968, guest speakers flew in, the city rolled out a blue-carpet welcome at the airport, and a capacity crowd assembled at the convention center to praise Reagan High.

The message rang loud and clear. The educators got it, the kids got it, and if the parents didn't get it the newspaper spelled it out for them:

"The selection of school districts plays a significant part in home-buying decisions, and no section in the city is better served by the schools at all levels than University Hills in Northeast Austin," the *American-Statesman* proclaimed in the late 1960s. "A family buying or building in this area can know that its children will have outstanding educational opportunities."

Now the associate superintendent wanted a tour. Dr. Glenn Nolly was a good bureaucrat, entrenched and politic, charged with supervising all the high schools in the district. He was worldly, he was charming. He spoke French. He liked to be called Doctor Nolly.

Dr. Nolly had been principal at Reagan High back when the Raiders were still making the football playoffs. In 1990, when he took the job, census workers counted twenty-three thousand people living in the school's zip code, only 1,417 of them foreign-born. The median household income was $30,930, slightly above the national figure. The Reagan yearbook carried senior photos of about eighty white kids, fewer than thirty Latino kids, and about fifty black kids, including the Homecoming king and queen. Tracking was the big concern in policy circles at the time, so Dr. Nolly had talked about getting more black kids into college prep courses. In hindsight, that debate seemed like a luxury: You had to believe there was a good path within the school to think your kid was missing out. After a while Dr. Nolly had run into bigger problems. One time he had to suspend a couple of white coaches for calling some football players lazy niggers. Maybe that was when things started to change. Pretty soon those white coaches were gone, but so were a lot of black faces, his among them.

By the first decade of the new century, nearly a third of the kids at Reagan were learning English as a second language, almost twice the state average. Fewer than 5 percent were taking classes for gifted and talented students. The mobility rate, a measure of unstable home lives, reached 40 percent. Nearly one in ten students dropped out, almost three times the state average.

At the front of the classroom the numbers weren't much better. Young teachers came to work off educational debts. Five years at a school designated "low income" could erase thousands of dollars in student loans. For the first five years, teachers at Reagan got paid more than the state average. Then they got paid less. Then, often, they left. On average, they had two years' less experience than teachers at other schools.

The hardest numbers were the ones the state didn't track. Behind the main office, two dozen infant children of current students played at a day-care center with a yard full of plastic toys. Little Raiders, they were called.

And some troubles defied statistical description: There were sex assaults on campus. Some football players broke into a liquor store. A sophomore stabbed a girl to death in a stairwell, drawing national publicity for the first time since President Nixon had declared the Raiders national champs. Pretty soon people thought of the school as the place where that girl got stabbed. On Friday nights, alumni from Dr. Nolly's era posted Facebook messages saying sure, go watch the football team lose if you want to get stabbed.

Nobody called the neighborhoods by names like University Hills or St. John's anymore; now the whole section of the Eastside was just the Two-Three, after its zip code. The stigma of failure was setting hard. On Dr. Nolly's watch, A. S. Johnston High School had already missed test scores, lost good teachers, obsessed over raising test scores, and labored on the last stages of the reform movement's downward spiral. Now Reagan, his onetime posting, was on the block. After the super's photo op, he stayed behind to size up Anabel. He'd seen the volunteers in the blue T-shirts, heard about the missionaries moving into the neighborhood: These people seemed to think Anabel was really going to save the school.

Dr. Nolly had some skin in the game. The district was promising his new boss a $22,500 bonus tied to raising test scores at Reagan. The love and expectations business looked like a big distraction. Time was short. Other numbers loomed large, bigger numbers. Census takers said the forces that had hit Reagan were only getting stronger: Families from the Yucatán Peninsula, Honduras, and Guatemala; sons and daughters of lawn cutters and housemaids conditioned for employment, pregnancy, or both by their teenage years were streaming into Texas. Of the thirty thousand people living in the 78723 zip code, one in four were foreign born and 39 percent spoke a language other than English at home. They brought home a median income of thirty-four thousand dollars. Fewer than forty-five hundred owned their homes. Their own kids had no time for sports, for yearbook making, for any of the starter responsibilities that make a high school the proud center of a place. Maybe nobody did anymore.

Anabel led Dr. Nolly past rooms full of kids trying to learn enough English to join regular classes or at least enough to take the standardized tests. She told him they were giving wrong answers to questions they seemed to understand conceptually. "Like a math question about sliding down a banister," she said. "I'm from South Texas: What's a banister?"

"So," Dr. Nolly said, following her down the hall. "It looks like the school is becoming less African American and more Hispanic?"

Anabel kept a clipped pace. Dr. Nolly knew the answer, and Anabel knew he knew, and he knew Anabel knew he knew. After all, it had been his signature on the letter announcing her appointment, the one that said she came equipped with "extensive experience working with both English language learners and students from economically disadvantaged backgrounds." Everybody knew that meant Latino and black kids both.

He'd been trying to help her out, writing that letter. The rap on Anabel made her the face of the new Eastside majority, *la exploradora del barrio* coming in to tear another city neighborhood from its traditional black roots. She was from the border: What else did you need to know?

Anabel Iris Perez left Brownsville behind but Brownsville caught up fast. At college orientation she walked into a twin-towered dormitory populous enough to merit its own zip code, looked around for people she recognized from the Valley, and there he was instead: Ramiro G. Olvera Jr., green eyes, high cheekbones, and a strong jawline, a Brownsville boy the likes of which she'd never seen. Not a boy: at last a real man.

"He's so beautiful," she thought. "He's going to be my husband."

For a first date Ramiro asked her out on a run. He called it a short five-mile run. Anabel liked sports but she wasn't much good at them. Halfway through the run she felt as if her organs were going to jump out through her nose. She kept running to impress him. Something did.

Ramiro liked sports a lot. He wanted to be a teacher, mostly so he could also be a coach. He wanted a family too.

They both found jobs at the mall. The city wasn't big but it was bigger than Brownsville. Anabel had one dress, red with big white polka dots, to wear for pictures or a night out. She studied literature, dance, and photography. She worked at Dillard's. Ramiro studied science; he worked at Oshman's Sporting Goods. That's where the police recruiter found him. New cadets made about fourteen hundred dollars a month with benefits and a pension, lifetime security for a young couple starting out. Ramiro dropped out of college and enrolled at the academy and graduated with the 67th Cadet Class in February 1984 and six months later they were married.

Ramiro's career took off. The white cops called him Junior because they couldn't say Ramiro right but they all wanted to be his partner. One time he chased a pair of gas station burglars clear to San Marcos going more than a hundred miles an hour with beer cans flying back at his patrol car. One time he got shot in the chest but a bulletproof vest saved his life. One time he shot and killed a man swinging an axe around a housing project. He jogged ten miles a day. He won a gold medal in the police karate tournament. He won nineteen commendations on the job. In 1986 the Coalition of Law Enforcement Agencies of Texas named him officer of the year. He got assigned to an elite task force with a name the department would eventually have to change, the Hispanic Crimes Unit.

Anabel kept up her studies. She worked at a YMCA, at a bank, in the capital office of the Brownsville state representative. She started taking more practical classes. One was called Practical Phonetics. Most of her other classes were about teaching. One was called Classroom Organization, Management, and Discipline. She earned a degree in education, the classic fallback for girls with big dreams. *National Geographic* wasn't going to happen. She was in love and real love was not the stuff songs were made of, but it was all right and maybe better.

Anabel and Ramiro took in a pair of shelties, practice kids. Ramiro coached Pop Warner football; Anabel drove the players to practice in her Corolla. They had to move one time when threats from friends of the axe-swinging guy Ramiro had shot got scary, but otherwise life was life. In 1987, when she was twenty-five, Anabel applied for a job teaching high school Spanish. She listed her health as excellent and her experience as student teaching. She described herself as qualified to oversee Spanish clubs, history clubs, cheerleading squads, dance teams, student council meetings, and the publication of a school newspaper. Then she scanned the rest of the form.

Name of teaching certificates you hold:

She left that blank.

Other teaching in public schools (full time):

She left that blank.

Other teaching in public schools (part time):

She left that blank.

Professional references:

She listed some friends who were teachers, in Austin and in border towns. Her manager at the bank. A police sergeant.

With what community organizations are you associated?

She wrote "Austin Police Support Group."

The fourth page of the application asked for a personal statement.

"I decided many years ago to make the field of education a life-long career," Anabel wrote in loopy cursive. "I plan to graduate in May 1987 and have made Austin my home, so plan to remain in the area permanently. Throughout the years I have tried to remain active within the community and working with youth. I greatly enjoy working with people and I look forward to teaching in the Austin School District."

Two months later she got a congratulatory letter from the district. She was pregnant again, on purpose this time, but the congratulations weren't about that. Her new job paid $19,450.

The baby looked a lot like his daddy, minus the black eye he was wearing at the maternity ward that day from kickboxing. They named him Ramiro Alejandro Olvera, the third Ramiro on his daddy's side of the family and the third Alejandro on hers, so Anabel called him Trey for short. Sometimes she called him *Colitas*, Little Heinie. His first Christmas she took him to Brownsville a few days early to see her family. Ramiro had to work so he was still in Austin when the swollen blood vessel on the right side of his brain burst after twenty-seven years of not bursting and he fell down in a driveway a few blocks from their apartment, dressed in his jogging suit. He had just canceled his life insurance policy to save eleven dollars a month.

Anabel had never been to a funeral before. She didn't know how to behave. Maybe she would explode; that seemed possible. She didn't want anybody to touch her and it turned out that was what people did to other people at funerals, especially to young widows. She didn't want anybody to sit in her row so she got up and stood beside the coffin like some Vanna White of Sorrow. She listened to the Reverend Juan Canales and she listened to Psalm 23 and Romans 8 and she listened to her dead husband's cop partner saying, "Good-bye my friend and *vaya con Díos, hermano.*"

Amigos en Azul solicited contributions but day care alone cost four-hundred-some dollars a month. Anabel taught more Spanish. Every year she got a P6 pay-grade scale raise and Trey got bigger. His childhood health took after his mother's: He had seizures and once stopped breathing. Anabel took in a boarder who watched Trey while she drove to San Marcos to get a night-school master's.

"She stuck turbo chargers on," her sister said. "What better way to grieve than to just keep moving?"

In 1993, Anabel filled out a new application, this time for an assistant principal job. Now she had an advanced degree, references from inside the district, and memberships in the Hispanic Women's Network, the Muscular Dystrophy Association, UNICEF, the

March of Dimes, Ballet Folklorico, and the Drug-Free Schools Program. For hobbies she listed reading, music, and travel, though she had only been to two states and Mexico. The fourth page of the form asked for a new personal statement. This time her answer was more candid.

"As far and as hard as I tried to run away from education, here I am," she wrote. "I believe that education will always be a part of my life. I love my students and I believe that if provided with the right environment, all students can learn. The role of an administrator plays a great part in the growth and development of our children. I plan to pursue my career in AISD and help facilitate the belief that I hold dear: Learning is a lifelong process."

Anabel got assigned to a middle school. The administrative job paid $34,333. She worked with kids bused in from the Eastside. She didn't like the way they were treated and said so. She applied to be principal herself. Instead she was transferred to an elementary school, sent to a classroom with no books, and assigned the title "helping teacher." She took a two-thousand-dollar pay cut. An official from downtown announced her demotion in a letter concluding, "We wish to express our sincere appreciation for the service you are rendering the children of Austin and solicit your best efforts and cooperation in your assignment."

Soon Trey was starting school. For a while Anabel kept teaching Spanish, or, in the official rendering, helping to teach it. In July 1997, she interviewed for a job as assistant principal at Mendez Middle School, where graffiti covered the walls, dealers worked the halls, and street gangs recruited their corner lookouts. She walked in with her hair in a French braid. The principal warned her, "A lot of our children have had adult experiences."

Anabel took over discipline management. She drove around

rousting kids out of bed. She took young teachers to see the conditions their students lived in. She talked about showing up no matter what. When Trey got in trouble she made him serve his suspension in school. She told him: "If I were to die, my funeral would have to be arranged at night if you want to go, because you have to be in school during the day."

Anabel showed up and stayed late. She supervised after-school clubs. She learned to laugh again. One time a boy unscrewed a bunch of lightbulbs and when she asked for his mom's number he spelled out 444-4444 and she dialed it even though she'd ordered from Domino's before. After a few more years Anabel got married again. Humberto Garza was a health teacher and a coach, just as Ramiro had wanted to be. Life was funny that way sometimes.

In the summer of 2004, the middle school principal recommended Anabel for an experiment the district wanted to run, a new academy for immigrant kids. She'd been impressed with the way Anabel handled kids in trouble.

"It wasn't, 'pobrecito mijo or mija,'" the middle school principal said. "It was, 'Okay, you got yourself into this, how are we going to get you out?' Anabel is someone who is able to establish relationships even with people who don't want to have relationships."

At the academy, six teachers and 140 students crowded into the outbuildings of a regular high school. Some of the kids had crossed the Texas border with smugglers. Several had never seen a pencil. One had actual work experience as a shepherd. There was no history to rally around. The best she could do was to tell the kids: "You never surrender. You never surrender. You keep fighting to the death."

The job at Reagan came open in 2008. Anabel's friends warned her to stay away. The headlines in the paper told of a district in turmoil, a respected superintendent resigning early, A. S. Johnston High faltering, and little hope for Reagan, which was next on the state's list. Anabel knew the score.

"If you have a school like this, are you going to bring somebody who has the very best experience or has no experience?" she said. "If you say, Mr. Successful Principal with twenty-five years' experience, everything you touch turns to gold, are they going to come here? The accountability system is like a land mine."

But she didn't have much to lose. Trey had graduated from high school. By her own count she had applied for jobs as a principal sixteen times over the years.

And here was a place people loved, or used to, a place with a foundation, no matter how deeply buried. In the fallow courtyards she planted shrubs, wildflowers, and tomatoes. She wrote her own letter to parents in the neighborhood, which they received around the time of the district's letter informing them of the right to take their kids out of Reagan. Hers took a defiantly upbeat tone: "I would like to THANK YOU for helping to make this school a success. Reagan can be a great school, but we have a long way to go."

As she worked on the test scores that first year, Anabel also set out to shore up her leadership. She sat through meetings. She reassured ministers. She drew lines. She got home at eight, ten, twelve at night. Her version of gardening involved stopping at Lowe's, buying some flowers, depositing them in the soil on her way to the front door, and then dancing with her daughter on the way to the laundry machine, all without breaking stride.

The long hours paid off. She won over the president of the parent-teacher-student association, Jacqueline Chatham, a black woman who'd worked in military intelligence. She enlisted Allen Weeks, a white community organizer. Together they wrote a twenty-point plan to address items called Improved Teaching, Improving

Attendance, School Climate, Pregnant Teens, Marketing and Com-
munications, Supporting Families, and Changing the Law. In other
words, everything all at once. By accident or design, their plan itself
even hinted at deeper divisions, with separate categories called English Language Learners and African American Students. They
opened their manifesto with a poem by a graduating senior, Jermiah Wooley:

Now we hit the low point.

Closure.

Closure means the state is going to close down Reagan

Bye bye school reunion

There is no school just an open field

My brothers can not go here

The people who live around this neighborhood have to be
bused across town just to go to another school

All the people who went here before us they're going to be
forgotten

The only thing people will remember is another school closed
down on the eastside

The plan drew some support. On a Saturday in November 2008,
more than a hundred people marched on the state Capitol waving
signs for Reagan. The showing bought Anabel some time.

When the morning of the standardized test arrived, she rented a
minivan with a GPS device. A school employee named Larry
Johnson, given the title parent support specialist, gathered a stash of

spare clothes in teenage boys' and girls' sizes. At 9:45, Anabel programmed the GPS with the home addresses of twenty missing students, kids with otherwise solid attendance records. Johnson took the wheel. Driving around the Eastside, they found kids who were stuck for a ride, handed out clean clothes, and headed to school for the test. They only looked for kids with solid attendance records. Why make the extra effort for kids who didn't care, kids who would only drag down the average? "That's dooming the school," Anabel said. "They'll shut us down."

Still, the science and math scores fell short of the "required improvement." That summer, Anabel started driving west to clear her mind. She got as far as Denver and then turned home. In July, the letter from the state commissioner arrived: Reagan would have one more year to shed the label "academically unacceptable."

One more year, then: Education consultants had already taken their turn trying to fix Reagan High, with theories and analysis financed by the charitable foundation of the computer boss Michael Dell, whose office park on the far outskirts of the city had played a considerable role in depleting enrollment in the first place. Reformers and profiteers were waiting in the wings.

The numbers would not come easily. Lawmakers had set a trip wire, a legacy of the postsegregation era. To keep schools from coasting on the scores of privileged white students, state officials used a system of cells based on race, poverty, and other factors. If one cell missed the mark—say, ninth-grade low-income Latino science students—it could render the whole school academically unacceptable.

But for one more year, perhaps the last, the school would become what it had always been, what every American high school had once been, a wild, confused, and conflicted ecosystem of aspiring athletes, musicians, scientists, mathematicians, auto mechanics, doctors, lawyers, janitors, housewives, programmers, criminals, maids, pilots, writers, financiers, nurses, et cetera, a population suspended in midmetamorphosis, hormones raging, teeming with divisions of race and class, religion and ambition, money and no money, united in an increasingly fragmented age by accident of geography, thrown together to receive the sculpting blows of four awful, unforgettable, and dizzying years.

Again the buzzer sounded, a staccato electronic demand. The superintendent was gone and the associate superintendent too. Anabel walked the halls.

"Let's go, let's go, let's go, Reagan," called her assistant principal, Rick Fowler. "Don't be late. First day of *escuela*. Don't be late."

In the interval before the last class period of the first day of maybe the last year, the courtyard swelled. Kids slapping five, kids asking directions, kids. Then the bell sounded again and Fowler made his move.

"Uh-oh!" he yelled, pointing toward the cafeteria. "Tardy sweep!"

The lazy and the lost corralled in the cafeteria, taking down up-turned chairs from the lunch tables. Some argued excuses, some accepted their fates. They sat for a lecture, an assembly more than fifty strong, the impromptu largest class in the school, tardy sweep.

"Okay, I'll be honest with you," Fowler began, his voice re-sounding off the concrete walls. "I thought when we had this tardy sweep, it'd be all freshmen in here. For those of you that go to Reagan, it's a pivotal year for us. It's a pivotal year for you too, because you have to get to class on time."

Somebody laughed. Fowler spoke to him in low tones: "Turn around, boy. I don't like talking to the back of your head."

Then he addressed the crowd.

"When that tardy bell rings, if you are tardy four times in six weeks, you will start to be sent home. If you are not interested in going to school, let me know now and we can find someplace else for you. If you are not interested in being successful, let me know now and we can find someplace else for you."

Then he dismissed the freshmen. Some older kids tried to sneak away, without success. Fowler raised his voice. "Do not start out the year this way," he said. "I promise you I will not waste time with you. And if you think I am not serious, test me. This is the first day of school, and you are late already."

Again he lowered his voice and singled a boy out. Ms. Turner, the in-school suspension lady, was nodding furiously.

Fowler said: "If you act like a buffoon, I will treat you like a buffoon. If you act like a mature individual, I will treat you like that."

"Don't be late."

"Don't be late."

"Don't be late."

"Don't be late. Don't be late. Don't be late. Don't be late. Don't be late. Don't be late. Don't be late. Don't be late. Don't be late."

Then: "Go to class."

The kids rushed out. When the last buzzer of the day sounded they turned out across the parking lot, back into the F-150s and junkers and crazy things with neon lights and tinted windows and wrong-way doors jacked up on hydraulics. Back on foot past the La Palapa cantina, through the Exxon station, and under the highway overpass, some pushing strollers, some sending text messages, and some looking scared to death.

When they were gone Anabel gathered the teachers in the library. She counted down from five, calling for quiet. She announced the morning roll call, only 639 students compared to last year's enrollment of 923. There were other problems too.

"The superintendent was here this morning, unfortunately at the same time the girls from 'da club' stepped out of the car in leopard-print dresses," Anabel said. "It was X-rated, and she definitely let me know."

The teachers laughed.

"I didn't dress them."

Then Anabel asked the teachers to put together afternoon attendance counts before going home to prepare the next day's lessons. It would make for a late night, but she needed the numbers. Next to standardized test scores, dropout rates would come in for the closest scrutiny from state officials. Anabel circulated a clipboard, directing a less-than-subtle message to anonymous complainers.

"Make sure you identify yourselves," she said, "so we can fix your problem."

Three

D-day-VUSS!
will-say-VUSS!
D-day-VUSS!
will-say-VUSS!

In the back of his mind Derrick Davis could hear it still, rising from these same wooden bleachers, resounding off these same Columbia blue and white cinder-block walls, carrying across two decades from his own high school triumphs. He could still see the crowds, the parents and the girls, chanting. He could still feel that couplet's lazy rhyme, save us, Davis. Save us by the grace of the jump shot handed down as your birthright, bequest of a hood legend, prodigal son of the Eastside.

At the moment Derrick wasn't looking too salvational. Antsy, more like. He was standing in front of the bleachers, twirling a whistle around his wrist, shifting his weight from left to right, right to left, giving the boys a minute to settle down. Squint and he could almost be one of them, 175 pounds filling out the five-foot-eleven-inch frame he'd trained to elevate, aim, and (legs together now, pebbled leather rolling across the index finger) release. Team photos from his own senior season at Reagan looked like somebody had launched a harpoon with mild acne through a blue Raiders jersey. They'd called him Little Pee-Wee because of his dad. Even now, with the class of '90's twentieth reunion approaching fast, Derrick could still rock a newsboy cap and sneakers with a gray linen suit. But his thirties were ticking away, no denying that. The NBA had never called. The hip-hop labels had never called. Now his fallback job was on the line, and nobody was calling him Little Pee-Wee anymore.

These boys called him Coach. He watched them tie their shoes, these almost-men, his not quite two dozen prospects turned out for basketball class on the first day of school. They knew what people were saying about Reagan; they knew the stakes; they knew what one year meant. Why pile on to that? As things stood, there were just enough heads to round out varsity, jayvee, and frosh squads if he didn't make any cuts.

And he wouldn't, of course, make any cuts. Derrick had been recruiting these boys almost half their lives. They were sixth graders the year he started coaching at Reagan, in 2003, playing together as the Pirates of Pearce Middle School and off-season AAU. Most of them had deep roots on the Eastside, but Reagan was a hard sell that year. As these boys and their parents and the whole country knew, 2003 was the Year of the Stabbing, the year Reagan High reasserted itself into national headlines, this time as the place where a fifteen-year-old girl called Ortralla Mosley was attacked by her estranged boyfriend. The incident cost Ortralla her life, the estranged boyfriend a forty-year prison sentence, the district hundreds of thousands of dollars in legal settlements, and the school newfound notoriety as the setting for an episode of *America's Most Wanted*. In its immediate aftermath, a pack of lawyers commissioned to examine the state of affairs at Reagan found elevated levels of aggression, inconsistent disciplinary enforcement, and, in a deflating bit of understatement, "a limited degree of positive school spirit or attachment among students, parents, and staff."

So recruiting wasn't easy, but Derrick hadn't seen much other choice. Recruiting was the new way. The old way was: You go where your big brothers and sisters went because that's where you live and where you're from and where your friends go and part of who you are and what you're becoming. Derrick had gone to Reagan because there was nothing finer you could wear to Highland Mall on a crisp Saturday afternoon than a Columbia blue letter jacket, and also just because of the map.

It wasn't the old way anymore, not in the crumbling inner rings of the first American suburbs. Not since Garnett and Kobe and LeBron made high school the new proving ground for the draft. Not since Division I colleges started offering delayed scholarships to eighth graders. And not since education reformers started singling out schools "identified for improvement."

His first month on the job, Derrick got in tight with Marlon Vincent, a junior playing center on the team. Marlon was manifestly gifted. Even after skipping freshman ball, he'd made the varsity as a sophomore and right away started dunking on the big white boys out at Westlake. He was a loyal and generous teammate too, the kind who would recite all the other players' names when a sportswriter from the local paper came around. But more important, Marlon had a little brother, Malcolm, a double-digit scorer who was on his way to regional all-star selection.

Malcolm wasn't necessarily better than Marlon, but that wasn't the point. Prevailing upon Marlon to stay meant acquiring Malcolm and all his little homies. It meant reasserting the traditional order of things: You go where your people went, the neighborhood school. You build something together and that thing builds something in you too.

And Derrick's plan worked, at first. Marlon and Malcolm won his program some respect, threw a scare into archrival LBJ High, competed for the district title, and gained a postseason entry. But the next year, parents started getting letters home from the district: *The No Child Left Behind Act (Public Law 107-110) . . . School Improvement Status . . . Adequate Yearly Progress . . . the option to request a transfer of your child to another public school within the district that is not identified for school improvement status . . .*

Malcolm promptly transferred to LBJ, a betrayal Derrick had to take with the cold comfort of knowing the Vincent family supply of untapped basketball potential was running low anyway. The next few seasons were a slog, Derrick dragging his players out to get their asses handed to them not just all over town but on the road in Houston, La Marque, and even Elgin, a semirural outpost better known for barbecue-oriented tourism than for sports. He'd play any team that would put The School Where That Girl Got Stabbed on its schedule, an approach that brought the Raiders to the far-flung home gyms of no small number of powerhouse squads looking to pad their records by teaching some Eastside thugs (who didn't look so scary getting off the bus way out in Pflugerville or Dripping Springs or BFE Wherever) a thing or two about hard fouls and the ad hoc laissez-faire jurisprudential philosophies of exurban hometown referees. It was around then that basketball scouting sites stopped posting statistics from Reagan. And it was around then that Derrick finally got JQ.

．　．　．

JaQuarius Daniels took his place on the bleachers. The other boys made room. A junior three weeks shy of his eighteenth birthday, JaQuarius was about the biggest kid in the school, six foot five with a full-grown weight lifter's physique and a fluid athleticism. He was used to being accommodated. He was used to being watched.

For JaQuarius, high school was passing in an orderly rotation of seasons, from football to basketball to track and back to football, his own true love. Settling into fourth-period basketball class on the first day of school, months before any actual basketball games were scheduled, with a full autumn of football spread out before him in the meantime, JaQuarius projected ease.

Everywhere he went, JaQuarius projected ease. Disarming ease, uncanny ease, and sometimes otherworldly ease. Disengaged ease. Unnatural ease. He was like Black Fonzie standing there.

Of course he could attract D-1 football scouts to watch the Raiders suffer another humiliating beatdown at Nelson Field; he was JQ. Of course he could walk down the hall holding the hands of two girls at once; he was JQ. Of course he could improvise sound bites every time the local paper sent a junior sportswriter out to find some uplifting good news from the Eastside school that was going to get shut down ("'I'm proud that people around here can look up to me,' Daniels said. 'I like being a leader.'"); he was JQ. And of course he expected to earn a business degree, which of course he wouldn't have any use for until his triumphant retirement from a storied NFL career, at which point of course he would deploy his hard-earned acumen toward the management of his image, his wealth, and his endeavors to give back to the community. He was JQ.

And being JQ meant letting it all hang out. His momma came from a West Texas hick town: So what? His sister and his two brothers all came from different daddies: Whose didn't? None of the daddies had stuck around: Whose had? He was quarterbacking a football team that couldn't catch, didn't block, and seemed allergic or perhaps even conscientiously opposed to tackling? All the more reason to admire his singular devotion.

Because all those things—if you wanted to be JQ, as opposed to just another oversize and athletically gifted Eastside kid— all those hard things had to look easy. So when his sister got hauled to the principal's office, when his stepdad turned up on the sidelines looking all wild man, when the family car broke down yet again, JaQuarius could always be seen gliding across the courtyard the next day, conspicuous grin conspicuously subdued, earbuds in, head above the crowd, nodding up and down just enough to show he was agreeing in principle with every thunderous downbeat. Also, he had a 3.4 grade point average.

"He looks like he's doing it effortlessly when I watch him," his football coach had said on TV sophomore year, when the local CBS affiliate pronounced JaQuarius athlete of the week for rushing 317 yards to score four touchdowns in a single game. "The sky is the limit for this young man because of his attitude, his work ethic. He's got his head on right."

At the moment JaQuarius had his head on straight forward, chin up, clocking Coach Davis. Maybe his mind was on football, but his basketball shoes were tied.

D id everybody get their physicals? Jerold, Josh, Willie, Corn? What about the juniors: Malcolm, Rodrick, JaQuarius, Jordan, Brandon, James, Alex? This was a big year, Coach Davis was saying. The Raiders were coming off their strongest season since the Vincent brothers. Last year they won third place in the district among AAAA schools, the second-largest classification, to qualify for a playoff run that ended with a four-point loss to (who else?) LBJ in the regional quarterfinals.

For the most part, the same squad was back to play this year. The problem was next year, and the year after that and the year after that. With just a handful of freshmen sitting on the bleachers (Derrick didn't say this part out loud; the boys could count), the team badly needed a strong season to attract middle school recruits to the school, assuming there would still be a school.

Anyway, big announcement: Letter jackets would be provided to the varsity squad free of charge.

"I was hustling to get this," Derrick said. "Got a business guy who took an interest. All last year he wanted to give us money. When you're successful, people want to be part of it."

Derrick sized up his varsity selections, seven of them better than six feet tall. Others he'd have to play up, boys who could use another year on the jayvee, but the team GPA was above 3.0 and that mattered too. He was building a machine that built futures. The No Pass No Play policies of the 1980s had guaranteed athletes would make their C's and D's one way or another, but then what? You couldn't even get into UT with that junk anymore. And beyond the players themselves, what kind of message would it send if the hoop squad could do better, even just a little bit better in class than necessary? It was only a game, true, but it was also true that here today sat eleven young men poised to embody the school to the Eastside and the whole of the city. They were here not by chance but by years of investment. They were the fruits of his labor, of long seasons spent making his case to Coach Parish after practice in the Pearce Middle School gym.

"Give me a chance," Derrick had told the middle school coach, invoking his playoff run. "You saw what we did in '05."

At first Coach Parish resisted sending his players to Reagan, and not just because of the stabbing and the school closure talk. Something bigger gave him pause: school ties. Coach Parish himself had been a standout player at LBJ some years back; sending his middle school charges to Reagan would amount to a betrayal.

But Derrick pressed his case: Year after year, Coach Parish was taking a new group of eleven-year-old boys, infusing their raw talent with discipline, teamwork, and muscle memory at no small cost, nurturing them through eighth grade and then sending them up to ride the bench at LBJ. Derrick promised court time, but he also spun the troubles at Reagan as an opportunity.

"There's something special about being part of something bigger than you," he said. "You give more to receive more. It's a biblical concept."

Derrick knew he was asking a lot. This squad was special to Coach Parish. This squad had the cohesion Brandon and Jerold and little Willie Powell had built season in and season out. It had JaQuarius, who even in seventh grade towered over the other kids at Pearce, who excelled on the court even though his heart was really in football, whom Coach Parish had set straight after a night in jail, and who'd eventually come to describe Coach Parish as a father figure. And this squad had Coach Parish's namesake son, Alex, among the youngest and smallest of the boys.

In the faces staring back at him from the bleachers four years later, dressed in sweats of Columbia blue, Derrick could still make out traces of the children he'd brought to Reagan with Coach Parish's endorsement. There was JaQuarius, still the biggest; Alex, still the smallest; Brandon, Jerold, and Willie, who always claimed to want the ball in his hands at the buzzer.

Derrick kept his welcome talk brief. He talked about district. He talked about area. He didn't say much about regionals. He didn't talk about state. Ambitions aside, the Raiders were still a AAAA squad at the school everybody said was going to get shut down.

The boys knew their schedule was stacked by design, a trial meant to prepare them for the pressure of everything a winning season could mean this year. In the coming months they would ride the bus up to Harker Heights to take on the hardened military brats from Fort Hood, enter four tournaments around the state, and confront the class AAAAA Chaparrals of Westlake High, all before the start of district play. And district play, starting just before Christmas break, would finally present two chances to take revenge on LBJ.

In sports there are only four stories—winning, losing, cheating, and getting hurt—but within them are contained all life's coiled treasures and sorrows. Coach Derrick Lamont Davis surveyed his charges, these almost-men, his varsity hoop squad, the Raiders of John H. Reagan High School, of the Two-Three, of the St. John's/ University Hills section of East Austin, Texas, USA, maybe, but he hoped not the last of the Big Blue.

"What did I tell you guys last year?" he said. "We gonna do some things different around the gym. Gonna try to get you guys travel uniforms."

Four

She'd been awake half the night, praying on it. The video she'd finished editing at a coffee shop early that morning, queued up from her laptop to the overhead projector, was supposed to make these kids look beyond their own concerns.

Still, she had her doubts. Maybe she was in over her head. There was always the medical school idea. *Dr. Candice M. Kaiser, Pediatrics:* It sounded nice, helping kids and getting tangible results and even getting thanked. Or maybe she'd just go back to nannying. That had been one way to use a degree in human development all right, building a résumé full of accomplishments such as "carried out developmentally appropriate activities that centered around the children's interests," earning references from corporate-lawyer-slash-guilt-ridden moms who could afford the services of a glorified babysitter with a higher education and the student loans to show for it. Nannying had always left plenty of time to party and some to volunteer, with College Bound and then with the Red Cross after Katrina, enough at first to satisfy her craving for something she was still trying to define. And the work? Sometimes all you had to tell a toddler was, "Use your words," and the lines of communication would open right up. Magical, compared to spending her whole day enforcing the three rules so important and yet apparently so impossible that she had to post them in big block letters on her classroom wall:

BE ON TIME

BE RESPECTFUL

NO ELECTRONICS . . . EVER

Candice made her way around the ring of desks, pushing in the extra chairs she'd borrowed to accommodate spillover crowds. She needed them, no matter how many times she'd been told no moving furniture. Science was where the scores had to come up; science classes were always packed. Call it the chicken and the egg, but from the front of the classroom it meant that even during the worst recession in three generations, at a school district facing a $7 million budget shortfall, in a school facing closure due to a whole other set of complex socioeconomic factors, nobody was talking about laying off science teachers. Science, math, special ed: You were golden. The district was even defending recruitment and retention bonuses. The new superintendent had to answer to the same set of numbers.

Candice was just warming to the job. She was only twenty-six. She had options. In the last few years, she had learned the hard way how the assortment of options available to a college-educated white woman in twenty-first-century America could be confounding, dizzying, even paralyzing. In her mind, they added up to a debt. Her bachelor of science degree from the University of Texas had afforded her the time and instruction to ponder not just the chemistry relevant to her current trade but also language and government, nutrition and tennis, family relationships and African American history, masterworks of literature, the psychology of sex, and contemporary moral problems, an intellectual smorgasbord unfathomable to many of the developing teenage minds of those who would soon fill the extra chairs she was presently pushing into the back of each of the desks in classroom 133 of the science wing.

So far, her efforts to narrow her options had led through Texas Teaching Fellows, a six-week summer program for aimless college grads (motto: "Think big. Become a teacher.") willing to get by without the thirty-nine-hundred-dollar tuition garnished from their starting salaries ($38,190.08 if you taught science on the Eastside), which had in turn led to Reagan. She'd been at it just long enough to see how teaching at its finest served the unending human quest for knowledge, how teaching at a public high school felt more like a key metric, and how teaching at Reagan meant bringing your own sense of purpose. She took hers from the hip young evangelists at the Stone Church, not from the teachers' union.

Tying an apron full of pens around her plain black dress, Candice made her rounds as first "Reveille" and then "The Star-Spangled Banner" sounded from the loudspeakers. From the wall by the periodic table of the elements, Old Man Einstein was staring down at the slight figure she cut, God's grasping servant in sandals and hairpins. One by one she peeled off Post-it Notes, smoothing her finger over the adhesive to mark each desk for homeroom, a strictly alphabetical assemblage designed to meet only once, on the first day of school, as a sort of student holding pen. When her first student arrived, Candice asked his name.

"Me?" the boy said, in a tone that suggested she ought to know.

Then it hit her: Grouped alphabetically, every student in home-room was named Hernandez.

"I mean, your first name," Candice said.

Hernandez after Hernandez trickled in, talking low in Spanglish, staring ahead, fingers drumming. Who needed to borrow a pen? Just about everybody, it turned out. Again and again Candice reached into her apron, and the kids signed her schedule cards: "Hernan-dez," followed by Felipe, Jasmine, Christian, Horacio, and so on.

"Okay, let me introduce myself. My name is Ms. Kaiser, and I teach chemistry and forensics this year."

Right away some joker asked whether bombs were made in her class. Yes, Candice acknowledged, a small explosion took place at one point last year but we're not talking about that now. Then she started picking up the unclaimed schedule cards. Only seven stu-dents had shown up. It was early yet. Roll call, known among teach-ers as the warm-body count, would not take place until second period, a policy meant to raise attendance rates by counting every last tardy student as present. Out in the hall some girls went by, gig-gling, finding their way, or not. Candice started collecting her pens.

"What if you want to buy one?" a boy asked.

"From me?"

"Yeah."

"Why don't you just go to H-E-B?"

"It's too far."

"Oh. Okay. You can totally buy one from me."

The dull hum of the loudspeaker sounded. The principal's voice cut through. The superintendent's visit, it seemed, had not gone well.

She is specifically giving us instructions to enforce the AISD dress code, the principal was saying. *Tomorrow you will be sent home if you are not dressed appropriately.*

When the speaker fell silent there was still time to kill. Candice tried to make conversation. Hey, where did everybody live? Off the big thoroughfares of Cameron, Rundberg, St. John's? Did they know she lived here in the hood too? Anyway, who's excited about the football season? Nobody? Hey, who rides the school bus? Nobody?

"Walking to school is good," Candice offered. "It gives you time to think. It gets you ready for college, because you have to walk everywhere in college."

"College?" somebody called. "Who's going to college?"

Ha-ha. Finally the bell issued its mercy. A new group arrived for first-period chemistry. The black kids chose seats by the window; the Latinos filled the inner ring. A new voice through the loudspeaker intoned: *One nation. Under God. Indivisible.*

Then Candice laid out her rules.

"You giving me your cell phone number means if there's an issue, I will call you first, before calling your parents. Next I call home. If I get, 'doo-doo-doo, not a working number,' I come to your house."

Her voice dropped to a whisper.

"It's called a home visit. Last year, a student told me, 'Ms. Kaiser, you have no life.' Those of you who know me know I don't have a life outside school. Y'all are my life."

The kids filled out forms. For the most part they were quiet, respectful, and without electronics, taking a cue from the star athlete. JaQuarius sat up straight and tall, as always, his grin framed by a neatly trimmed track of facial hair running ear to ear, the center of attention in a striped polo. Girls leaned over each of his shoulders, their curls finely braided, earrings neck-low, flirting over their laboratory safety contracts.

"There's Spanish and English on it," Candice said distractedly, fiddling with her laptop. She called for the lab contracts and cleared away the screen saver and clicked on the video program, then let her finger hover above the button for a second. She looked around the room. Several of these kids already knew about her trip, the summer she'd spent volunteering at a Christian school in Nairobi. Brandon from the basketball team knew; he came to after-school Bible study. Sometimes JaQuarius came, even if he was just doing it for Ashley. DeVonte came, proclaiming his agnosticism and rattling off questions. All right, she asked: Who could tell the class where their teacher went this summer?

"Africa!" a girl called.

"You went to Cancún," JaQuarius teased.

Ha-ha.

"I've never been to Cancún," Candice said. Leaving out the details about the missionary group, the Bibles she'd handed out with medicines, and anything else that might cross the line for classroom talk, she introduced her video.

"The video is about Kenya, and they have a slum there," she said. "Does anyone know what a slum is?"

"Ghetto!" somebody called.

"It's like, what you said, times ten."

"Ghetto ghetto ghetto ghetto . . ."

Ha-ha. Enough. The children in Africa, Candice said, had asked her how much it cost to attend school in America.

"I almost cried when I had to tell them it was free."

The room fell quiet. Candice saw her opening. Meet them where they're at and draw them forward. The job of a public school teacher, distilled. She drew a breath. Why, she asked, do you think the African kids study so hard?

"They're paying for it."

Not exactly.

"They don't take it for granted."

Right. But why?

"They want out."

Now she had to show them. Now it was out of her hands. Now it was grace that had brought her through this far, through all the partying, all the nannying, all those suffocatingly comfortable dangers, toils, and snares and into this classroom on the Eastside, where her unpainted fingernail now tapped the keyboard. Images scrolled across the projector screen: piles of trash, a barren landscape, and yet eager young faces.

"Four hundred students in an area the size of the 130's wing of the West Mall," her homemade video reported, making the comparison to Reagan distinct. Captions told of HIV and head fungus. The Kenyan students waved at the camera, offered greetings and love. The soundtrack played "I Am Blessed to Be a Witness."

Candice flipped on the light. Somebody clapped, then stopped.

"Hey what time do we get out of here?" a kid was asking when the bell answered, but Candice made everybody sit back down. She scanned the room, a new set of minds nestled inside highly distracting corporal vessels, ready to get on with whatever came next.

"I love you all," she said. "Have a great day, bye-bye."

Five

Hello everybody! Thank you, thank you. Thank you,
everybody. All right, everybody go ahead and have a seat.
How is everyone doing today?
—President Barack Obama, in a National Address to America's
Schoolchildren, Wakefield High School, Arlington, Virginia

In America, how everyone was doing was angry. By Labor Day
2009, people were out of work in numbers unseen for a quarter
century, losing their homes and debating the merits of public enter-
prise. All summer, from Tampa, Florida, to St. Louis, Missouri,
tempers had flared in town hall meetings on health care, where
people shouted insults, pushed and shoved, called in death threats,
invoked Nazi imagery, and even strung up a congressman in effigy.
The hard feelings centered on the "public option," a proposal to
more deeply involve the federal government in the medical insur-

ance business. Supporters on the left said it would reduce costs; opponents on the right said it would reduce standards of care. For a diverse society 300 million strong, founded on a document that sought to promote the general welfare in its preamble and limit the role of government in its addenda, the dispute was a vigorous part of the great American experiment: In it together for crime, fire, and picking up the trash, with everything else on the table.

But the education reform movement, more than any other public policy campaign, was emerging from a history so muddled, passions so personal, and stakes so high as to upend traditional notions of left and right. This was people's kids. Both sides derived their positions from the colonial-era thinker Cotton Mather, who'd written that "a Good School deserves to be call'd the very Salt of the Town that hath it: And the Pastors of every Town are under peculiar obligations to make this a part of their Pastoral Care, That they may have a Good School in their Neighbourhood."

Three centuries later, as the postwar dream of the suburbs rounded a corner, Americans still didn't much care to live near people of different means or skin tone, but they didn't want to fall behind in the global economy either, so considerable responsibility still fell to the "Pastors of every Town" to foster good schools in their neighborhoods. The federal government had all but given up on busing, tacitly accepted resegregation, and let the states hash out new proposals to enforce standards of equality, including subsidies paid to poor school districts in Texas and overtly racial districts drawn in Omaha, Nebraska. Having failed to spread resources around evenly, the U.S. Department of Education was spreading around the consequences of standardized tests instead.

As the reform movement gathered force, though, the endgame was changing. Public schools, financed by the people, run by the people through their governments, and open to educate all young people, seemed to be marked for extinction. The only real debate concerned the nature of their replacement. The usual opponents of taxation and spending on the political right found themselves promoting vouchers, which would give parents some money to pay tuition at private schools. They didn't get much traction, but then the usual supporters of government service on the political left came around promoting their own plan to deal the government out. They wanted to turn schools over to anybody who could show results on the standardized tests. As first proposed, in Minnesota in 1991, these new charters would go to devoted teachers, but the economics soon favored charismatic fund-raisers and profit-making corporations (in most states, charters came with some government grant money for salaries but nothing for buildings). Companies with names like White Hat and Imagine Schools presented themselves as education test kitchens marinating the classrooms of the future. They chose students by lottery. They offered to replicate their trademarked systems, for a price.

Politicians on both sides cast public-school teachers as listless bureaucrats punching the clock at the expense of American kids. Philanthropists and documentary directors made heroes of such figures as Michelle Rhee, the Washington, D.C., superintendent who was closing down dozens of schools; Arne Duncan, the education secretary who was dangling reward money in front of slash-and-burn governors and superintendents; and Geoffrey Canada, the Harlem visionary who was raising hundreds of millions of dollars (his Web site accepted Visa, MasterCard, American Express, and Discover) to expand his Promise Academy Charter Schools. Closing ranks behind their union leaders, teachers countered every criticism, no matter how legitimate, with a demand for more resources all around. And so it was on, the Race to the Top.

. . . And we've got students tuning in from all across
America, from kindergarten through twelfth grade.
And I am just so glad that all of you could join us
today . . .

The day after Labor Day, President Obama, who had enrolled his own young daughters in the private Sidwell Friends School, took the stage at Wakefield High School in Arlington, Virginia, before a blue banner marked My Education, My Future. Wakefield served South Arlington, another working-class, racially mixed inner-ring suburb crowded with new immigrants on the wrong side of a high-way. Its principal, Doris Jackson, a former guidance counselor, was carrying on the work of Marie Shiels Djouadi, who'd quit the Sisters of Charity to devote her career to public education. Over the course of two decades, Djouadi had improvised a blend of language-immersion classes, arts instruction, athletics, and senior class projects to lift spirits and academic performance, not miraculously but respectably. *The Washington Post Magazine,* noting the absence of a Hollywood-ready story line at Wakefield, wrote that successful school revivals "are often pure luck, propelled by the serendipitous presence of smart and resourceful people above and below the principal at the right moment."

Not that anyone noticed. President Obama, on hand that day to deliver what the White House billed as a "National Address to America's Schoolchildren," ended up speaking to a television audience of "certainly a large segment of the nation's 50 million public school students," in the estimation of the *New York Times.* Many students tuned out, conscripted into a boycott of parental design.

The boycott, the last flare of that long raging summer, had taken hold after Secretary Duncan suggested some lesson plans based on the speech. A Republican Party official had responded with a written statement: "As the father of four children, I am absolutely appalled that taxpayer dollars are being used to spread President Obama's socialist ideology."

How much of this derived from the new president's standing opposition was a matter of opinion. His education policies, popular in theory across the political spectrum, did imply an exertion of federal power in their proposed execution. But his speech itself was standard pep-talk stuff, praising the example of studious young people from around the country with diverse-sounding names like Jasmin, Antoni, and Shantell. The White House released the text in advance: not much different from remarks President George H. W. Bush had made to a previous generation of schoolchildren. Nothing about education policy.

Still, some parents ordered their kids to sit out the lunchtime address in empty classrooms. Others kept their kids home all day. Some school districts refused to screen the speech. Protesters waved signs: "Mr. President, stay away from our kids." Boycotts or their absence dominated headlines across the country. U.S. Trade Representative Ron Kirk (Reagan High, class of '72) watched from his daughter's high school in Dallas, telling reporters: "There are few moments in my life when I'm embarrassed to say I'm from Texas. This is one of them."

. . . And I want to thank Wakefield for being such an outstanding host. Give yourselves a round of applause . . .

In Texas, graduation rates consistently fell below 75 percent, not the worst in the country but bad enough to envy Kentucky. SAT scores ranked near the bottom, though only about half the students in the state even made it as far as taking those.

Some chalked it up to stinginess: The state only spent about $9,200 a year on each student, ranking 37th in the country. That was about $10,000 less than it spent on each prison inmate, a figure that also came in well below the national average. Teacher pay averaged $48,000, about $7,000 below the national average.

No doubt immigration placed an outsize burden on the border states. By the estimate of the Census Bureau, some 7 million Texans, or 33 percent of the population, spoke a language other than English at home, compared to 19 percent nationwide.

But whatever the trouble, it clearly wasn't any lack of accountability-style reform. As far as the reform movement was concerned, Texas led the nation. Its legislature set up a numbers-based reward-and-punishment system in 1993 and then strengthened it a decade later, as Congress replicated it on a national scale. By 2009, 208 schools were rated academically unacceptable, including 75 high schools. Eleven had been on the list for three years, which meant the state commissioner could shut them down. Thirty schools, some of them overlapping the state targets, were listed in the worst possible Stage 5 of the federal accountability system known as No Child Left Behind.

. . . And no matter what grade you're in, some of you are probably wishing it were still summer and you could've stayed in bed just a little bit longer this morning . . .

At Reagan High, Anabel Garza had sent notes home to parents about the national address to America's schoolchildren. No one had objected, but then, no one had responded at all, a fairly typical result for notes sent home to parents of students at Reagan. The reasons were various and complicated, but that hadn't stopped the state education agency from trying to express them as a percentage: "limited English proficient, 33.3%," "economically disadvantaged, 83.6%," and "at risk, 86.8%."

Changing those numbers in any meaningful way would take a generation if it could be done at all, so Anabel was starting small. On the third day of school, she convened an assembly in the theater. The topic was rules. Her audience, having engaged in and witnessed near-daily fights between blacks and Latinos, some of which had escalated to mass brawls requiring the sort of makeup days other schools call only for blizzards, looked skeptical. Right away, a girl in the audience refused to remove her cap. Offered a second chance, the girl refused again and then there were handcuffs. As school police officers dragged her off to the Gardner Betts Juvenile Center, Anabel addressed the crowd: "This just shows you that there's justice for all. You can't just act crazy and expect us to tolerate it."

. . . So I know that some of you are still adjusting to being back at school . . .

Anabel could do tough, sure. In her first year at Reagan, she had suspended 275 students and expelled another 52, exceeding her predecessor on both counts. Most of the infractions constituted what the district called "abusive conduct," under subcategories ranging from "rude to adult" to "gang-related act."

But back in her office, Anabel dropped the tough talk. "I can't tell you how close to not okay we were. You could have had four hundred students rampaging," she said, letting the image drift away. Tough could only take her so far. History's littered with restless, hopeless places tamed only to recoil on their ambitious tamers. And in education, the selective charter groups getting so much attention for their numerical results were the first to concede the limits of tough talk. The most famous one, the Harlem Children's Zone, knew the importance of resources. Its Promise Academy boasted in promotional materials of a $75 million budget to provide "the Baby College parenting workshops," "the Harlem Gems preschool program," "the HCZ Asthma Initiative," and "an obesity program to help children stay healthy."

No public school could match the fund-raising power of the charter groups and education services firms, but Reagan High did have its share of nonprofit agencies providing social services. Austin Voices for Education and Youth, with supporters ranging from a hip west side movie chain to the Robert Wood Johnson Foundation, offered mentoring for students and training for parents. Communities in Schools, a national group financed by large corporations, did more of the same. Project Advance, funded by the Dell Foundation, counseled students to prepare for college. Anabel welcomed anybody willing to pitch in.

. . . But I'm here today because I have something important to discuss with you . . .

From a converted classroom on the second floor, Danielle Chatmon set out a lunchtime spread of hot dogs and chili. Culinarily speaking, her only competition came from the cardboard pizza served free in the cafeteria to anybody living near the poverty level, meaning just about everybody. But her meal came with a price: You had to listen to some advice and maybe fill out a form. Last year she helped sixty-four Reagan students successfully apply to college. For the coming year her budget was cut by a fifth, but she could still afford chili dogs and talk.

Chatmon, who drew her paycheck from the school like a traditional guidance counselor, shared the space with Wilton Harris, Reagan class of '81, who worked for one of the outside nonprofit groups. Harris displayed a list of rap stars with diplomas as a recruiting poster for his XY Zone—XYZ as in the final stages of learning; XY as in the chromosomes. He was out to teach teenage boys to act like young men. No question it was a job their fathers should have been doing at home, but it was no small job under any circumstances. Was it a job for the school? Maybe it had to be, if you expected teenage boys to do anything so judicious as absorbing scientific, mathematical, cultural, and literary concepts that might or might not come in handy years down the road, or even if you just wanted them to sit still long enough to fill in some bubbles on a multiple-choice test. Teenage boys don't do that on their own, not anywhere, not ever. Left to their own devices, teenage boys start fires, throw rocks at cars, play guitar all afternoon, play basketball or video games all night, and chase teenage girls.

Even back when parents had (or took) more time to get involved, like all those "mesdames" shelving books in the new Reagan library back in the midsixties, public schools played a role in molding young citizens. They had to; that's where kids spent at least half their waking hours. And to hear Wilton Harris tell it, Reagan had shaped him into a man.

"The teachers and principals had been here a lot of years," Harris said. "It was a place you wanted to be. The climate was different. The camaraderie was different. We were very close. We were Reagan. When you met students from other campuses, they were like, 'Man, I wish I went to Reagan.' I look back on those times, and I think of how close we were. Everybody played a sport. Even if you weren't good, you got out there anyway."

The teachers he remembered brought in diving gear for lessons on oceanography, dressed as Ben Franklin for history class, and gave pre-HIV-era straight talk about sex and relationships. The coaches prescribed a certain way of carrying yourself. An assistant principal once pulled him aside and said: "You got two options in life, son, state pen or Penn State. Make a choice. I got to pay taxes for either one."

Maybe distance had brightened his memory, but the tangible result was that here he sat in this converted classroom with his jacket and tie and his tough-love talk and his poster of educated rap stars, ready to exert that same effect on a younger generation of kids, anybody who walked in off the street from University Hills and St. John's. He'd argue with them. He'd scold them. He'd drive them around. He'd make them read *Forbes*. He'd take them to NASA, the Texas Supreme Court, a small farm. Keep expanding perspectives, keep raising the bar: nothing different from what his own teachers had done, only Wilton Harris wasn't a teacher. The actual teachers were drilling standardized test questions. Private donations paid for his services, which he characterized this way: "You can come in and knock down Reagan and build a Wi-Fi Reagan with teachers who have won all kinds of awards, but if you don't have students who have decided they want to learn, it don't mean nothing."

. . . Now, I've given a lot of speeches about education.
And I've talked about responsibility a lot . . .

It was working: Just look at Arturo Garcia, blazing through senior year with some college credits on his transcript, taking AP classes along with auto mechanics (don't call it a fallback—that'll pay the bills while you work toward a degree), arts electives, and public speaking. Public speaking! For the shy kid who could hardly look Harris in the eye when they first shook hands. Last year, when the new Latino police chief came to visit, Harris made Arturo give an introduction. Arturo turned red and started rocking on his heels, but he got through the speech and it was the start of something. Pretty soon he was asking the new principal tough questions in an interview for the school newspaper. He helped organize the big march on the Capitol and even addressed the crowd: "How can the TEA say Reagan should be closed? Tests are just tests. I see a lot of committed people at Reagan." Now Arturo was applying to college, no small thing for the oldest son of a maintenance worker and an out-of-work maid. He wanted to study American history, which he described as the struggle of a long series of underdogs to reap the benefits of freedom. He told people Austin Community College was his first choice. He worked a summer job at Rosewood Rec and was hoping Harris could help him get a job at Walmart or Target, something he could do on the weekend and still help his three little brothers—a sophomore, an eighth grader, and a fifth grader—with their homework after school. They were all going to Reagan too if Arturo had anything to say about it.

It wasn't working: Just look at Jesse Martinez Jr., who wrecked his credits following a girl around and skipped class for two years until he got written up (by Ms. Kaiser) and sent (sentenced?) to the Alternative Learning Center detention camp and eventually dropped out. Jesse's dad was around and even had a good job at the credit union, but the math questions on the Texas Assessment of Knowledge and Skills (TAKS) exam still didn't make any sense to him. Jesse was into hip-hop, especially the dancing, but the educational achievements of Lil Wayne, Ludacris, and Common ("attended Florida A&M University," the XY Zone's poster informed) weren't enough to make a classroom an appealing place to spend an afternoon. There was only so much Wilton Harris could do.

. . . I've talked about teachers' responsibility for inspiring students and pushing you to learn . . .

Inside her science classroom, Candice Kaiser kept order with brief, whispered asides, denying troublemakers the spotlight. Her students sat clustered in that twilight of adolescence where facial hair, curves, and tattoos counterpose backpacks depicting Spider-Man and the Incredible Hulk, vestiges of childhood betrayed in their posture, shoes half off, minds deep in concentration or its opposite. They'd been occupied filling in bubbles since third grade, starting with spring reading and math tests and then other subjects depending on the year. The state tested science proficiency in fifth, eighth, tenth, and eleventh graders, dividing all of human understanding into five "objectives." Parents received a report scoring performance on each objective as "commended," "met standard," or "did not meet standard."

Though she knew about the state's algorithms for "required improvement," Candice set herself a goal of 100 percent passing and wasn't shy about saying so. When a woman from the state education agency came to visit, Anabel called her into the meeting and said: "Ms. Kaiser, why don't you tell her your goal this year?"

So she did, and the TEA lady said that it had never been done before, and Candice went home that night thinking, "Did I really just tell that woman from TEA that I was going to have all my kids pass?" Later she figured Anabel must have had a reason for putting her on the spot. Anabel had heard her say the 100 percent thing before. Maybe Anabel was forcing her to believe in it. Anabel was always up to something.

*. . . I've talked a lot about your government's responsibility
for setting high standards, and supporting teachers and
principals, and turning around schools that aren't working,
where students aren't getting the opportunities that they
deserve . . .*

Candice called for quiet and counted down from five. Christian Hernandez was walking in late to second-period chemistry, bringing to thirty-one the number of kids clustered around her twenty-one classroom desks. At this rate they'd be lucky to get through lab safety contracts in the first week.

"All right, time's up, I'm going to come around," she called.

*. . . But at the end of the day, we can have the most
dedicated teachers, the most supportive parents, the
best schools in the world, and none of it will make a
difference, none of it will matter unless all of you fulfill
your responsibilities, unless you show up to those
schools, unless you pay attention to those
teachers . . .*

Candice worked the floor, bending and turning and stamping papers and muttering: "It really is crowded in here." Some boys at the lab table in the back were messing with the faucets.

"What are we talking about today?"

"Lab safety," one of the kids suggested.

Candice asked for a show of hands: How many think this is important? Ten arms went up, hesitatingly. She demonstrated the chemical shower, the fire hood, and the extinguisher.

"I can see all of y'all playing with your electronics, so please put them up."

. . . I want to start with the responsibility you have to yourself. Every single one of you has something that you're good at. Every single one of you has something to offer. And you have a responsibility to yourself to discover what that is. That's the opportunity an education can provide . . .

Candice fluttered her hand under her nose, demonstrating the proper method of smelling chemicals.

"When diluting acid—this is on the TAKS test also—you should always add the acid to the water."

She dimmed the lights and passed around worksheets. Talking. Another five-second count.

"Excuse me," she said, addressing the boys back at the lab tables. "Our class is a community, and you're taking time away from it."

. . . And no matter what you want to do with your life, I guarantee that you'll need an education to do it. You want to be a nurse or an architect, a lawyer or a member of our military? You're going to need a good education for every single one of those careers. You cannot drop out of school and just drop into a good job. You've got to train for it and work for it and learn for it . . .

Candice paced the room, giving out high-fives for correct answers. Just before the bell rang, her door opened. In walked a kid with a shy smile and a Mohawk, a senior new to the school, student number thirty-two for her chemistry class. He took a seat by the window with the rest of the black kids. In the time she had left, Candice used an egg to demonstrate the effect sulfuric acid could have if it got in your eye.

. . . And this isn't just important for your own life and your own future. What you make of your education will decide nothing less than the future of this country. The future of America depends on you. What you're learning in school today will determine whether we as a nation can meet our greatest challenges in the future.

Back to school was tough; even the president said so. Candice didn't like to think about the way her classroom would get more manageable as kids dropped out. She was serious about her 100 percent passing rate. And the kids had already surprised her once. She was just trying to jolt their little worlds with that video of the African school, but some of the Post-it Notes that came back in response amazed her. She taped them on the wall at the front of the lab where the kids could be reminded all semester:

"Give my money"

"Help pay for their school"

"Tell other people about them"

"Appreciate my education because some people don't have it free"

And this one:

"Go to Kenya"

. . . So I expect all of you to get serious this year. I expect you to put your best effort into everything you do. I expect

great things from each of you. So don't let us down. Don't let your family down or your country down. Most of all, don't let yourself down. Make us all proud. Thank you very much, everybody. God bless you. God bless America.

Six

At night the glowing *R* planted on the dun brick facade backlit the numbers '67, '68, and '70, beaming a Columbia blue reminder of ancient seasons clear down Cameron Road to the Whataburger. Those state football championships meant something powerful in Texas, where the Dallas Cowboys were opening a new billion-dollar stadium and the Longhorns were within striking distance of another national title. The name of Reagan High invoked a dynasty to stand alongside Abilene, Southlake Carroll, Odessa Permian, and just a handful of others. For decades Reagan had turned in winning records, setting the citywide standard for the most successful coach by victories (Wally Freytag, '74–'78) and by percentage (Travis Raven, '65–'70). Even in the late 1980s, when the draw of the new exurbs took hold and enrollment fell to twelve hundred, Coach Dennis Ceder fielded an undefeated class AAAA squad, advancing to the third round of the playoffs. On the fortieth anniversary of the school's first state championship, thirty-six old-timers showed up for a reunion. Some wore varsity letter jackets. The local paper sent a photographer. "Once a Raider, always a Raider," the tight end said.

But in four years on the state's list of academically unacceptable schools, Reagan had won only seven football games. Friday nights at Nelson Field the bleachers were nearly deserted. Banners advertised a minor-league soccer club wholly unaffiliated with the school. Now just twenty-five kids showed up to practice, including sixteen starters from last year's 2–8 team. In his note to scouting services, the most optimistic Coach Paul Darby could sound was: "The Raiders need improvement throughout the lineup, but they should get it as players get older and gain experience."

The quarterback, JaQuarius Daniels, only a junior, was already one of the returning starters, six five, 210 pounds, and needing, in Coach Darby's estimation, "to improve significantly on a learning season."

The school principal had bigger expectations for JaQuarius.

"I don't know what has made JQ JQ, but I see leadership potential in him," Anabel Garza said. "He doesn't see it in himself yet. He's doing it for himself . . . He doesn't have to be a man of many words; he just has to communicate to others."

But JaQuarius wasn't used to communicating to others. He was used to watching. He'd learned a lot that way, by watching. He'd watched his older cousins play football. He'd watched his mother, LaDonna Cummings, give birth to his younger sister while LaDonna was still a teenager herself, then to two more boys in the next four years. Moving the family from Abilene to Austin, where her own mother lived, she'd found work as a home health aide, taken up with a roofer who wore a cheek tattoo, and enrolled her children in the public schools.

New to the Eastside, one of the biggest kids at Pearce Middle

School, JaQuarius had starred at running back. Trouble noticed soon enough. The summer before seventh grade he got arrested in a big brawl at Highland Mall, where somebody was showing around a pellet gun. As he told it, his night in jail was a turning point: His mom was mad and hurt, and from all that sitting and watching he knew she'd been struggling all her life and he shouldn't have been adding to her troubles.

JaQuarius didn't figure all that out on his own, though. Coach Parish, who'd been trying to get him to join the Pearce Pirates basketball team for a year, started talking about what a shame it'd be to waste great talent with bad decisions. The compliment connected; JaQuarius joined the Pirates, where Alex and Brandon and Jerold and Willie already had a tight bond. JaQuarius elevated their game with his size and athleticism, but they were all going to Reagan, where Coach Davis was promising playing time. JaQuarius had to think it over. Football was his first love, and most of his football teammates were going to LBJ High, where the Jaguars had just made the playoffs with six athletes selected first team all-district. The LBJ freshman squad was bound for even bigger things, stocked with kids who would eventually sign to play for Georgia Tech, Texas Tech, and the Air Force Academy. And LBJ was rated academically acceptable, so there was no risk of getting shuffled across town just when scouts were starting to notice.

On the other hand, maybe JaQuarius could stand out playing against LBJ. And of course there was Ashley Brown.

D on't follow me. Do what you got to do, and I'll do what I got to do." That was what JaQuarius had always told her, all the way back to junior high. Ashley usually called him JaQuarius, not JQ; she had high expectations for him too. That was why she'd agreed to go out with him even though he was a year younger and, she claimed, not very handsome. Their first encounter was less than romantic. The girls were playing basketball against the boys in the Pearce Middle School gym, things got out of hand, and he gave her a slap. She told the girl he was seeing, Dominique, that she'd better get her man in line, but Dominique didn't respond in a manner she found satisfactory, so the next time the girls and boys played basketball, Ashley gave JaQuarius a slap herself. Ashley would remember it all vividly for years; JaQuarius would just say he was pretty low in seventh grade.

Later on, at a party, one of her girlfriends passed along the information that JaQuarius liked her, to which Ashley said: "I don't care; he's ugly." She thought little of it until JaQuarius and a boy named Michael each asked for her phone number in close enough succession that she suspected they'd made some sort of wager. Eventually she gave the number to JaQuarius. She liked the athletic body type for sure, and JaQuarius seemed ambitious. She liked that too.

There was never any question Ashley was going to Reagan, even though her freshman year in 2006–07 coincided with the state labeling the school academically unacceptable. Her mother, La'Quisha, had graduated with the class of '93, and her aunts and uncles were Reagan alumni too. The Lady Raiders track squad had won state in 2000, and Coach Leslie Riggins, who'd been around since the 1990s, was still taking girls to the big meet most years. Coach Riggins had noticed Ashley, who loved to race the neighborhood boys in Craigwood, and had a word with her mom.

Being an athlete made Ashley popular, and being a pretty one made her more popular, not that she cared about any of that. She cared about the feeling she got when she was running: stress-free. Grades came pretty easily, but running was the only time she stopped stressing about whether she was going to see her dad again, or when, and other stuff. She had developed an attitude problem, she was the first to admit. People called her Tough Cookie. She'd get mad about something and the anger would just spray out before she could aim it at the thing she was mad about. Still, she was off to a great start at Reagan, passing the standardized tests, making good enough grades to run track, and even qualifying for state in the 4×100 relay freshman year. So no matter what he said about not following each other, JaQuarius enrolled the next year at Reagan too.

The weight of history rested lightly on his shoulders. When JaQuarius spoke of Reagan "back in the day," he meant the depths of 2003, not the glory of '67. He wasn't carrying on anybody's dynasty. He was out to set his own legend, or at least his own course. His devotion was pure enough. Before bed he did a hundred push-ups. Off-season he lifted weights. Hurt, he performed his assigned rehab. Even in that dispiriting 2008 season as a sophomore, when scouts ranked the team 927th in the state (and 11,258th in the country), he'd thrown eleven touchdown passes to make first team all-district.

By junior year, football looked like his best chance to go to college, the first one in his family, setting an example for his little brothers. His mom understood how things worked. When JaQuarius offered to get a money job, she told him to concentrate on schoolwork and sports. The sports part came easily. Football led to basketball led to track, and when nothing else was going on he joined the golf team (he shot in the low hundreds). Schoolwork came less easily. Sometimes math problems looked as if they were written in a foreign language, but he worked hard for his 3.4 grade point average, and his confidence was improving. None of that made him a leader, not yet, not at the level of the expectations set when the newspaper put him on the cover of its sports section: "Star Daniels Could Revive Reagan Athletics."

The new season wasn't starting out as much of a revival. In the heat of August, the Raiders traveled to Taylor, an exurban outpost of fifteen thousand, to lose 52–0 to the middling Ducks of Taylor High. Their next five opponents ran up 245 points (Texas does not adhere to the mercy rules some states use to protect fatigued players) to the Raiders' 26. All season the losses came by thirty-five points or more, except for the hardest one. Playing at home against the winless Vikings of Lanier High, Reagan lost by a margin of less than a touchdown.

When the game ended, JaQuarius dropped to his knees on the turf, ashamed of his team. Where was the dignity? Where was the courage? What had he gotten himself into? In the next few weeks the Raiders would lose the rest of their games. They would lose 48–7 to his old middle school teammates at LBJ. The college scouting reports would mostly notice, with no small measure of sympathy, how he was throwing off his back foot all the time, scrambling away from unblocked defenders. When JaQuarius looked up that night in the middle of the Lanier celebration, Anabel was standing over him, right there on the field, pulling him to his feet. He didn't commit her words to memory, but she did: "The minute you look like you've been defeated, we have no hope," Anabel said. "Because people are looking at you."

Seven

The next-door neighbors, glancing through a six-foot chain-link fence with a sign that said Beware of Dog, made their way across a dirt yard and past an assortment of toy plastic cars and real rusted ones to a minivan, where they loaded their offspring and drove away without complaint.

A noisy crowd was gathering on the other side of the fence in front of 6915 Carver Avenue, a tan American Foursquare off St. John's Avenue just east of the interstate, six blocks from the campus of Reagan High School. More than two dozen teenagers sat around a concrete stoop framed by rosebushes. Wind chimes trilled on a light September breeze. Several of the girls held babies. In the driveway Cornelius Cammock, a senior forward on the Raider basketball team, dominated a frenetic game of three on three, with a group of girls calling next. One of them got her hands on the ball, a flirtatious struggle ensued, and then the boys resumed their game. The girls fell into a circle, singing:

Big booty big booty
Aw yeah
Booty to the ten
Ten to the three
Three to the six
That is you and you are . . .
Out!

Corn sank a jumper, fourteen feet at least. Somebody argued the score, Corn handed off the ball, and his teammate missed the rim entirely.

"See!" came the taunt from the girls at the top of the driveway, who'd given up on joining the game. "That's exactly why we don't win at basketball."

A cheering section formed: "Blue! White! Raiders fight!"

More cars pulled up, unloading more teenagers. They made their way around a Keller Williams sign raised on behalf of the owners, speculators from Petaluma, California, who'd found few prospective buyers since the real estate bust had stopped the creep of gentrification around the old airport. All the better as far as rent was concerned for their tenant, Candice Kaiser, who, despite her own high school cheerleading experience, was struggling to master the pattern of handclaps her students were demonstrating to complement the half-court basketball game in her driveway.

When the game broke up the crowd moved to the backyard, where lighted Christmas strands colored the twilight. The sound of hammering down the block punctuated the low roll of a bass line. Four girls practiced a step routine. Plates of spaghetti, salad, biscuits, and brownies went around with lemonade. Nijalon Dunn, sophomore class clown and younger brother of a high-ranking Crip, offered a blessing: "Let us come together and celebrate, without the drama with the mamas, and enjoy ourselves like you want us to, through your son, Amen."

"Amen."

Candice stood in a corner, holding somebody's baby girl, scanning the scene: That kid was in her chemistry class. That kid should've graduated by now. And that kid . . .

"What's your name? Are you Roger?"

"Ummm . . . no."

"Liar! You're supposed to be in my class. You skip my class all week, but you come to my house?"

The kid gave her a few lines about reenrolling. Candice let it go. Her house, shared with a cast of roommates including Lindsey Griffin, a teen pregnancy counselor, was becoming the biggest Reagan hangout since Highland Mall. It wasn't just about the food either. The Carver house was a safe place to hash out misunderstandings, air jealousies, confide troubles at home, and complain about schoolwork. On nights like this, the house also served as a center of ministry, as evidenced by the young adults wearing T-shirts that said "I can do all things through Christ who strengthens me."

Christian groups have a long history in American public high schools, where courts generally protect their work on First Amendment grounds. Young Life, which reports ministering to 646,395 students a year at 2,364 high schools, says in promotional materials that its program "began in the early 1940s in response to an emerging adolescent subculture, the center of which was the world of the high school. Kids' lives revolved around their school; the first Young Life leaders realized that to reach kids who had no interest in organized religion they would have to understand and be present in that world."

Financed by charitable gifts, banquets, and golf tournaments,

Christian high school ministry groups expanded their memberships along with their roles over the years, as states slashed the budgets for drama clubs, student publications, and other extracurricular activities. From the poorest quarters of the cities to the most overstimulated exurbs, college students and other volunteer mentors organize sporting events, field trips, and drug-free gatherings, usually in nondenominational (but unmistakably Christian) settings off the school grounds, offering separate Bible study to students who express an interest. The biggest group, the Fellowship of Christian Athletes, reported attendance of 1.4 million at the thirty-three thousand events it sponsored in 2009. FCA promotes general Christian values, while lesser-known groups focus on specific issues such as sexual abstinence (True Love Waits), prevention of drug abuse (Teen Challenge), and promotion of school prayer (See You at the Pole).

For decades, the abundant supply of volunteers from the University of Texas had given Young Life a strong presence at Reagan High. But the dynamics had been changing since the neighborhood caught the eye of Matt Carter, an ambitious young preacher from the East Texas town of Athens. In evangelical parlance, Carter "planted" the Austin Stone Community Church in 2002, giving sermons on Sundays in a rented room at a middle school in South Austin. In an official church history, Carter wrote that he had initially resisted a friend's suggestion to move to Austin because "the city was not spiritually sensitive or open," but before long he was proclaiming a vision "to build a great city, renewed and redeemed by a gospel movement, by being a church for the city of Austin that labors to advance the gospel throughout the nations." He started drawing thousands of worshippers, hosting four services every Sunday and outgrowing his second rented space in a high school near downtown.

In an interview with *Mission Magazine*, Carter said he had been on vacation one day, reading the book of Amos, when he asked God:

> "Are we being a blessing?" This led to me confessing to the Lord that if He desired me to, I would move our church to one of the poorest parts of Austin. This area is called 'St. Johns' and it is incredibly under-resourced. Literally three days after this heartfelt prayer, our land broker who was helping us look for land to purchase called us and said 'I have a piece of land for you. There are fifteen acres in the heart of Austin, but I don't think you're going to want it.' I asked, 'Why?' His reply, 'It's in the St. John's neighborhood.' Needless to say, we bought it. This has begun a long journey for us of getting a massive group of mostly young people to think outside of their middle class sensibilities and consider the poor.

Candice had been raised nominally Catholic, the daughter of a retired cop and an insurance worker who divorced and each remarried more than once, producing a scattering of half siblings and a formidable rebellious streak. Growing up in a prosperous suburb of Corpus Christi, she balanced drunken excursions into Mexico with smart/popular-clique obligations such as cheerleading, running for class secretary, and dating the principal's son. Middle-class sensibilities all the way.

She moved to Austin partly to defy her dad, who was pushing her toward the conservative campus of Texas A&M University. Also, she followed a boy. Candice was going to be a pediatrician, or something, but there was always another party in West Campus. When her parents cut off the tuition money, suggesting community college in Corpus, she went to the financial aid office in tears, signed a letter disavowing financial ties to her family, and qualified for student loans and grants. The partying stopped, for a while. She earned a 4.0 grade point average to prove she could, then went feral: Padre Island, recreational Adderall, five nights a week at Cain & Abel's. She still graduated in four and a half years, making the honor roll four times while nannying three days a week to pay the bills. Everything was easy; nothing satisfied. Medical school started to look like a real commitment. You couldn't just do it for the prestige.

Part of it was just being twenty-three, restless and reckless. She did some tutoring, the usual résumé-building stuff, and after graduation she got more into volunteering. The aid groups were all looking for help with Hurricane Katrina then. It was hard for anybody to miss certain sociological truths made plain in the storm's aftermath, especially hard for anybody who visited the refugee camps, and close to impossible for anybody who also made a living as the glorified babysitter to a lawyer's kids. Thanksgiving 2005 Candice went to visit her dad and his friends in Tennessee, somebody dropped the n-word, and she freaked. Growing up in Texas you hear it from time to time, mostly from old people, and no matter how much you tell yourself they'll all be dead soon enough, you still have to wonder how much generational dilution it takes to get meanness out of the bloodstream. The next day Candice was on a plane back to Austin with even more defiant ideas. She filled out a Peace Corps application, went for an interview, and asked to go to Africa. Then she got a new boyfriend and stopped following up with the Corps. Casting about for ideas, she thought back on her favorite childhood toy, a dry-erase board used to "teach" her grandpa lessons from school. Why not? The Texas Teaching Fellows sent her to interview at Reagan, and the place felt dry and dead and hopeless: perfect. Candice was going to go in and save everybody, mostly so she wouldn't have to deal with herself.

In the interview she talked about hope. Totally Hollywood, but she probably could have said anything with that science degree. Thirty minutes later she got a call on her cell and took the job. Told her friends she was going to work with "the underprivileged." Her first year, 2006–07, was scary. She made $38,190 teaching ninth-grade physics and chemistry, with more than forty kids to a class. She didn't save any of them. She saw big fights, gang fights, group fights, near-riots. The kids couldn't believe it themselves. A few years later, one of them would ask her, "Ms. Kaiser, remember when I threw that chair at you?"

And Candice was a mess. She was dating a fellow teacher and another guy too, lying to both of them. She got a thrill from it, and hated herself for getting a thrill from it. Ashley and Princess and Sasha, the freshmen she thought she was going to save—she started to think maybe her example was doing them more harm than good. Most of June, Candice traveled around, second-guessing the whole teaching thing. Were these kids just bad? Or not bad necessarily, but had they learned behaviors she'd never be able to change? And who was she to be fixing anybody else's behavior? Back in Austin, she moved into a house in the fashionable Bouldin neighborhood with a guy she'd met in Tennessee and some other roommates. She taught summer school at Austin High, where the west side kids had different kinds of problems. They could afford hard drugs. One of them stole her wallet. Some of the girls cut themselves. To her, they seemed deceitful, as if they were hiding the same kind of animosity the Reagan kids wore front and center.

It took another six months and a trip to Big Bend, gazing out over the Chisos Mountains, to convince Candice she was the biggest fake of them all. To show her how small she was. On the way back, her roommate Jenny got out to attend a Stone Church service, still grungy from hiking, and a few weeks later Candice asked to come along. At first she felt awkward, out of place, put off by the charismatic hand raising. But nothing else in her life was working, and snippets of the sermons started to stir the emotions she'd felt at Big Bend. Mighty. Grand. Words like that. The preacher spoke of God chasing you down with rod and staff like an old-time shepherd, and Candice took his words straight to heart: *You can go your own way, you can choose your own life, but if you are a child of God, He will come after you. He will do whatever it takes. Break your legs.*

For reasons she couldn't explain, that image gave her comfort. That God would let her go her own way and screw everything up and get hurt, but in the end He would come for her, with consequences and with love. That He would use whatever it took, even the world and darkness and sin, to break her and to bring her to Him. Candice started going back to church every week. When the preacher mentioned living in sin, she swore off premarital sex (but didn't move out). She told Jenny at dinner, and a few nights later she broke the news to her boyfriend, who declined her invitation to the Stone Church.

Candice started to feel as if God was chasing her down. Every sermon seemed to speak directly to her. She felt the Holy Spirit taking root. She felt God moving in her life. Another friend converted to Christianity; that felt like a sign. A student asked for help starting a Fellowship of Christian Athletes chapter; that felt like a sign. She found an old letter from her grandma quoting Romans; that felt like a sign. She'd cashed the check and set the letter aside, but now she looked up the passage: "And we know that all things work together for good to them that love God, to them who are the called according to his purpose." Sitting alone in her classroom, Candice broke down and cried. Had she really only cared about the check?

In March 2008, two months after her first visit to the Stone Church, Candice submitted herself for baptism. The timing felt like another sign. The pastor was pushing his congregation toward a missionary role on the Eastside, where she was already teaching. As Matt Carter went into contract on the land for his new church, nearly two dozen of his followers moved into the neighborhood. Candice told a church official that teachers could use help in their classrooms, and soon hundreds of volunteers showed up at Reagan to tutor, demonstrate résumé-writing skills, and donate classroom supplies. Some of the teachers resisted, but the new principal, Anabel Garza, hired a volunteer coordinator to organize all the help.

Still, Candice stayed in Bouldin. Teaching at Reagan suited her new ideas about serving God, as long as she could cross the highway before dark. There weren't any trendy coffee shops in St. John's. And maybe she was overthinking this, but wasn't it pretty clichéd to be the girl who finds Jesus and breaks up with her boyfriend? Instead she slept on the floor, waking up in the middle of the night to listen as he talked in his sleep. She thought maybe she could change him, even though she knew there was a term for that: missionary dating. The harder she fought, the more she became convinced that God wanted her whole life.

In the fall of 2008, not long after her twenty-sixth birthday, Candice drove around St. John's with her roommate, Jenny. An elder from the church had told them members lived on every street but Carver Avenue. When they saw the For Rent sign on a house built in the speculative frenzy of the mid-2000s, Candice and Jenny pulled into the driveway and prayed over a passage from Isaiah:

> If you do away with the yoke of oppression, with the pointing
> finger and malicious talk, and if you spend yourselves in behalf
> of the hungry and satisfy the needs of the oppressed, then your
> light will rise in the darkness, and your night will become like

the noonday. The Lord will guide you always; he will satisfy your needs in a sun-scorched land and will strengthen your frame. You will be like a well-watered garden, like a spring whose waters never fail. Your people will rebuild the ancient ruins and will raise up the age-old foundations; you will be called Repairer of Broken Walls, Restorer of Streets with Dwellings.

L iving a few blocks from the school, Candice started spending more and more time with her students. She gave them all color-coded assignments tailored to their shortcomings on the standardized test objectives, but some came to depend on her in other ways. They bummed a lot of rides, mostly to basketball games but sometimes to school or even the doctor's office.

In May 2009, Candice finished her third year at Reagan, the point when 25 percent of American teachers quit. State officials issued preliminary standardized testing data indicating that Pearce Middle School, where the basketball team had come together, where little brothers and sisters still looked up to Reagan, would probably be closed. Reagan would remain under threat of closure, on the list of academically unacceptable schools, for another year. But Candice's identity was getting caught up in the school. She signed a new three-year contract.

A week later, Candice finally boarded a plane to Africa, but not with the Peace Corps. She raised twenty-seven hundred dollars to join a Mannah Worldwide mission, the kind often derided as poverty tourism. Connecting in London, she watched her roommate nod off to sleep, put a Francis Chan sermon on her iPod, "What God Can Do Through Ordinary People," and started scribbling in her diary.

Hopeless situations throughout the Bible. Lazarus sick—waited—dead for days—Glory to Him. It's not over; let me show you My Power. . . . Do we worry about the things that will matter in the end? God is still on his throne. Hopeless out of our vocabulary.

She underlined that word, "hopeless." She wrote of the joy Jesus brought to her life, thanks and praises, but also desperate pleas.

Day One, and all I want is you—Rock my world—whatever to sanctify me, Lord . . . Only you are worthy of worship, Lord. We worship other things, Lord, why? Why do we fall from your glory and your joy? O praise Him, He is Holy . . . Lord, let us be broken for those who don't know you—Lord they need you—more than water . . . Lord we know the darkness exists. Lord but you are conqueror of all darkness. Lord, you can break us. Break me. I love you Lord and I lift my voice—wish I could on this plane. . . . Let us be your light. I remember singing this @ camp, before you orchestrated so much in the school I teach in.

In the notorious Kenyan slum of Kibera, Candice took dutiful notes on the prevalence of disease, but visiting a school prompted her to pull out her video camera. That night she filled page after page in her diary:

6-11: They said, "What is the answer to this question, #45," to test me. They knew the flow of blood in the heart better than my kids and some teachers, including myself, on the spot. They were brilliant, loving. They shared. I asked them: Do you share? Stupid question. They looked @ me like I was crazy. "Yes?!"

When I walked in the room, they were all using one book + one pen—crowded around like they would give their left arm to see the page—but helping each other—not copying—oh my! This was where I wanted to teach—Here! This place was a beautiful experience—It was amazing. This school—the kids were so attracted to any information I could give them. Paper was used more than once.

Their questions—What did kids in America pay to go to H.S.? Did they have to buy their utensils? What did my rent cost? How much American $ was their tuition? Would I come back?

How, Jesus, will I survive seeing this? I need you. Show me your control over their lives—please give me peace. I can't go back without your peace. . . . Please wipe away their tears . . . Jesus, I am torn apart. I am trying to muffle my cries of pain.

After three days, the group moved on to Tanzania.

Lord, take the selfish, inconsiderateness away. Please purify my heart, mind, soul . . . Show me how to love, like you love.

Candice visited mud houses. She ate freshly slain goat. She let her mind wander back to Texas.

Lord, let me not be angry at my children, for they know not what they are doing. Lord, let me take back your truths—Lord, you will show them truth and where their lives should Δ . . . You Lord, not me. Only You.

Again and again she watched the video images from Kibera, imagining how her own students would react.

They have broken families, disease, lose family yearly, live in mud houses, get sick and have no way to get medical care, have little chance of a future—Yet give it all @ school—Rarely miss.

After a month in Africa, Candice returned to her rental house on the Eastside, halfway between the church construction site and Reagan High, ready to abandon—what did the preacher call it?—her "middle-class sensibilities."

We live in isolation—they open up their houses—make you feel at home—not just welcome—Community?

Now the crowd fell silent. The kids were waiting for SaulPaul, a Christian rapper who promoted his hip-hop act as "Entertainment, Inspiration, Education," but Jesse Martinez Jr. stood up first.

"Most of you know me, my name is Jesse. Last year I was supposed to graduate. I was doing my own thing, smoking weed. I ain't gonna lie to you. I got sent to ALC."

Jesse didn't call Candice out by name. Everybody knew who'd written him up and gotten him expelled to the Alternative Learning Center.

"Over the summer, I made a promise to myself, to God, my parents. I'm gonna finish what I started. I'm done with the games I played last year. I just want to start over. Be a brand-new person."

The kids gave him a round of applause, then turned to watch SaulPaul. Music was a powerful force at Reagan, more than sports and religion combined. The Public Offenders, led by Chris Ockletree, who performed under the name Gator, sold hundreds of albums around the Two-Three. People paid attention to Ockletree because he could emcee. When he was elected student body president a few years back, he put butcher paper up on the walls and got kids to write about race relations instead of going straight to the fists (or worse). More recently, the new school music director was remaking the marching band as the Soul Raiders, a show band-style act capable of Strauss in competition but more likely to play "All I Do Is Win" at halftime. Membership outnumbered the football team by a wide margin (even Jesse joined, on cymbals).

Perched on the back of a chair, SaulPaul called for applause, first for the current senior class of '10, then the classes of '11, '12, and '13. Nobody cheered for the freshmen.

"N-O-W: What's that spell?"

The kids just laughed.

"Let's do that again," he said, "like a TAKS retest."

"Now!"

SaulPaul spoke of the perils of hustling, street life, the game, prison.

"You was born on purpose, with a purpose," he said, warming up to a call and response.

"If your mind right, then you shine right."

"Now!"

"Tight right."

"Now!"

"You bright right."

"Now!"

"Now!"

"Now!"

"Now!"

He urged everybody to read the Bible carefully, drawing a comparison to faking your schoolwork.

"It's like with the TAAS test," he said, "you be pretending to be studying, reading, and then you can't do it."

The kids caught his mistake immediately: TAAS was the old standardized test, replaced by TAKS.

"They stopped the TAAS when I was in second grade," somebody yelled.

SaulPaul laughed it off: Only the name had changed. He sang:

To God be the honor
To God be the praise
To God be the glory
For all of my days

A chorus of voices joined him, with harmonies emerging and a soprano adding gospel interludes, voices hesitant and sure, husky and lilting, rising together into a wordless moan like a Wurlitzer over a four-chord vamp with the Christmas lights twinkling and the dogs barking down the block and the metronomic punctuation of the neighbors' motion detector, then turning to a chant:

We gonna praise
We gonna praise
We gonna praise
We gonna praise

Eight

Back when Tom Sawyer "did play hooky, and he had a very good time," Aunt Polly suspected him of swimming away a school day, so over supper she asked "questions that were full of guile, and very deep—for she wanted to trap him into damaging revealments."

Somewhere in America, probably, teenagers were sneaking away from a high school campus in the first weeks of September 2009 to savor the last wonders of childhood. Maybe they even went for a swim.

But in East Austin, Anabel Garza did not stand to profit by asking a lot of guileful questions. There were procedures. Like everything else in the reform era, the playing of hooky received scrutiny in numerical terms. The key figure, the completion rate, measured the percentage of each group of ninth graders on track to graduate in the allotted four years. To qualify as academically acceptable, a school had to show a 75 percent completion rate among all students, as well as among African American, Hispanic, white, and economically disadvantaged students.

For schools labeled academically unacceptable, the district had a protocol in place. Flush with grants from the Dell and Gates foundations, its consultants had designed step-by-step countertruancy procedures and personnel assignments, from guidance counseling through court action.

At Reagan High, rounding up dropouts to achieve the required improvement toward the completion rate was becoming a frantic annual ritual, with a deadline of September 25. Anabel delegated much of the responsibility to Eric Sanchez, a former medical supplies salesman whose qualifications included inner-city volunteerism, fluency in Spanish, and a rugby-toned physique. His formal title, dropout intervention specialist, merely hinted at the demeanor he affected on assignment, where he signed off e-mails with a quotation from Victorian poetry:

I am the Master of my Fate

I am the Captain of my Soul

By the letter of the district's guidelines, Sanchez was supposed to investigate students incurring multiple absences, then to "focus on 12th graders who haven't pass [sic] the TAKS test and work on getting them to return to their school." For investigative purposes, the district had suggested "Additional resources to explore: Juvenile Justice Center, Child Protective Services, Summer School graduation list, Telephone Book, Internet sites, Myspace.com, Dept. of Human Services, Local churches."

On September 3, Anabel summoned Sanchez to plot strategy. The completion rate stood at 70.6 percent, measured by the class of

2008, the year before Anabel arrived. Stalking Highland Mall on weekends, Sanchez had been bringing in dropouts, including the kids whose attire had shocked the superintendent.

But his success was causing more serious problems too. If the kids stayed, they were bound to depress scores on the standardized tests. More immediately, Anabel had to figure out what to do with those who had earned all their credits but failed the standardized tests. Qualification for a diploma required a score of 2,100 or higher on the TAKS, so no matter what their report cards said, those kids counted as dropouts. Over time, making classes more rigorous might close that gap. But technically, to make the numbers for Reagan, Anabel just needed a place to put those kids.

"They just have to be here for one day, but me personally, I have a problem with bringing them in for one day and saying, 'Thank you, good-bye,'" Anabel said. She'd heard about a school in Houston that would award diplomas for $250, "no questions asked." It was only two and a half hours away by car; maybe they could drive the kids who'd passed all their classes out there. TAKS or no TAKS, the diplomas might qualify the kids as graduates for the purposes of their job and community college applications (and as non-dropouts for the purposes of Reagan's completion rate). Sanchez asked for details. Anabel wasn't sure; she'd heard about it from some kids.

"If you were a student and you could just go to the Baptist school and pay and get on with it, what would you do?" she asked. But aside from the ethics of that proposition, Anabel knew the $250 would be a deal breaker. Talk turned instead to assigning the TAKS-deficient kids a special code to attend all-day test prep sessions in the library. Was that against the rules? "Maybe the less questions we ask, the better," she said.

For now, the completion rate deadline was first priority. Anabel and Sanchez talked about posting a list of names at Highland Mall or the La Michoacana Meat Market on Cameron Road. With year-book photos? What about a reward? Cafeteria ice cream? What if they could fix the autodialer to call parents every time an unexcused absence turned up? Would that even help? Would anyone answer? Was anybody free to organize the list of missing students? How about the guidance counselors? The XY Zone guy? Ms. Turner, the in-school suspension lady? She was grumpy, but she knew the neighborhoods . . . All told, 147 kids counted as dropouts, including 27 last-chance students who should have graduated with the class of 2009, crucial to the state's evaluation system.

"We need to move," Anabel said. "If we don't move, we won't make the deadline."

The summer's heat was starting to lift. A cool gray haze settled over the courtyard. A janitor's cart clattered, a cop's walkie-talkie droned, a shuffling straggler pulled on a shirt deemed more appropriate for school than the one she'd arrived in. Military recruiters roamed the halls, looking to staff two foreign wars. Domestic job prospects were hard to come by, parents were out of work, and the same forces depressing the completion rate worked to the advantage of the U.S. Army.

Along the perimeter, teachers herded kids into Advocacy Class, the weekly sessions intended to monitor progress on TAKS objectives. The school librarian, Jordan Grams, finished his TAKS interrogation and then offered books, but the kids with night jobs wanted to catch up on sleep. Grams understood. He'd worked nights too, supplementing his paycheck with the 11 p.m. to 7 a.m. shift at a diner. For a table near the bathroom, the prostitutes would leave a twenty-dollar tip on toast and coffee. "They had scars and every-thing," he told no one in particular as the kids drifted off.

Over in the science wing, Candice Kaiser was handing out work-sheets. The knowledge she had been hired to convey, over the course of nine months, was supposed to border on the profound. "An un-derstanding of basic chemistry concepts," the state teaching manual said, "helps students understand their world and enhances their lives."

Candice, dressed in a blue polo (her wardrobe contained little besides the school colors), watched Cornelius Cammock stroll back to the lab, where she allowed him the privilege of sitting away from the class, one of countless tiny pieces of leverage she used to keep order. The other kids bent over their desks, clutching pencils marked with star stickers to identify them as Candice's property. The room fell quiet. The kids converted years to seconds, seconds to days, days to seconds, and years to days. Corn finished the exercise, flipped over his paper, and opened his phone. A girl with heart-shaped ear-rings opened a novel called *His Woman, His Wife, His Widow.*

Next Candice passed around a graduated cylinder filled with oil and water, soap and glue. She asked what was going on inside, then interrupted herself: "I can't let you sit back there if you're going to play on your phone," she told Corn. "You're back there be-cause I trust you."

Candice collected the various explanations for the behavior of the liquids in the cylinder: "They're separating because they have different reactions" . . . "Glue is the heaviest, oil is the lightest" . . . "The molecules are different" . . . "Density" . . . "Glue is the most dense" . . . "The molecules are negative of each other."

She called for a show of hands in favor of each response. "Den-sity" won the most support. Consensus soon rallied around density.

Density, the kids agreed, was what was going on in the cylinder. Did that mean they understood the word? The concept? The objective? Candice could not be sure.

On to mass, weight, and volume. Candice handed one girl a brick wrapped in plumber's tape, asking for a description. The girl offered: "Heavy."

"Rico, heads up," Candice called, tossing an identical-looking block across the room to a kid in a Junior ROTC uniform. Rico flinched and put up his hands. A collective gasp sounded. The block bounced harmlessly off Rico's palms, Styrofoam in disguise.

"Damn," one boy said. "I thought she was going to break his head."

Same volume, different weight. Lesson learned, or at least demonstrated. Candice moved on.

"Buzzword, buzzword," she called. "Density."

She put the words on a projector screen: Mass. Volume.

"Y'all remember these words on the TAKS test."

"Miss, can you tell me what matter is again?" Christian asked.

She did, and then she explained density again, this time with a demonstration of water displacement and a call-and-response exercise.

"You know the *Titanic?*" she asked. "Not the Leonardo Di-Caprio movie, but the ship?"

Somebody said it sank. Nobody knew why. Candice said why: "Density." On the projector screen, she displayed a list of liquids and solids, asking which ones would float on water.

"The TAKS test will give you this kind of question," she said.

From gold, copper, aluminum, oak, balsa, mercury, oil, and antifreeze, the students made their selections. Most chose correctly. When Candice asked why, one girl called out: "Because I've seen wood float on water."

Okay. Candice looked around for something more tangible than a buzzword. She found bling.

"How many of y'all have gold? How many of y'all brought gold today, on your bodies? The way to tell if it's fake or real is by the density."

She gave the formula, she demonstrated.

"Please calculate the density. You have twenty seconds. Go."

A girl called out her answer, forgetting a conversion step.

"Y'all are getting ahead of yourselves," Candice said. "That's what happens on the TAKS test."

Demonstrating the technique, she went on: "I see y'all do that, you say, 'I'm just going to multiply. And do they have those kinds of questions on the test? And do they put that on there? They do, for the kids who say, 'I'm just going to multiply.' They do and you get it wrong."

Candice took a deep breath. She couldn't throw fake bricks at their heads in the exam room. Before she could say much else, the loudspeaker sputtered alive with the principal's voice asking teachers to prevent underclassmen from leaving for lunch. Candice's accomplishments of the hour felt less than profound, but then, somebody would have to brace the TAKS average against the downward tug of the completion rate campaign. She dismissed her class: "Bye-bye, love y'all, have a great weekend."

In place of questions full of guile, Eric Sanchez had Section 25.094C of the Texas Education Code, establishing failure to attend school as a class C misdemeanor punishable by a five-hundred-dollar fine. After documenting ten unexcused absences, he could file a complaint at the courthouse.

On September 15, ten days before the deadline to count heads for the completion rate, Sanchez sat in his office in the shop build-ing, down a hallway ornamented with Columbia blue lockers, a portrait of President Obama, and a tackboard celebrating the achievements of Mr. Ramos's Auto Collision Repair and Refinish-ing Tech class.

Sanchez wore a guayabera and a thick mustache, with his salt-and-pepper hair trimmed into a wave. He looked like he'd stepped out of a buddy cop movie, from the back half of the ampersand. Framed by rugby photos and the trifold flag from his father's mili-tary funeral, he gazed across the desk at a girl named Samantha, who was talking about bullies. Her mother sat by her side. Her brother sat outside the door, seething, watching a small gecko cross the floor. Samantha said she was afraid to reenroll at Reagan; her tormentors remained. Sanchez spoke of tempers, jail, school, and the problem of working for minimum wage the rest of your life.

"You need to listen," Samantha's mother said. Out in the hall the boy's temper boiled over. Exit the lizard, three quick stomps, guts under Nikes. Sanchez didn't look up.

"I understand," he told Samantha. "People used to pick on me too. If you let them get the better of you, they'll just keep doing it. You need to turn away."

He listened some more, then offered to call about a slot at a dif-ferent school.

"To avoid filing on her," he said, "I have to have her registered by this weekend."

The school improvement facilitator, newly hired from a middle school, started wiping up lizard remains with a paper towel.

"I didn't want to kill it," the boy said. "But it was just sitting there on the floor like it wanted to be dead."

Samantha left without making any commitments.

"Okay, let me know," Sanchez called. He wasn't far behind her.

In the parking lot he started his Land Rover, opened the sunroof, and put the stereo on loud. Since the meeting with Anabel twelve days ago, nine more kids had been added to the list of the missing in the most pressing cohort, students who should have graduated with the class of 2009. Of those thirty-six, he'd tracked down sixteen. Of the sixteen, he'd reenrolled three. By September 25, he needed to enroll twenty-five, bringing the roster of the unaccounted-for down to eleven. He turned past a check-cashing place and the Discoteca Universal onto St. John's, driving past houses of crumbling wood, shotgun shacks, yards of dirt, and upturned refrigerators. A sign depicting a pit bull said: "I can make it to the fence in 2.8 seconds—can you?"

Sanchez parked and made his way past discarded cans of Budweiser. Before he could knock, the door swung open. A man in a black T-shirt stood blinking into the sun. Sanchez said he was looking for a girl called Arecel. The man sat on the porch by a plastic swing. A boy of perhaps five curled up beside him. Sanchez asked again.

"¿Por qué no es Arecel en la escuela?"

The little boy cuddled the man's arm. The man professed to know no one named Arecel. His older teenage son skips class now and again, the man said, but not today. Sanchez handed him a card. Maybe this was a misunderstanding. A data entry problem. Maybe so.

Driving back to the school, Sanchez passed two kids skipping class, hanging out on the outskirts of the campus. They didn't count as dropouts yet, and it was too soon for a court complaint. He didn't stop.

His office computer confirmed it: The man's son had been counted present at attendance, and the man had no daughter named Arecel. Arecel was his wife's name. His daughter was Bianca. Sanchez got the man on the phone. Oh yes, he was told. Bianca. Bianca was at work. Sanchez had heard this before: The boy needed an education, the family needed money, and so the daughter was at work. In Spanish, Sanchez said: "Reagan has a program where she can work part of the day and go to school the rest of the time." If the man would bring Bianca in to talk, Sanchez promised, he wouldn't file on her in court. The man wouldn't say where Bianca was working.

Back in his Land Rover, Sanchez drove south past the Casa Grande Meat Market into Windsor Park, along the outskirts of the old Mueller Airport. Developers with considerable tax incentives had refashioned the site into a "mixed-use urban village," advertising access to McCallum High School on the west side. District maps placed much of the Mueller development in the feeder pattern of Reagan High, but the policy granting automatic transfers out of academically unacceptable schools made their advertisements true enough.

Sanchez had no business at Mueller. Instead he parked at the Berkman Court Apartments, a fortlike structure with a banner that said Cable Gratis. He climbed the stairs, knocked on a door, knocked again, and left a business card behind.

Back up north, past the school, Sanchez turned at Rundberg Lane, where the police were working to install the city's first video-surveillance system. He drove past a taquería, a fire station, and a sign offering goats for sale. He parked at the rental office of a gated apartment complex.

"I'm from Reagan High School, and I'm looking for a kid called Daniel Vasquez."

"He's a kid?" the receptionist asked.

"Yep."

"How old is this kid?"

"Eighteen."

The receptionist scanned a computer screen. Sanchez looked out the office window. They had a pool out there.

"This is a nice apartment complex you've got here."

The receptionist didn't look up. If the kid wasn't on the lease, she said, he wouldn't be in the database. Did Sanchez want to take it up with the manager? Yes, if she didn't mind. Sometime later, the manager appeared.

"I'm from Reagan High School, and I'm trying to track down a kid who lives here so I don't have to take him to court," Sanchez said again. "If I could just get a name of a parent I could follow up with—"

The manager shook his head.

"The only thing about that, sir, is that because of the privacy act, we really can't give out any information."

Sanchez handed the manager his card and turned to leave. There wasn't anybody out swimming in the pool.

Nine

There weren't any brown faces on the recruiting flyers. Long before the start of the school year there had been talk about making the parent-teacher-student association more inclusive, but nobody ever changed the flyers, so the flyers still showed only black kids smiling over textbooks, only black parents volunteering, only black families doing all the little things that make a neighborhood school come together. Jacqueline Chatham, president of the PTSA, brought a fistful of the flyers to Back to School Night, the orientation dinner that doubled as a sort of annual trade show for the various parties out to help solve and/or profit from the troubles at Reagan. She offered the flyers around evenly, but it turned out there were few parents around to be recruited anyway, and hardly any Latino ones. At the front of the cafeteria, Wilton Harris had his XY Zone boys on hand to open the door for women. They weren't getting much practice.

"It just goes to show you," Harris was saying. "If you said, 'We're closing the school down tomorrow,' you'd pack this place. But Back to School Night?"

He shrugged.

"It just goes to show you the disconnect."

Deborah Warren, sitting beside him at the PTSA table, thumbed a stack of *College-Bound African American Student Guides*.

"I'm here," she said.

So a crowd peopled mostly with teachers watched as Anabel Garza, decked out in white, took the microphone in front of a banner that said Celebrate—We're On Our Way.

To the accompaniment of PowerPoint slides, Anabel gave a numerical accounting of her first year. She started to explain the system of cells used to determine the school's fate but soon cut herself off with, "We have a lot of work to do."

Forget the standardized tests: The basics of instruction were bewildering enough. Years of exodus by the most promising students had overlapped years of efforts to jump-start test scores, leaving behind programs layered on top of programs. A few years back, a "High School Redesign Team" financed by the Gates and Dell foundations had, in the words of one consultant's résumé, "conducted extensive market research and implemented identifiable brands for Small Learning Communities to bolster student ownership at Reagan High School." What that meant seemed to be grouping dance, theater, yearbook, and all the other creative stuff into a unit called AOL, the Art of Learning Community; grouping most shop classes into LEAD, or Leadership in Engineering, Architecture, and Design; and grouping other classes into MASH, or Medical Arts, Sciences, and Health. Without much subtlety, Anabel had been adding groups of her own to address the more immediate concerns of her split constituency. MAC, the Multilingual Academy of Culture, handled students who were actually just unilingual, only in the wrong language for the standardized tests. And AHA, the Audacity of Hope Academy, handled students who were "struggling."

From the stage, Anabel called out all those acronyms, along with room assignments. The teachers and parents cleared out, leaving behind a crowd of vendors. The credit union had a booth, Goodwill had a booth, and the air force had a booth, but nobody had turned out in greater numbers than the private tutoring companies, which could bill the federal government for every student they signed up at an academically unacceptable school. To companies providing "supplemental educational services," in the government's rendering, troubled schools were big business. Back in 2002, when the No Child Left Behind Act became law, a fast-growing company called Edison Schools announced its move into the tutoring market, with designs on $22 billion in government appropriations. Since then, the market had grown beyond even Edison's wildest ambitions. Every year, reformers demanded more extensive standardized testing. Every year, lawmakers ratcheted up the stakes. And every year, the authorities added more schools to their lists of the academically unacceptable, expanding the pool of new customers for supplemental educational services.

Around the Reagan cafeteria on Back to School Night, representatives from Elite Academics stared down reps from One on One Learning, 1to1 Tutor, Group Experience, CZ Education, PE&C, The Comedi Tutoring Company, Applied Scholastics (with learning materials based on the works of L. Ron Hubbard), Babbage Net School, Wonder-Space Mobile, Alpha Academics, and College Nannies & Tutors, whose sign bluntly advertised, "Beat the TAKS!"

Every few minutes more of them arrived, looking for parents and spotting the competition instead. A woman from Click2Tutor muttered, "The principal or somebody needs to explain how they can take advantage of this. It's for their benefit."

At last, as time ran out on Back to School Night, Jesse Martinez Jr. sauntered up to the first booth he found. He was serious about the vow he'd made in Candice Kaiser's backyard. It was all the tutoring company people could do to keep themselves from jumping him.

Jesse didn't need help with language, at least not in the way the immigrant kids did. He didn't hang with that crowd. English wasn't his second language. He'd grown up on the Eastside, following his black friends from middle school to Reagan. He was tight with DeVonte Sanders, a junior cornerback on the football team. They were both into hip-hop dance and poetry, which was one big reason Jesse was back in school, playing cymbals in the Soul Raider band and trying one last time to make sense of the standardized math tests. The kind of language help he needed had more to do with deciphering the test questions. For example, one question from the Exit Level TAKS exam administered in April 2009 asked:

Mr. Ugalde has an 80-acre farm.

- 38 acres are used for planting corn
- 18 acres are used for planting soybeans
- 10 acres are used for planting wheat

The remaining acres are used for planting oats. Which of the following graphs best represents these data?

Plenty of TAKS questions used imagery more familiar to city kids, like cell phone bills, fast-food joints, bus schedules, part-time jobs, and electronics stores. But after years of drilling, Jesse still had trouble with questions like this:

Carl was asked to solve the problem shown in the box below:

> A certain type of cube has 2-inch edges. What is the maximum number of cubes that can be put into a box that measures 2.7 feet by 3.2 feet by 4.1 feet?

Which of the following could Carl do to solve the problem correctly?

    F. Add the dimensions given in feet
    G. Multiply each dimension given in feet by 2 inches
    H. Convert 2 inches into 24 feet
    J. Convert the dimensions of the box from feet to inches

What? Which box? The box the question is in, or the one the cubes are supposed to go into? And converting two inches into twenty-four feet doesn't even make sense—is that a trick answer? Jesse took another flyer and kept walking. "There's so many words on there," he said, "I'd probably be just, like, 'Whoa, okay.'"

B ack to School Night wasn't a total bust. When the first PTSA meeting convened on a Tuesday evening later in September, two Latino families showed up with young children in tow. Anabel, ever the optimist, set up five long rows of blue plastic chairs across the cafeteria. A color guard from the JROTC held the American flag straight up and the Lone Star one dipped as the speakers played the same tinny canned overture the kids heard every morning.

Anabel stood across from the flag bearer, hand over her heart, staring deeply into his eyes or possibly just trying not to faint. Her blood pressure hadn't dropped to a reasonable level in three days, despite prescription drugs. She was under doctor's orders to turn herself in at the hospital if things didn't improve by the weekend.

For now, she'd assigned herself the task of translating all of the black PTSA officers' remarks into Spanish. When "The Star-Spangled Banner" finished playing, she walked to the side of the stage, in front of a mural depicting her students' artistic rendering of city history: a burning cross, a broken chain, and a thick barrier marked "IH-35 East/West." She translated as Joe Warren, treasurer, reported a bank balance of $6,455. She translated as Deborah Warren reported an increase in membership, to ninety-seven from twenty-nine since the big march on the state Capitol last year. She translated as Deborah announced, "Our goal is 100 percent membership; I'll repeat that, 100 percent," turning to the two Latino families to add, "I see some new members here, and I thank you." She translated as Allen Weeks, the community organizer, talked about starting a social services center. She translated the results from the fund-raiser, even when it became apparent her translation probably wasn't all that necessary.

"¿Cómo se dice 'golf'?" she asked at one point.

"Golf," one of the Latino dads called back.

When it was her turn to address the meeting, Anabel rambled a bit about breaking up lunch periods, leaving less time for the kids to get into fights. Glancing at the clock, she tried again to explain all the academic programs, all the standardized test measurement systems, and some of her own ideas about love and expectations, but she'd promised to wrap up the meeting by seven.

"It's very, very complex," she said, "but we only have this one year, so time is pressing."

Pointing out the free dinner, she ceded the stage to a guest speaker, Kenneth D. Thompson, a past president of the school board up in Pflugerville, whom she did not introduce as a sterling example of black flight to the prosperous exurbs. Thompson related memories of his own Eastside childhood and told of his son's job in the Obama administration, all achieved in a generation.

"I think it's a shame that they're talking about closing Reagan, which was one of the most powerful high schools in all of Texas," he said. "Never surrender, and always keep the faith. . . . Don't let anyone tell you that good things don't come from East Austin. As parents, don't let anyone, any institution, take your dreams away from you, and don't let them take them away from your kids."

Anabel translated that into Spanish too, just in case a pep talk was what either of the Latino families in attendance needed, then opened the buffet.

B ianca was working, just like her father had said. Eric Sanchez found her a few days before the deadline for reporting dropout statistics. Her job title was food production specialist, her employer was the Austin Independent School District, and her workplace was the cafeteria over at LBJ High School.

"Here we are looking for dropouts," Sanchez said, "and they're working for us."

Though she was already eighteen, Bianca agreed to reenroll at Reagan as a sophomore. Half the day she went to class, the other half she scooped out taco pies to the kids at LBJ.

On his rounds, Sanchez had learned to lead with a promise: *Su hija todavía puede ganar dinero.* Your daughter can still bring home her paycheck. Sometimes it was the only useful card he had to play, better even than threatening to file charges in court. "It really bugs me," he said. "As Hispanics, we're becoming a majority now, and we're not doing what we need to do, taking advantage of the opportunity to get an education." But he'd studied enough psychology in college to remember Maslow's hierarchy, in which physiological needs come first: food, water, air, and sleep. Until those are fulfilled, you can't move on to the next level, safety and security. Next come social needs like love and affection, then self-esteem, and eventually personal growth, if you have the time. Judging by the tall fences and menacing dogs of St. John's, Sanchez judged most of the parents he encountered to be hovering somewhere around level two. He looked at the kids hanging out on campus long past dark through the same framework. Playing Ping-Pong in the cafeteria might be safer than going home, and when the PTSA is serving pizza you've at least got level one under control. "Give them food and shelter and security and they'll flourish," Sanchez said, "because everything else is built on that."

But food, shelter, and security weren't part of his portfolio. His boss, Anabel, was mounting a big attendance campaign. She wanted him to get more aggressive. As she saw it, kids like Bianca weren't just passing up an educational opportunity. In the reform era, they could bring down the whole school. "We need to have people on Facebook and Myspace," Anabel said. "We can't do that at school because we're blocked. We need to be in the malls. We need to greet people in the morning and say, 'Have you seen these kids?' You either go that route, or at the end of the year, those will be the kids that sink you, and game over."

So Anabel told Sanchez to file charges against kids after five absences. The law didn't require filing until ten days, but it didn't say she couldn't either. She found another loophole too: Section 25.085(e) of the state Education Code said she could "revoke for the remainder of the school year the enrollment of a person who has more than five absences in a semester that are not excused."

It also didn't say she couldn't make their parents take a training class to reenroll. "In a lot of single-parent homes in the Hispanic community—not all—as soon as the child hits eye level with the mom, he's the boss," Anabel said. She'd seen it under her own roof. When Trey was suspended from school some years back, she made him serve the punishment at the Alternative Learning Center instead of at home, partly to scare him straight in the company of real delinquents and partly just to send a message: *You will be in school, mijo, no matter what.*

Aside from getting the parents' attention, dropping those kids wouldn't hurt the school's numbers either. If they didn't reenroll, they'd vanish from the denominator in Reagan's completion rate, not to mention the TAKS average. That was the plan, at least. "I'm going to run it till somebody stops me and calls me on it," Anabel said, "and then I'll say, 'What are we doing instead?'"

Of the 232 kids who should have graduated the previous spring, Sanchez resorted to filing charges against 76. He eventually dismissed the cases against about half a dozen who reenrolled. By Thursday, September 24, the day before the deadline, he figured he could account for 74.3 percent of the cohort to the standards of the state Education Agency, meaning that all those kids certifiably came back to the school, moved to another school, got expelled, graduated, earned a GED, or died. The standard for an academically acceptable school was 75 percent, and the agency only rounded up by a decimal point, but Sanchez's numbers were in the range to meet the year-to-year required improvement, earning Reagan a reprieve. As it turned out, he'd underestimated his work. The final tally came to 177 "completers" and 53 dropouts, good enough for a completion rate of 76.3 percent. Eric Sanchez did his part. He brought in the kids.

. . .

Now came the hard numbers, the knowledge and skills. Candice Kaiser spent the last weekend of September at a coffee shop, bent over her laptop. Across a spreadsheet, she plotted each mistake made by each of her eighty students on the TAKS practice exams. The exit level retest was coming up in less than a month, the crucible for seniors, second-year seniors, and the "dropouts" who'd passed all their classes, failed to meet standard on a TAKS objective, and wandered off into the world diploma-less. Only twenty-one of the seventy-eight kids in Candice's classroom had arrived with scores on track to pass the exit-level TAKS, and this was *honors* chemistry. Based on the data, Candice assigned each student a set number of hours to marinate in specific TAKS objectives with tutors drawn largely from the ranks of the Stone Church congregation. Her color-coded spreadsheet looked like a poorly drawn subway map crossed with an NFL playbook, but in the reform era it amounted to lesson planning (though she still had to make traditional lesson plans too).

There's no other way to describe what she intended to do: teaching to the test, on an elaborate scale. The phrase had become shorthand for everything wrong with American education. Decades ago, holdouts against the early reform movement called the practice one of the worst pitfalls of standardized testing. "Flaws in the current system," an official of the New York state teachers' union declared in 1991, "go from the extreme of testing for things students have not been taught to the other extreme of teaching to the test." More recently, a sense of realpolitik had crept into the debate. Prominent education researchers, despairing of any chance to turn back the tide of the reform movement, had started to draw distinctions between drilling specific test questions obtained in advance (cheating, in other words) and narrowly coaching students on the test material (the "Beat the TAKS!" mentality). At Reagan, Candice's boss was encouraging teachers to play the numbers game in the short term. "Years back, they aligned what kids should know to the test," Anabel said. "So if you're teaching to the test, that's not a bad thing. It's the test we have to take. How are you going to pass the driving test if you've been taking a cooking class?"

On Monday morning, Candice waited through announcements concerning Homecoming royalty and a school play. Last year, the theater director had to borrow students from LBJ and McCallum high schools to get a production of *Dreamgirls* onstage. But the sisters-doing-it-together story line had rekindled some interest in drama club, drawing people to the school, so Anabel was announcing all kinds of new clubs. She had clubs for community activism, environmentalism, dance, martial arts, filmmaking, spoken-word poetry, music production (Beatlab), a literary magazine, Raiders' Project Runway ("get the instruction you need to turn your fashion visions into real-life threads"), model rocket building, and even croquet. The clubs wouldn't all take off, but it meant something just to announce them. In the long run, maybe a good reason to come to school could replace criminal charges for not coming.

Of course, none of those pursuits would count before the judgment of the state education agency, so when the announcements ended, the kids in Candice's chemistry class were looking at a color-coded spreadsheet.

"Do y'all know how many questions are on the TAKS test?" Candice asked. She answered her own question (fifty-five), letting the kids get a look at their scores up on the projector screen, organized by student ID number. "I'm about to give you a file folder with your data laid out," she said. "In your face, basically."

The kids cracked open their tutoring orders, looking a little like undergrown spies contemplating a next mission.

"Do I want you guys to study objective one if you got a ninety-eight in objective one?" Candice asked.

Objective one was: the nature of science. In the state blueprints for the exit-level TAKS exam, seventeen of the fifty-five questions generated each year would concern objective one. State teaching guidelines dictated the proper way to prepare for objective one: "The student, for at least 40 percent of instructional time, conducts field and laboratory investigations using safe, environmentally appropriate, and ethical practices."

Scanning their color-coded tutoring assignments, Candice's students called back in a hesitant chorus: "No?"

"No," Candice said. "Because that's ridiculous."

She waited for that to sink in.

"I will ask a lot of you, because I want one hundred percent passing this year. You know how they say in the military, we leave no one behind? Wouldn't that be great, if we could show the district and the people in suits that we can do it, that we can teach and you can learn? Because the problem isn't me, and it isn't you. And if we did that, one hundred percent passing rate, what would that mean?"

"Stay open," somebody called.

"Stay open," two more kids repeated.

"I don't know if it will mean the school will stay open or not, because they look at a lot of other things. But it will mean that you will graduate."

Candice passed around a quiz designed to mimic a section of the TAKS. Missing one question, she said, would spell failure. The kids got to work. Candice stalked the room with her grading pen. The timer chirped.

"All right," Candice called. "The point is not to get you, but sometimes that's how I feel the TAKS test is set up. So I'm sorry if you feel that way. I'm just trying to get you ready."

The education reform movement's good intentions had been memorialized in the lofty language of the state teaching guidelines: "It is essential for teachers to expose students to science content in a variety of ways. Teachers must also help students make connections among the science disciplines by showing the natural integrations among the life, earth, and physical sciences. An example of this might be when students study different soil types (earth science) and learn how nutrients (chemistry) in the soil affect the types of plants (biology) that grow there."

From her position at the front of Science Room 133, Candice could see the sense in that proposition. Wood floating on water made sense to her students. Gold jewelry made sense. A fake Styrofoam brick made sense. Science, in other words, made sense, and yet many of the perfectly good minds arrayed before her had never once met standard in their entire academic careers.

Candice projected the quiz up on the screen. Which was more dense, she asked, a can of Coke or a can of Diet Coke? A debate ensued.

"It may be true," Candice said, shouting over the din, "that there are more calories in a Coke than a Diet Coke, but because they don't tell us that, you can't pick it. This is one of the gotcha questions."

She went for the light switch, turning her back. Somebody tossed a ball of wadded paper across the room. On the projector, Candice presented a sample TAKS question: "Do you agree or disagree with the following statement: When electricity charges the neon gas in a neon sign, there is no change in the state of the matter and therefore no physical change."

But when she read the statement aloud, Candice accidentally

skipped one of the negatives, reversing the answer. Even the teacher, it turned out, was prone to getting turned around in the TAKS language.

"It says there is no change, but that's not supported, so there is a change," Candice announced.

"I put disagree," one of the kids said, "so I'm right. Right?"

The whole thing was a muddle. Some kids in the back of the classroom smelled weakness. A boy shook up a soda bottle. A girl hissed at him: "You're like a seven-year-old who likes to play with the damn sink." Candice split them up, but the chatter carried on. She ignored it for the moment.

"What was the objective today?" she asked.

Rico started to read it: "Distinguish between the following types of matter . . ."

But now things were out of hand. Candice heard something she couldn't ignore. She loudly thanked the kids who never cursed or spoke a negative word, and then she changed her tone.

"You are at a high school, and these are my four walls," she declared. "I recognize that when you curse, it comes into my life as something negative and it comes into everyone's life as something negative. If you go into a job and use that kind of language, your boss will fire you. That kind of stuff, it makes you sound so unbelievably ignorant. It makes you sound like you don't know how to express yourselves without using curse words. I know we learned it from TV, I know some of your parents talk that way, and I'm sorry. I heard it from my parents when I was growing up, and I didn't like it. So if you understand what I've just said, raise your hand."

She stared and the kids stared back; this went on for close to a minute. She went around the room that way, staring until every glare melted, until every giggle subsided, and every last hand was raised. Then she allowed herself half a smile.

"It's because I love you," Candice said. Next she asked her students to please assemble a chart describing every kind of matter in the known world. They were boys and girls, after all, schoolchildren no matter how streetwise, and she was their teacher, assigned to enhance their lives through a basic understanding of chemistry.

As long as anybody could remember, Wednesday night had been prayer meeting night in the South. On this Wednesday night, a few weeks after the concert in the backyard of the house on Carver Avenue, some of the kids wanted to follow up with Bible study. Candice was leading the female session. Ashley Brown, Briana Fowler, and Princess Ohiagu all signed up together. They were all seniors. They ran track together; they ate lunch together; they did everything together. Ashley was raised Baptist, though not particularly churchgoing, and she'd known Candice since freshman year, though not particularly fondly. Candice was always on her about homework and her attitude. But since the first day of school this year, after seeing that video of the kids in Africa, Ashley had been asking to go. Not to Bible study: to Africa. Briana and Princess too, of course. Candice had told Ashley her attitude would need more work before they could even talk about flying halfway across the world. Bible study was supposed to help. Candice assumed Ashley would drop it, but Ashley had time on her hands. She'd passed the exit-level TAKS on her first try junior year, so school didn't have much left to offer. The teachers mostly had to work with kids who hadn't met standard. Track season wouldn't come until spring, and everything else in her life just seemed stressful. She hadn't seen her dad since he dropped off a card for her sixteenth birthday; that was stressful. JaQuarius didn't tell her what he was feeling and she didn't know how to ask; that was stressful. Africa was a long way from the Two-Three, and for the moment that was enough.

Before meeting with the girls, Candice helped pick up the boys at the football field (not alone—she had a strict policy against male students riding in her car without adult male supervision). George Warren was there, of course, the boy everybody counted on. George turned out for football, baseball, and track, and he never demanded to be the star. When the basketball team needed an equipment manager, Coach Davis called on George. Bible study was nothing new to him. George had devoted his life to Christ at age fourteen, and since then he'd improved his grade point average more than anybody in his class, coincidentally or not. Jesse Martinez wasn't there, no matter what he'd said in front of the crowd at the concert. DeVonte was there, but he disclaimed any knowledge of Jesse's whereabouts. Candice dropped the boys off at a house on Bennett Avenue, a block west of her own place in St. John's.

Inside the house, several members of the Stone Church had set out paperback Bibles and a buffet spread with chicken salad, Doritos, and juice. They were white guys, recent UT grads, living on the Eastside near the land the church was acquiring for its new building, which was to be called the For the City Center. They were planning to lead the Bible study sessions together until Candice showed up with Chase. Chase was thirty-four, a former IT consultant working as a tutor at Reagan. His first name was Errol, but everybody called him Chase. Chase had some street cred. He claimed to have been in trouble with the law some years back in New York, though the state prison system up there had no record of him. The kids knew him from Reagan, and also he was black, so the guys who lived in the house let Chase talk first.

When the boys finished eating, joking around ("You texting your boyfriend?"—"I'm texting your mom"), and raiding the morning paper for coupons, Chase led them out to the small concrete porch. Under a rattling fan and a sign that said Longhorn Country, they passed around mosquito repellent. At first the four boys were outnumbered by their prayer leaders, but then Candice reappeared. "I found Robert walking," she said, leaving it at that.

When Chase asked for introductions, the boys fumbled around about how to behave at a Bible study. James tried extreme formality ("I'm a student athlete, raised in East Austin, Texas"), while Alex went the opposite route ("I like to eat lunch all the time, y'know, I like to eat chicken . . .").

"Why do y'all think you're here tonight?" Chase asked.

They went around the circle:

"Learn about the Word."

"Increase my knowledge of the Bible."

"I'm here to have a good time and eat."

Chase said God wanted him here. Then he said a prayer. Then he asked: "What's love? It's an open floor. What's love?"

DeVonte said it depends: "There's different kinds of love. Brotherly love. Relationship love. Loving the job. Love of the school. Different types. Basically love is all around."

What about strong love? Passion? DeVonte said he had passion for hip-hop dance and choreography. The other boys said they had passion for sports. Chase said passion was defined by a willingness to sacrifice. Nobody said anything to that. Chase called out a boy named Alex.

"I really don't know," Alex said. "You can love football. And he said 'dancing.' You can have love for a girl. I really don't know."

George said he loved his parents, plus a couple of girls he'd known. And football. Chase asked the other boys whether they knew their parents. Not both, the boys said. Chase told of a time when he'd gotten caught cutting class and his dad had gotten a parking ticket coming to pick him up and then his mom had spanked him. It was painful but it set him right, he said. That's what God does, he said.

George told a similar story: Trouble at school, a whupping right before bed, a lesson learned. His story sounded made-up to please Chase, with hardly enough detail to distinguish it from the one he'd just heard. Chase returned to his theme: "When man lets you down, God doesn't."

Chase asked about grudges. George spoke up again.

"I can't say I hate the cops, but when they get me for doing something I hadn't done, I don't like it."

"All right, I shouldn't have gone there," Chase said. He asked why God loved the world. No one had an answer. One of the white guys read from Corinthians. Chase asked whether love comes with conditions.

"I just love God, family, and sports," said a boy named James. "I don't have a female to love, and I'm not looking for that right now, so there are basically no conditions."

"What about friends?"

"I play for Reagan, and our football record is not all that. The scoreboard can have a hundred to zero, and that's not what I came to Reagan for. I came to Reagan to make a difference, so I'll still love my bros," James said.

The night was warm and the mosquitoes were still coming. One of the white guys asked: "All right, are you all buying it?"

The boys looked at each other and then at Chase. Christianity, the guy meant. The call of the Holy Spirit. DeVonte said: "It's not convincing enough, and it hasn't happened to me yet. They say when God sees you in a struggle, he'll send help, and it hasn't happened to me yet."

Nobody interrupted him. The boys knew there were people

who'd tried to help DeVonte. DeVonte sometimes described himself as a momma's boy, oldest son of a hairdresser, but he didn't live with his mother. He was crashing at Jesse's sister's house that month. Now he told about the death of his father, when he was six. "I just started going crazy. I didn't do anything to lose him, and I don't know if he did something to lose his life, but still, I'm lost without a father."

One of the boys tried to tell DeVonte things happen for a reason. DeVonte leaned back in his chair and draped his hands loosely across his borrowed Bible.

O n a cloudy Saturday in October, while much of the city tailgated in anticipation of the Texas Longhorns' first conference football game, Christian charities took over the parking lot of Reagan High School. Under a banner marked Festival de Esperanza, Stone Church members directed hundreds of families toward a rock-climbing wall, a bounce tent, and ponies to ride, which the families mostly ignored. Musicians set up their instruments too, though hardly anyone paid attention. Instead, a long line formed in front of an RV where doctors were giving checkups. A longer one led to the gym entranceway, where nurses were giving vaccinations. Inside the gym vision screeners, dental hygienists, domestic violence counselors, and more offered their services. Most of them were volunteering their time, and Allen Weeks got a five-thousand-dollar grant from Bank of America to pay for the rest of the setup. Recruiters turned out with their booths too, from the tutoring companies and the military. Transit authority workers took a survey, asking whether you'd prefer less service or higher fares for the same service (better service was not an option). The whole scene looked like a temporary fairground of basics taken for granted across the highway. Every passing hour brought more families, a sea of brown faces, enough to convert any nonbeliever, not necessarily to Jesus but certainly to Maslow's hierarchy. As long as the Festival of Hope banner flew, late into the afternoon, Reagan High School remained the most important place on the Eastside.

A few weeks later, Anabel stood in the cafeteria again. Her audience was bigger, not astoundingly but noticeably.

"If we continue on this trajectory," she said, "we should be clear. Reagan has a good feel right now. If you come during the day, our kids are studying, they're learning."

She talked about test scores, but not only test scores. She talked about spirit. She talked about the Soul Raider marching band scoring a one in competition for the first time in two decades. She talked about football: "You take the good with the bad, but I'll tell you what we have out there. We have kids that love each other; they love the game and they love what they do."

She talked about planting tomatoes in the courtyard. She talked about painting. And she talked about the future.

"The school is more beautiful," she said. "It's appealing. And the question is always, 'Are we getting it ready for somebody else?' And the answer is no. We're getting it ready for you, because you deserve this. The challenge isn't over yet. We have the rest of this year to go. There's a lot of hard work to do, but we're on an upward trajectory. We started out the year with, 'Reagan is a choice,' and I'm staying to stand up for my school."

Ten

Football season couldn't end soon enough, and it didn't. The Raiders lost their last game, by fifty points, to the Knights of McCallum High School. JaQuarius was devastated. He'd expected to lose to LBJ, where his middle school teammates were playing. He'd gotten over losing to Lanier, where the principal had to pull him up off his knees. But 70–20? The Knights scored so many touchdowns they had two kickers trading off extra-point duties. JaQuarius kept his cool on the field but not on his Myspace page, where he called himself the one "that shot or shank a nigga."

Losing to McCallum would have hurt no matter what the score. It wasn't because the Raiders had a chance; they didn't. Reagan was ranked last in District 26-4A, behind the sorry Lanier Vikings, behind the hated Jaguars of LBJ High, and hopelessly far behind the first-place Knights, which had made the playoffs every season for the past seventeen years.

It wasn't because the Raiders were the sentimental favorite; they weren't. Since the McCallum head coach had died of a heart attack at sixty-three (an occupational hazard of Texas high school football as real as any concussion), the Knights were fixed for pep talk fodder, magnets for maudlin sports page copy, and playing the way only teenage boys wearing a dead man's initials on their helmets can play.

And it wasn't because the Knights were a traditional rival; they weren't. McCallum kids looked forward to playing Travis High every year for the right to keep Old Locomotive Bell No. 988 in the school trophy case. Reagan kids looked forward to the annual showdown against LBJ at Nelson Field, the home stadium they begrudgingly shared.

It wasn't really even because of football.

It was because McCallum was choking Reagan to death.

Reagan High was used to losing talent to the far-flung exurbs, academic and athletic alike. The most striking example was Reggie Brown, a star linebacker in the 1990s who earned a scholarship to Texas A&M, signed with the Detroit Lions, and then bought his mother a house north of town in Pflugerville. His younger brother, Michael Johnson, played for Pflugerville High, not Reagan, before going on to the Super Bowl with the New York Giants.

Black flight wasn't much different from white flight. Families that could afford to move out of the city took their property tax dollars with them. The district had to spread around the budget impact, and come Election Day the mayor had to deal with it and the city council and everybody.

But McCallum was just three miles west, drawing kids with good TAKS scores, ambitious parents, and reliable transportation right across the interstate. The trickle became a stream in 2006, when the state education agency pronounced Reagan "academically unacceptable." McCallum wasn't just winning money and resources by producing high-caliber students. McCallum was winning high-caliber students by producing money and resources.

And so on a warm Friday night in November, with a light breeze blowing south across the field, the Knights of McCallum—the academically acceptable home of the city's Fine Arts Academy, where teachers earned $1,896 more on average than Reagan's for their fourteen years' average experience to the Reagan staff's nine, and where twice as many students were enrolled—beat JaQuarius Daniels and the Raiders by beating Reagan High School, first at the TAKS, then in the pay stubs, then on the real estate brochures, and finally on the field, by seven touchdowns, each more humiliating than the last.

A week later, with another winless season on the books, Anabel Garza walked the halls in a Columbia blue polo. Kids growing up in the Two-Three had considerable experience discerning patterns of affiliation from shirt colors, and she meant to send a message. Smiling wide, she stopped to inspect a big green tomato growing in the courtyard, then walked on to a history class, where she handed a boy in the front row a hall pass to her office.

"We got some talking to do?" the boy asked. "I'm in trouble?"

Turning on the heel of a sensible flat, Anabel gave a wink but no explanation. Her next stop was a TAKS prep class for kids who'd already fulfilled all the other requirements for graduation. She selected two Latino boys for hall passes, again moving on without comment. Outside she came across a football player called Morgan showing off to some girls.

"Don't make me break this up," Anabel said, handing Morgan a hall pass. She was gone by the time he understood he'd been summoned.

"Aw, I don't want to go talk to Ms. Garza," Morgan complained.

Anabel gave JaQuarius a hall pass too. She didn't say anything about what he'd written on his Myspace page.

Back in her office, Anabel found the campus police. They'd caught five kids hanging out across the street. The meeting she'd planned for the morning would have to wait. The cops were already deep into it.

"When's the last time you smoked?" one of them was asking a boy named Frank, emptying his backpack.

"Last night."

"It's on your hands, it's fresh, it's on your person and clothes."

The cop kept searching. Anabel knew some things about police work.

"I need to see the whites of your pockets, and give me your purse," she told one of the girls. "First, is there anything I'm going to find that you're not supposed to have?"

"Uh-uh."

Anabel opened the powder and the cream and all the lip glosses.

"Why were you late today?" a cop was asking a kid named Dominick.

"I just woke up late," Dominick said. "When I wake up late, I got to catch two buses."

Anabel went to her desk. There was a book there called *Using Data to Close the Achievement Gap* and another one called *101 Ways to Make Your Classroom Special*. She looked up attendance records on the computer. She started calling parents. Nobody answered. She left messages. She turned to a boy called LV.

"So, now, you're missing a lot of class. LV, you don't want to be here?"

"Yes I do, ma'am."

"I don't see the burning desire here on the screen."

"You wouldn't understand. Or maybe you would."

"I probably would."

"I go to my classes."

"But you're marked absent."

"I ain't gonna lie to you and say I go every day, but I go to my classes. When is a convenient time I can come talk to you about this?"

"Me? You can come anytime."

Anabel printed out LV's attendance record.

"Now, after ten absences, I can drop you. So count."

LV started counting.

"I'm pretty disappointed," Anabel said. "Who do you stay with now?"

"My teammate."

"Who?"

"Nah, I stay with my momma."

Anabel dialed the phone again.

"This is Anabel Garza, I'm the principal at Reagan High School. Frank was just brought in . . . At ten absences I'm dropping people . . . Fourteen, fifteen, sixteen, seventeen . . . I'm just counting absences in the last two weeks . . . He's been absent more than he's been here."

She held the phone out: "Frank."

Frank did a slow march to the receiver in basketball shoes and no socks. By way of greeting he said: "I just woke up late."

Anabel sized up a girl called Keisha. Keisha had moved away from the neighborhood but she was still enrolled at Reagan and skipping class, and Anabel wondered why.

"My momma said we've always gone to Reagan," Keisha said. "She doesn't want to go through all that."

"But it's better to go to a school you can get to than get taken to court . . ."

Anabel trailed off and took the phone back from Frank. She told Frank's mother about the cigarettes and listened for a minute and rang off. She looked at LV again.

"What are you doing?"

"I need to get a pass."

"No, it's a bigger question than that. You're not coming to school. What are you doing?"

LV mumbled some promises. Anabel shuffled the kids off to class.

As they walked out the next group walked in, the ones she'd rounded up with hall passes. Anabel wanted to hear their ideas for improving the school, but mostly she wanted to plant some ideas in their heads. These kids were role models to many of the others, for better or for worse.

JaQuarius was carrying a bright red backpack. He grinned and he had good posture, like athletes used to. He loomed half a foot over the next-tallest kid and nearly two over the principal.

Anabel passed around candy. Mondays and Thursdays at the boot camp gym were supposed to be bringing down her blood pressure, but getting rid of her Halloween stash probably wouldn't hurt. Life was full of numbers to be made.

"*Gracias*," said Morgan.

"*De nada*. Now you can pass the Spanish part of the TAKS."

Seven kids sat around the table, four Latino and three black, two girls and five boys. There was no Spanish part of the TAKS but nobody laughed. There was a business-looking lady in the room with them. Anabel nudged one boy's elbows off the table and mimed the removal of headphones and said, "Yeah, doesn't work for me."

The kids ate her candy. Anabel talked about how the teachers had been trying for four years to make the academically acceptable numbers and yet here they were. She said maybe you kids have some ideas. She introduced the woman from the state education agency, as an "observer."

"Here are the topics, and just fast and dirty," Anabel said. "Our attendance is bad, and if people aren't in classes we're not going to get better. Our benchmarks are ten percent better than last year, but we will have to cross the finish line together. So the ones who are doing better have to help the others along."

She looked around the table. The kids kept eating candy.

"Oh, and another issue is our interracial tension. It's brown and black tension all the time. We don't understand each other. And if we don't cross the line together, none of us win."

She looked around the table again. The candy was almost gone.

"How many Hispanic players on the football team?" Anabel asked.

"None," said everybody.

"How many black players on the soccer team?"

"None."

Morgan said, "But that's just because they can't play."

Anabel started over.

"As a school, if we can't make it, if we can't pass a test . . ."

She started over again.

"If somebody doesn't want to go to class, it turns into a school problem; it turns into your problem; it turns into a community problem. How do you think people look at Reagan High School?"

Morgan said, "Stupid. We're killers, because of something that happened in 2003. And we're bad. Because the school is here in St. John's."

"Okay, that's three things. When you look in the mirror in the morning, what do you see?"

Nobody answered. Anabel started to ask another question but

then Morgan addressed the first one, sort of. He didn't talk about the bathroom mirror.

"Every time we're in the news, it's because the school is going to get closed down or they're having a community meeting to save Reagan," he said. "If they would show something more positive, then maybe more people would want to come here."

"But who is 'they'?" Anabel asked. She talked about the power to influence your own friends. She talked about attendance again.

Morgan said, "Like, you got to make it fun for us to come here."

"Fun? What does that mean? I'd have to have a party every day for you to come?"

"No. Just make it more interesting. Something different every day."

Anabel said to brainstorm the race thing for a minute. JaQuarius and Morgan did rock-paper-scissors to see who would talk first. JaQuarius won. JaQuarius usually won.

"When we're in class," JaQuarius said, "don't just let us pick what groups to be in. Let the teachers pick the groups, and put the different races together. And make them get along with each other."

Anabel was taking notes. These were not new ideas. People had taken them to the Supreme Court more than once.

"JQ, what makes you want to do well?" Anabel asked.

"Seeing my momma, how she struggled when she was younger."

She went around the circle. All the kids repeated JaQuarius's remarks, inserting their own mothers. One of the boys said: "We're all divided, Hispanic and black, and that's wrong. They don't do a thing to us and we don't do nothing to y'all, so why don't we hang out together? And the other thing is, teachers can't control the classes."

JaQuarius said, "Sometimes it's not the case of teachers not wanting to teach the class. They're just scared to say certain things to the students. Sometimes I think the teacher makes it worse. They just fail them, and they don't go up and talk to them, and so the student just keeps it up."

The TEA lady said, "This is all good information."

Then she said: "What happens with the school, whether it gets to stay open, rests on your shoulders, all of your shoulders. It's not just the teachers and it's not just the parents. It's up to all of you. And it's a real critical time for Reagan and the community. And the more I listen, the more I'm convinced it needs to stay open, because there's a lot of good students here. And I think you can do it. I want you to tell your friends, when you're seeing them acting up in class, 'This is a critical time, and you're under a lot of scrutiny from the state. And this could turn into a bad situation.'"

Anabel cringed a little. She said, "That's a lot of pressure to put on students."

Then she talked about how high school was an important time in their lives and how quickly it would pass and how a bad decision could ruin things.

"You are very powerful," Anabel said. "You don't know how powerful you are."

The kids sat quietly, almost somberly for all the candy they'd ingested. Anabel said she believed in them. She said they'd always be connected to Reagan High.

"I didn't have that burden on me when I was in high school," Anabel said. "I didn't even know high schools closed. But financially, there's a burden on everybody now. And they're trying to push us toward excellence, which isn't a bad thing. But we didn't have it together last year, and now this is the year to make it happen. Those of you that play sports, it's like we're in the last few minutes, and it's, 'Are we going to make it or not?'"

JaQuarius picked up his backpack. Basketball season was starting next week. Coach Davis had a district bus reserved and they were going to Harker Heights to play the kids from the military post up at Fort Hood.

Cool Hand Luke was a war hero. What he did was he got all turned around one night and vandalized some parking meters, which wasn't right, but he didn't deserve to be in that prison work camp where the captain put him in the box over and over. You could tell there was something to him though because every time the guards hit him Cool Hand Luke got up again and after a while they didn't hit him anymore.

Wilton Harris was telling all this to a girl called Vanessa, who wore a black Everlast sweatshirt with the hood up and had her nails painted many different colors. They were sitting in the room reserved for all the social services groups. The social services groups worked in schools all over the country, not just Reagan. Some tried to do a job that teachers and coaches and band directors used to do back before the reformers made them all accountable and busy with other things. Some tried to do a job parents were supposed to do. Harris mostly worked with boys in the XY Zone, but Vanessa was there, so he was telling her about Cool Hand Luke. George Warren was there and a kid named Chriss Conway and a kid named Pedro too. Harris went on for a while about the movie. He left out the part about Cool Hand Luke getting shot to death at the end. He told Vanessa what he was driving at was that she had the keys to her own prison.

"You got to see yourself in a different way," he said. "See yourself as who you really can be."

Vanessa slumped on her elbow. She said: "Mmm."

Harris compared her present circumstance to a Lou Rawls song, to firefighting, and to several other points of reference with which Vanessa seemed minimally familiar.

"Here's an opportunity for you to take something and be a runner," he went on.

Vanessa mmm'ed again.

"You're a fighter, man."

Vanessa laughed. *Man.* She was a skater and a tomboy. Mister Harris was okay.

"You know what this school has?" Harris inquired. "Y'all are fighters. You can't be afraid to get hit. I can't tell you how much, as an adult, I get hit."

Vanessa was kneading her backpack. Danielle Chatmon, the counselor, walked in and asked what was going on.

"I failed the TAKS again."

Harris made no effort to catch her up on Paul Newman, etc. Chatmon gave Vanessa a hug.

"I missed by one. That's what happens every time I take that test."

Chatmon suggested redoubling her efforts with the graphing calculator.

"I know that calculator inside and out," Vanessa said. "I don't know why I can't pass it and get out of here."

"One point?" Harris said. "Don't let it beat you up. I know people who are miles away. One point? Pick that one area and go over it and over it."

Chatmon said, "Make it your boyfriend."

Vanessa might have blushed, under that hood. She said, "I just feel like I've been here forever."

"I know you must be frustrated," Chatmon said. "Feel like you've taken it over and over."

"I just want to get on with my life."

The counselors talked about finding Vanessa a new math tutor. Vanessa said the tutor would need to know about a cylinder inside a cylinder with marbles and a probability component involving dice, because that was what had given her trouble. A tutor by the name of Joe had helped last year, she said. He could relate to her because of skateboarding. Nobody knew Joe's last name or whereabouts. Vanessa clasped her hands together.

"I don't know, guys," she said. "I don't know."

Chriss Conway's problem was his car had broken down. He knew the part he needed and somebody had even given him the number for a salvage yard but there he sat. Harris spoke at length about this generation, how coddled, how short its attention spans. Conway suggested someone should make the call for him. George Warren looked up from his paper.

"You losing, Chriss," he tried to warn.

Too late.

"What do you do?" Chatmon asked Chriss. "Sit in that hallway and laugh and giggle. And then when I come to you and try to talk to you about how you need to handle your business, you act like this? You're wrong and you don't listen."

Harris said, "Listen, Chriss. It is better to be a man and say, 'I was wrong' than to be a teen and get defensive."

Soon they were all yelling, Chatmon the loudest: "Just go! Just go!"

Chriss slumped in his chair and kept up the back talk.

"Chriss, don't rob no bank, because you're going to argue with the teller and be like, 'I wrote in my note that I wanted fifties, and it was in the note, and that can't be wrong because I'm Chriss Conway,'" Harris said. "The cops will have time to show up, and you'll be on TV, and we'll all be laughing."

Chatmon failed to see the humor in that.

"It's called respect," she said. "It's called reciprocity. We're all supposed to sit here and listen to your attitude?"

Harris drew parallels to college, to football, to working at Dell, and so on. Chriss gave no reply. Harris talked about how adults let one another state their positions in an argument.

"You're turning on us trying to help you," he said. "This is something you need to think about so that if this situation comes again, and it will because this is life, you'll know a better way to deal with it. There's going to come a time when you're working for a major corporation and you'll need to know when to stand down and when to voice your opinion. When you're ready to learn, a teacher will show up. You've got to adjust those attitudes."

George Warren was nodding along, but Vanessa spoke up.

"Not everything is easy for us, Mr. Harris," she said. "We all have to walk our own walks in life."

Harris said he'd been through more than they had. He said everything was easy now: social promotion. Free tutoring. Day care. Dissecting virtual frogs on the computer in biology class. Staying enrolled even though they skipped class. When he was a student at Reagan, he said, kids had to keep up on current events. He said: "What happened up at Fort Hood last week?"

Pedro answered from the sofa: "That guy shot thirteen people."

"I just prefer not to know," said Vanessa.

Eleven

The video opens on an image of skinny Ashley Brown, camera-ready in braids, Daisy Dukes, and a red tank top, perched Indian-style on a swivel chair before a map of the world in an upstairs bedroom at the house on Carver Avenue.

"Hi, my name is Ashley," says Ashley, in a tone implying the disclosure of information her interrogator should already know.

"And where do you go to school?" asks the voice behind the camera, which belongs to Candice Kaiser, who knows the answer to that one too.

"Reagan High School," says Ashley, who has to suppress a giggle because this lady has been hounding her about science homework at Reagan High School for about three and a half years.

"Okay, so I might say, 'How do you feel about your life up until now?' and you'd say, 'Up until now, my life has been 'Blah.' You have to turn it into a sentence so they know what you're talking about, 'cause they won't hear me asking questions," says Candice, who has

made amateur videos before and even won an award for one in college. Candice lets the video run for cutting and then asks the first big question, which is really just a distillation of stuff she and Ashley have been talking about for months: *"Okay, why do you think you're here on Earth?"*

"The reason why I'm here on Earth is because God put me on here with a purpose," says Ashley, who has been insisting since the first day of school that her purpose on Earth suddenly involves going to go visit those kids in Africa.

"And what are some things you take for granted every day?" asks Candice, who had been hoping for a strong reaction when she played that video of her Kibera mission trip, just not this reaction. She had hoped to shame her students out of what Ashley calls "attitude" (Candice calls it "entitlement issues"). She had hoped to set a tone for the year. She had even hoped to make the kids, in her words, "feel connected to a community of children through a teacher."

"Um, what I take for granted every day is . . . not turning in work sometimes, not doing what I'm supposed to do, and hurting people that really care about me the most," says Ashley, who does, in fact, do a lot of what she's supposed to do. She's in the top 10 percent of her class. She went to state last year and finished eighth in the hundred-meter dash. She keeps in shape off-season. She watches her little brother. She's been dating the most popular boy in school for five years, and she's not pregnant. She passed the TAKS. She has started filling out applications to Baylor, Texas A&M, and Prairie View A&M. She's got a plan, one that's concrete enough to be called a goal and bold enough to be called a dream. She wants to be a pediatrician, which means studying biology. Just like Ms. Kaiser.

"What are some things you struggle with every day?" asks Candice, whose own trip to Africa was transformative, not just spiritually but professionally. She met children who crowded around a single sci-

ence book, responding to her questions about cardiac function with a debate on the finer points of blood oxygenation. She came back with a complex view of education policy in America, where reformers often describe a "culture of excuses" in public schools. She still isn't convinced that standardized testing will solve things, but she no longer believes that more money will solve things either. "The kids in Africa didn't have that," she tells anybody who will listen, "and they were enthusiastic about learning."

"One of the things I struggle the most with every day is reading. I hate reading. I hate English, so therefore, it's one of the things I struggle with," says Ashley, who really does hate reading. She has lost track of how many times she's seen *The Color Purple*, but she has no patience for Alice Walker. It's just not the way she relates to the world.

"Um, how did you feel when you saw the video of the kids in Kibera?" asks Candice, whose experience raising twenty-seven hundred dollars for her own trip has given her little cause for optimism in this endeavor. She figures it will cost sixty thousand dollars to return to Africa with a dozen Eastside kids and their chaperones. She hopes that this interview footage, spliced with a dozen others into a fund-raising video, will win over sponsors.

"I was sad and hurt. I got teary at it, because it's hard just thinking about what they go through, and being up here, we really don't go through all that and stuff, not having school supplies, we have it up here," says Ashley, whose own high school in America, in fact, does not allow students to take certain textbooks home due to limited supplies.

Ashley turns and points to the map, then addresses the camera: *"Kenya, yeah, East Africa."*

"How did you feel when you saw the actual pictures of the slum and what they lived in?" asks Candice, who has read up on the

drought choking the economy in Kenya, where there are fears of new violence to rival the 2008 election riots. It's never a good sign when a country's anticorruption chief is forced to resign. No matter how many waivers and permission slips get signed for this trip, Candice knows where the ultimate moral responsibility would land if anything were to happen.

"I was sad, 'cause they lived in filth, and it's not right," says Ashley, who actually seemed beyond sad when she watched the Kenyan kids on the video. She cried, and she talked to the screen. She said, "I love you all too."

Somebody trips into the camera. Candice has three roommates, and kids are always passing through to meet a tutor or hang out in the AC.

"So then, how do you feel . . . like, why do you think they're so joyful?" asks Candice, who has spent enough time with Ashley, and with Briana and Princess and Ebony and Kay Kay and Jesse and DeVonte and Nijalon, to know what it would mean if she of all people were to become another voice telling them something was impossible for kids from the Two-Three. She has spoken with the pastor in charge of missions at the Stone Church, who promised to screen the fund-raising video. All she needs, she has been telling herself, is for one door to close so she can say, "Okay, God, I get it, we shouldn't go."

"I think they're so joyful because it's their life, and they've been dealing with it all their life, so they should make better of it and have fun, because they really don't take nothing for granted," says Ashley.

"Why do you think they love God so much there?"

"Because God has helped them through a whole lot of things, and helped them move on and do what they got to do."

"I heard a story once that the kids we're going to visit had to get on their knees and pray for food, because for a couple months they didn't

have food. So, um, how do you feel about knowing that kids across the world have to get on their knees and pray for food?" Candice asks.

"I feel bad, 'cause shouldn't nobody have to sit there and get on their knees for anything in their life. So I felt very bad about it and wished that I could've helped them out," Ashley says.

"Do you think God is, like, at work in their lives?"

"Yes, God is at work everywhere, so . . . yes."

"How do you feel about your life, up until now?"

"I feel, about my life up to now, it's going good. Hopefully I'll be graduating this year and going to Baylor University to study to be a pediatrician. Once I become that, I would love to help Kenyans."

"What do you think are the most influential things that have happened to you in your life?"

Ashley tilts her head and swivels in the chair and gives no reply.

"Like, what are some things that have changed your life completely?"

"My life has changed a whole lot because back then I was terrible. I got into it with people, I always said stuff wrong that would hurt people that loved me the most. Now I've learned my lesson, and I have grew up. I learned from my mistakes."

"And what do you think, or, how has God worked in your life, like when you were a kid? Do you remember how God worked in your life when you were a kid? Do you remember anything?" Candice asks.

"He did change me a whole lot. Um, I did come down with my attitude," Ashley says. "If I was a lot like I was when I were younger, I probably would've ended up pregnant or in things. Now I'm doing good, not worrying about a whole lot of stuff and just worrying about my responsibilities and what I've got to do this year."

"How are you like the kids in Kibera?"

"They're kids. We love to have fun. We smile a lot."

"How do you think this trip will affect the rest of your life?"

"This trip will affect my life in a lot of different ways," Ashley says. "I'll learn how to deal with a whole lot of stuff, and going there to experience their life and the way how they live will teach me a lot about life."

"And how do you feel God is at work in your life right now?"

Ashley scratches her arm and smiles. Candice asks: "How is your relationship with God right now? Do you go to Him all the time, or do you wish you went to Him more? How do you feel your relationship is? How close do you feel to God right now?"

"I feel that I want me and God's relationship to get even closer, because right now I've been going through a whole lot with school and stuff like that and really haven't took the time out to just thank Him, so I wish it was closer."

"Okay," Candice says, "how do you think it's going to feel, because when I first went to Kibera . . . Do you remember the video, like, when I walk in through and we go through the gate and I shake that little kid's hand? That was the first kid's hand I shook, and it was like, I just remember that moment, for some reason it really sticks out to me, 'cause I could connect with him. But how do you feel, whenever you're going to get to actually make a relationship with these kids over those two weeks?"

"I'm gonna be happy, because, I feel it's gonna be fun meeting new people and just meeting new friends. It's gonna be fun. I'm very excited."

"What do you want to teach the kids over there?" Candice asks.

"Sports! I love running track, and I hope they're gonna love it too."

"So how do you think you're gonna teach them about . . . what do you think you're gonna do to teach them about track? What are some things you can do when you get there?"

"I can teach them how to get out of blocks. We can make our own *little blocks, have fun,"* Ashley says. *"And how to keep your knees up, and the good form of how you're supposed to run."*

"What do you think they can teach you?" asks Candice, who struggles every day to inhabit the lessons of her nightly Bible studies. When she has problems at work or when she needs to confess the desire she feels for Ryan, the new boyfriend she has met through the church, she still goes to her friends first. She knows that's wrong. She knows she has to learn to go to God. She can recite the mistake the Hebrews made—"They went after false idols and became false." She knows she needs to surrender to God. She talks about surrendering but she still worries about things, and she knows that isn't real surrender, isn't real trust.

"How to be grateful," says Ashley, who is already learning gratitude, without ever leaving the Two-Three. In the fund-raising letters to accompany this video, she calls her mother "the best thing that ever happened to me. She is a strong, independent black woman. I love her for that. God gave me a mother who has guided me. I am blessed."

"You can reword it and say, 'I think they're gonna teach me how to be grateful.'"

"I think they're gonna teach me how to be more grateful," Ashley Brown says, *"of what I have."*

Twelve

P EYTON—I NEED YOUR HELP."
Anabel Garza frowned at the block letters on the yellow slip of paper sent to her office from one of the special education classrooms known as Life Skills. She didn't have time for this. It was going to be tricky enough getting to both middle schools during the lunch break, when she could catch the eighth graders as a captive audience. She had a bus idling in the parking lot, and she could already hear the names of her chosen ambassadors being called on the intercom: *Emily Torre, Justin Coleman, Jesse Martinez, JaQuarius Daniels.*

But sometimes Peyton would respond only to her, especially when he got confused or scared, so Anabel held his note out like a divining rod, letting it summon her around the corner water fountain and through the double metal doors at the pace of a child told not to run around a swimming pool. She came to a Life Skills classroom where a teacher sat with a wheelchair-bound girl, but no Peyton.

The teacher asked to see Peyton's note. He looked worried, as if maybe Peyton had something on him. He said Peyton was probably playing a prank. Anabel said she'd check on Peyton herself, just the same. She had other places to look. Other Life Skills classrooms, for a start. There were 141 special education students enrolled at Reagan, 16 percent of the population compared with 9 percent for the district. Nobody made much effort to transfer disabled kids out to McCallum High, so Reagan ended up spending $1.6 million a year on special education, compared with $3.4 million on regular education and the sum of $443 on gifted and talented education.

Down the hall at another Life Skills classroom, Anabel stopped to greet a girl with Down syndrome, who strongly recommended seeing the movie *Snow White*. Anabel promised to put it on her list. On her way out, she was waylaid by the worried-looking teacher, who suggested that Peyton might just want a ticket to the volleyball game. Anabel kept moving. More Life Skills classrooms, still no Peyton. She stopped short, backtracked into the hall, stood outside the upstairs boys' room, and listened.

"Peyton, are you in there? Peyton, are you okay?"

Peyton, wearing a gray T-shirt and a distant gaze, shuffled out.

"I hope I didn't make things worse," he said.

Anabel provided assurances. Peyton disclosed the cause of his note: His student ID card was stamped with the wrong lunch code, and it was his belief that only the principal could alter the coding. Anabel made a show of taking notes: "Needs a fix for lunch," she wrote, and said aloud.

Then Peyton came out with the real problem.

"Also," he said, "downstairs somebody wrote something very bad on the wall."

"What?"

"Downstairs, across from the boys' bathroom, 'F-U-C-K you,'" he said. "And some other things I didn't understand."

Anabel suppressed a smile.

"That's okay," she said. "Sometimes it's better not to understand some things."

Peyton declined a volleyball ticket. He already had one. Deeming the morning's crisis resolved, Anabel hurried out to the bus, where the marching band had a solid rhythm going with mallets and drumsticks on the seat backs. She stood up front and counted heads. Her star athlete turned up in sandals.

"Where are your tennis shoes?" Anabel asked.

"I don't have any," JaQuarius said, joking.

"You're going to wear mine. You better wrap them around your feet. What size do you wear?"

"Fourteen."

Anabel passed around flyers describing Reagan's electives, meant for distribution to the middle school kids.

"We've got every sport but swim team," said JaQuarius, who was on four of those teams, counting golf. "We need a swim team."

Anabel said: "You want to be on it?"

The bus pulled out of the lot, its passenger manifest chosen by an imprecise amalgam of grades, profile, and charisma. The kids bounced in their seats, away from class for an hour. They rode off toward middle schools they'd once attended, on an errand to convince at least a few of the more capable eighth graders that Reagan High might have more to offer than four years of TAKS cramming and the avoidance of getting stabbed.

Anabel draped her arm across the seat back, tucking a leg to achieve that position at her stature, and surveyed her troupe. The band kids had been an easy choice, the drum line in particular. They drew a crowd wherever they went, from the Mueller parking lot to formal competitions; they'd been called up to play on the *Friday Night Lights* TV show; and this morning they'd dressed up their uniforms with headbands that said Soul in Columbia Blue.

Still, JaQuarius was the main attraction, Mr. Reagan High. On the football field he stood out just by showing up, an athlete among scrubs. Some college programs were looking at him, Baylor and a couple of bigger ones too. As he told it, that had been his plan all along, to shine against the backdrop of a fallen dynasty. But the lesson of the losing season was hard to miss: JaQuarius couldn't do it alone. "His delivery may seem long, but he is also having to throw off his back foot a lot, which leads to a lot of inaccurate passes," one college scout wrote. "When he has been able to stand up and deliver the ball, he looks like a different player."

And for all his devotion to football, JaQuarius was drawing more attention on the basketball court, with the boys who'd been together since middle school. The Raiders had made the local paper's preseason list of ten teams to watch, at tenth, and the sportswriter had said they "could surprise some people." Burned by the memory of last year's regional quarterfinal loss to LBJ ("L. B. Gay," some kids called it), the team was drawing crowds to its open practices, where there wasn't even much to watch but drills—outlet, shovel, bounce pass, layup, outlet, shovel, bounce pass, layup, with Coach Davis calling, "Stay low, stay low." The Raiders had opened their season up in Killeen, where people were still reeling from the shooting at the army post. Playing Harker Heights, a 5-A school with 2,536 students and a recognized rating from the state, Reagan had won by three points, 57–54.

When the bus driver parked behind the cafeteria at Webb Middle School, the drummers and dancers gathered their things. The band director went in to make arrangements. JaQuarius took the chance to give the principal a hard time.

"This is illegal, recruiting," he said.

"We're not recruiting," Anabel said. "We're showing off."

Then she changed the subject to standardized test prep, and JaQuarius stopped smiling. He had a solid GPA, but his first look at the exit-level TAKS was coming up. His girlfriend, Ashley, had already passed the tests her junior year. She was applying to Baylor and some places even farther away too. No TAKS, no college, and no college football.

"When I get to the test," JaQuarius said, "it doesn't translate. I act like I haven't been studying."

Anabel looked for some encouraging words, but a buzzer was sounding from the middle school cafeteria. The eighth graders were starting lunch. If she wanted to attract an incoming freshman class with good students to balance out Reagan's wealth of delinquents, special ed wards, and limited English proficiency cases, it was time to put on a show.

"All right, *chicas*," she called, giving the dancers a roundhouse wave. "Are you ready?"

The girls in their sparkling blue followed JaQuarius up the delivery ramp, past a sign tracking the progress of a Thanksgiving can drive, and into the cafeteria with their principal close behind, calling, "Where are my strutters and my dancerinas at?"

The bass drummer smashed an opening salvo, the echo resounded from the concrete walls, and somebody called, "Hit it, Reagan!" John Philip Sousa this was not, and "The Hey Song" neither. The drum line teased a march beat but soon dropped into a slow and low shuffle that might have resembled standard hip-hop if not for Jesse Martinez clashing those off-brand cymbals together in a tremendous racket with every muscle in his face straining and the whole band doing exaggerated tucks and chair steps. The Soul Strutters took to the floor below the stage, all hip-shake and crunk, and the drum line hushed to stick clicks for the call and response:

Everybody say . . .
RHS!

The drummers called their parts in voices as deep and sonorous as their teenage vocal cords could drop. The Soul Strutters did a suggestive twist, stopping now and again to fix the sashes of their frayed uniforms. The middle school kids perched on their cafeteria stools, rapt and maybe a little overwhelmed. Somebody introduced the woman responsible for this lunchroom spectacle, the principal of Reagan High School, Ms. Anabel Garza.

"We are hearing fantastic things about you at Webb," she told the eighth graders. "We hear how smart you are. We are here from Reagan today to identify our future Raiders."

She asked for a show of hands.

"And those of you who aren't coming to Reagan," she went on, "we hope we can change your minds today."

"I'm good," one kid called, and some others laughed. They were only thirteen, but they'd seen some things. They'd seen their middle school, named for the state's foremost keeper of history, go through the same desperate race to make the numbers. They'd seen their big brothers and sisters staving off a middle school closure order, and now this lady wanted them to come to an academically unacceptable high school for more of the same. Anabel went on with her pitch, introducing the band, the Strutters, the cheerleaders, the yearbook photographer, and the quarterback.

"As you can tell," Anabel said, watching the eighth-grade girls watch JaQuarius, "we have the best-looking kids in Austin, the most beautiful girls, the most handsome boys . . ."

The drum line took over, grinding hips and twirling sticks and building a great crescendo to a hard stop and:

Silence, frozen in a high step pose.

"Oh snap," called a middle school girl, and the band lurched back to life. Sweating and straining, Jesse counted off dance steps under his breath and clutched his splintered cymbals through bandanas for good grip and made a big big sound. The band played on, a deafening clamor in that unacoustical lunchroom. The Reagan kids worked the room, circulating flyers that told of auto shop and drama clubs and sports. The middle school girls competed for the attentions of this fine and towering JaQuarius, who made his way up and down each aisle before returning to his place by the stage. When the music stopped, JaQuarius held the door for the drum line, the Strutters, and everybody. Last came the principal. The middle school girls didn't stop staring until JaQuarius let the door close behind his back.

"I don't know what they see," Anabel said, shaking her head at JaQuarius, "in a boy with no shoes."

Back on the bus, JaQuarius passed around bags from the Reagan cafeteria. The burgers were cold, the fries soggy, the apples mushy, and the chocolate milk fat free. JaQuarius asked the driver to stop at Burger King. The driver did not. JaQuarius asked Anabel if she knew how many students left campus for lunch. Anabel said she knew how many didn't come back.

When Dobie Middle School came into sight, the Dobie alumni on board opened a spirited back-and-forth concerning the merits of various alma maters. The discussion ended when somebody yelled: "Your middle school don't even exist; that's how weak it was." The taunt was not precisely true. Pearce Middle School, where JaQuarius had grown up playing for the Pirates, had in fact been ordered to close by the state commissioner, but now the district was "repurposing" Pearce under the same name, a procedure that involved firing the principal, firing all the eighth-grade science teachers, and firing a lot of the other teachers too. It still operated as a neighborhood public school, but enrollment was at half capacity.

On the pavement outside Dobie, the delegation from Reagan waited for its cue. The Strutters discussed hair care; Jesse told a pretty good joke (Mexicans cross the border by twos instead of threes, the joke informed, because the signs say No Tres-passing); and JaQuarius asked Anabel to explain why she'd been refurnishing the classrooms at Reagan.

"There a lot of better things you could have spent a thousand dollars on than new chairs for us," he said.

"No," Anabel said, "Because we want to build pride. Why should other schools have the best, and you don't have the best?"

The wait went on. Cold burgers hadn't been all that filling. Anticipation was building inside the middle school too. When the Reagan kids finally made for the cafeteria, a seventh-grade class was watching in something like awe.

"Because y'all are in seventh grade," their teacher said as she led them away. "When you move up to eighth grade, then you can see it."

The drum line started setting up in the empty cafeteria. JaQuarius, dribbling a green rubber ball, took a seat at the front table, across from Anabel. If she really wanted to build pride, JaQuarius said, he had some suggestions. What about all those babies in the day-care center? What about birth control? Anabel turned the subject to relationships and marriage.

"I couldn't ever commit myself to one girl for the rest of my life," JaQuarius said.

Anabel said she had married young. JaQuarius asked why a person would do such a thing.

"You fall head over heels, and this person was the love of my life."

"And you're still married to him?"

"No, he died."

And then the bass drum gave its thunderous signal and the Reagan High School Show started all over again for another class of prospective numbers-makers bent over their milk and Jell-O. Anabel smiled big and took the microphone.

"We've been hearing a whole lot about Dobie," she said. "We hear that you are smart, we hear that you are talented, and we hear that you are the best-looking students in Austin."

The drum line and the Strutters and the cheerleaders again did their thing, and on the way out JaQuarius held the door long enough for Anabel to call back, "We can't wait to have you at Reagan!"

On the return trip, JaQuarius asked Anabel to level with him: Was Reagan going to close? She must know, right?

She started to answer but he wasn't done.

"Where would I go then? I would just drop out."

"It won't," Anabel said. "That's why we've got to do it. Just got to got to got to."

When the familiar red brick of their high school came back into view, Anabel rummaged in her purse for the cell phone paid for with that forty-dollar stipend from the district and started taking pictures of the kids she could see skipping class over by the city bus stop.

The first week of December brought just a trace of the snowfall the TV men had said to expect, but Anabel canceled *Little Shop of Horrors* rehearsal and all the after-school clubs just in case.

Many people in Central Texas have trouble driving on roads where it is possible ice could form. When the nonstorm had safely passed, the Reagan basketball team boarded a bus for a Tuesday night game against the Eagles of W. Charles Akins High, a 5-A school with 2,650 students and recognized status from the state education agency. The night was foggy, and the boys rode past gated housing developments and big-box stores to a parking lot with a special trailer painted up for the Eagle band. Akins was about 70 percent Latino, the same as Reagan, but not really the same. The census counted just 2,131 foreign-born people living in the zip code around Akins, or 8.5 percent of the population, compared to 25 percent of the population in the Two-Three. Seventy-three percent of people in South Austin owned their homes, and they made median household incomes twenty thousand dollars better than on the Eastside. Those numbers translated directly into the schools: At Akins, only 14 percent of kids were classified as "limited English proficient."

Including the big opener against Harker Heights, Reagan had compiled a 6–4 record traveling around the exurbs, to Cedar Park and Bastrop and as far south as San Antonio. Coach Derrick Davis was planning to enter the team in a tournament in Dallas, but Akins would be the last game in town before the start of district play. The Raiders had a decent turnout: Some of the players' parents, plus a couple of dozen kids who caught rides from Candice Kaiser and her church friends. Not bad for a school night sixteen miles across town in the fog and the cold, but the principal was conspicuously absent. Anabel, who tended to make an appearance at everything, would have to decide where to stand tonight. Her husband, Humberto Garza, was coaching the Eagles. They'd met in the mid-1990s, seven years after Ramiro Olvera fell dead on his jogging route. At the time, they both worked at Pleasant Hill Elementary, Humberto as a student teacher and Anabel as an assistant principal starting the decade-long odyssey toward the goal described on her résumé, "To obtain a position as a principal with the Austin Independent School District." They'd started dating when Humberto transferred to another school, and now they had a daughter nearing high school age. She'd probably go to Akins. It was closer to their house.

At the visitors' bench in the Akins gym, Coach Davis called a huddle. He had dressed for the game in a linen suit, canary tie, sweater vest, tasseled loafers, fashionably narrow glasses, and a newsboy cap. The boys leaned together and clapped in rhythm and on JaQuarius's count called, "Hoop Squad!"

JaQuarius had a height advantage but he lost the opening tip. Akins took the first lead. Soon Coach Davis was out of his seat yelling, "Shoot the ball!" He paced the floor and muttered, "We did this all day yesterday. What do we need? Motion." JaQuarius made a pretty reverse under the basket for a double pump layup, the tall senior Corn Cammock blocked a shot at the other end, and the Raiders were in the contest. Coach called another huddle and talked about defense while JaQuarius patted his back with a closed fist and then led a chant of "1-2-3 Defense."

By the end of the first quarter, Coach Davis had removed his jacket, unbuttoned his sleeves, paced a good half mile of sideline, argued more than one call, and taken to yelling, over and over again, "Motion!" Basketball coaching by tradition produces some of the most absurdly incongruous figures in the sporting world, men who dress like Mafia lawyers with the temperament of nap-deprived toddlers, and Derrick was claiming his humble place in that storied lineage ("As modern as I am," he once said, "I'm an old-school guy"). Basketball was his livelihood; Reagan basketball more or less his life; and arm-flapping, tie-pulling, double-taking cartoon indignation his style. On the court, at least. In practice, Derrick sought to re-create the Reagan of his playing days, the suburban feel of rules and consequences. He preached fundamentals. He taught ball movement, the key to any successful offense. He nurtured the team spirit formed at Pearce Middle School. "We play like white boys; we're just fast black kids," he liked to say. "We run drills, set picks, nothing different from Duke." In the gym and in his social studies classroom, where 93 percent of his students were passing the standardized tests, he valued what he could impart less than what he could make kids want to know. He told every class, "There are people that don't think you can. If I ever *just* teach you, I'm not doing my job."

Back on offense, JaQuarius went for a layup.

"And one!" somebody in the crowd yelled. No call. "Hey, ref, we gonna need that 'and one' next time."

Akins 17, Reagan 16. The boys huddled up.

"Listen, right here," Coach Davis said. "What did we say we were going to be doing? Dribble and drive."

But the Raiders were losing whatever composure they'd had. They bounced inbound passes off one another's shoulders like the Globetrotters, only not on purpose. The Akins boys stifled their every effort to penetrate the lane, answering with consistent perimeter shooting.

"Come on now, rebound!" somebody called from the bleachers, where Anabel Garza was taking a seat on the visitors' side. She wore a matching sweater and scarf, Columbia blue.

"Anybody on the floor with two?" Coach Davis asked the scorekeeper, managing fouls. He put JaQuarius on the bench. JaQuarius did not breathe hard but his dark tattoos rivered with sweat.

The score was 38–32 Akins at the half. Coach Davis took his squad to the locker room. Anabel's daughter fetched Gatorade. Anabel made small talk with her staff.

"I've got four of these guys in my first-period class," Candice was saying, "so whenever we have a Tuesday game, I know Wednesday morning I'm going to hear, 'Did you see that foul?' And I'll be, like, 'That's not chemistry.'"

Anabel laughed, then nodded toward her husband over on the Akins bench.

"I told him he's going to sleep in the doghouse tonight."

"If Akins wins?"

"No, either way."

Anabel joked about her crisis of allegiance, but after a while she disclosed the real reason she had arrived late to the game: The superintendent, who was planning to visit Reagan again before the end of the semester, had called her in for a meeting.

"I told her, 'I've been sitting in this same meeting for five years with people asking, 'How are we going to change East Austin?'" Anabel said. "You can't just shut a school down and reopen it with all different teachers every few years. We've got to address it across the city, at the elementary schools."

Candice nodded along. The Raiders took the court for the second half. Anabel took a position by the front of the bleachers at the bottom of the stairs, where her students could see she was on their side, even when her husband was coaching the other team.

On the court, Akins started to pull away. They double-teamed JaQuarius, but Corn managed to feed him the ball for a layup, with the clairvoyant sort of pass available only to teammates of many years standing.

"Let's go Raiders," Candice called from her place in the bleachers. Ashley Brown was sitting next to her, in a T-shirt decorated to say "Them boys ain't ready" on the front. On the back it said who they weren't ready for: "JaQuarius." Ashley was ready for JaQuarius, ready for him to talk about the future, about her, about his dad, but that wasn't happening. She was here anyway, in her JaQuarius T-shirt. She let Ms. Kaiser do the yelling.

Now it was 59–46 Akins. Coach Davis ordered a full-court press. The play started getting physical, and Reagan drew a charge from the Eagle point guard on the opening sequence of the fourth quarter.

"We deserve it to go our way sometime," a man yelled from the Reagan bleachers. "We always get the short end. We got to get the long end sometime."

JaQuarius sailed to the hoop and drew another foul. On the sideline, Coach Davis went similarly airborne. The Akins boys started making sloppy passes, faltering under the press. The Reagan cheering section was up and stomping. Coach Davis absolutely pogoed.

"They falling apart!" a woman was shrieking. "They falling apart! Come on Raiders!"

Reagan cut the lead to nine with six minutes to play. Akins put on a press of its own, and a furious transition game began, fast breaks end to end. The ball got loose and ten boys dog-piled it like a fumble recovery. The possession arrow said Raider ball: JaQuarius Daniels made a layup, then stole the inbound pass and made another, four points in less than a second. The Akins lead fell to five. The Eagle cheering section fell silent, with lots of folded arms.

At the front of the Reagan section, Anabel was shaking. The parents and the kids and the teachers and the teachers' church friends were up and stomping. The bleachers felt ready to come down at the riggings. Wild as the scene was getting, nobody could match the exertions of Coach Davis, who flailed around the sidelines like Little Richard on crystal meth and now called another huddle.

"All right. Listen. Listen! Right here. You've got them afraid. We've got a relationship. When 45 gets it, we go at him hard."

No. 45 was the scrawniest white kid on the Akins squad. On every possession he'd hole up in the corner, wait for the Reagan defense to double-team the ball, and then catch-and-shoot the open three. Coach Davis was serious about going at him. Both sides were fouling hard. One Akins player looked like he had a bloody nose, but the refs hadn't noticed and the kid wasn't saying. Corn got fouled next, but he missed the free throw. Coach Davis muttered an oath.

"He's still bleeding over there," somebody on the Reagan bench yelled. "That's how you get the swine flu."

The ref examined the Akins kid.

"It's been going on for seven minutes," Coach Davis called. The kid was benched. Brandon Golden made a three to keep Reagan in the game. Coach Davis called timeout. Anabel brought more Gatorade.

"Brandon," Coach Davis said, "be ready, 'cause we're gonna squeeze it now. Everybody know what we're doing?"

Down by nine with a minute and a half to play, Brandon stepped up for another big shot. Akins responded with a fast break, and the chemistry teacher's voice cut through the gym yelling, "Raiders fiiiiight," but it was too late. Reagan lost 87–79. When JaQuarius and Brandon walked into fourth-period basketball class late the next afternoon, an assistant coach demanded twenty-five push-ups each. It was thirty-five degrees out, about as cold as the city gets, and they performed their punishment by the open door. JaQuarius was wearing sandals. The other boys stood over him, yelling, "What's up, Captain?" Somebody in the crowd wanted to know whether the push-ups would nullify the tardiness for the purposes of report cards. They would not. "Do you want to be fair, or do you want to be on time?" the assistant coach asked, not waiting for an answer.

Coach Davis, bundled in a sweater, wool cap, and striped scarf, called the varsity into his cluttered office. The Dallas trip was coming up, but first he wanted to talk about what had happened at Akins.

"Now, guys, are we gonna get those funny calls, especially in

Austin? When we left the city before, we didn't see any of that. Now, when we get back to Austin, we're still gonna get those calls and that funny stuff because of the connotation of Reagan, and we just got to ball."

Coach Davis had a scholarly assistant and a street one. The street one, Nate Haynes, who taught health, spoke up next: "If they ain't from northeast Austin, they hate it. You're gonna get slapped in the face, and no calls. They want you to snap, so they can kill you out of the game."

Coach Davis told the boys to spend the period on homework. They were scheduled to play the Wildcats of Woodrow Wilson High, an East Dallas landmark that had produced more than its share of mayors and Heisman winners, at five o'clock Friday afternoon in the tournament. They'd probably keep each other up late at the Red Roof Inn win or lose, so better to get ahead now.

"There ain't no practice," Coach said. "I'm shutting the gym down. We got to get away from it."

The Dallas trip was bound to be rough, and meant to be. When they got back, the Chaparrals of Westlake High would be waiting up in the hills. The boys sat in silence. Coach Davis ran through team housekeeping. As it turned out, Coach himself had been the only "business guy" willing to help underwrite their travel uniforms, so most of the boys still owed their forty-five-dollar share. "I got kids too," he said, "so I want to get some of it back, especially with Christmas coming up."

The boys looked at the floor. Forty-five dollars. The janitor walked in for the trash. L. C. Bradley was his name. Coach told the boys to thank "the most important dude in the program." Then he asked if anybody had anything to tell the team.

"I want to apologize for quitting," Willie said. "I just want to hoop."

Coach told him not to worry.

"This is a family," Derrick said. "Hey, listen, after you go to your tutoring, go be kids. I'm shutting this gym down. Don't go shoot at another one. Let's step back and smell the roses, guys. You know how they talk about how they give you roses when you're dead?"

He told them to study hard and then called another huddle and the boys put their hands in.

"Hoop Squad on three. One-two-three."

"Hoop Squad!"

The boys turned out into the cold afternoon. Coach told the six-foot junior James Marshall to stay behind. James had e-mailed him out of the blue about a family trip.

"Why are you going to Atlanta for the break when there's games scheduled?" Coach asked.

James said he'd miss Westlake and one other game but that he'd keep up. Said he'd play pickup with his cousins out in Georgia.

Derrick was having none of it.

"Where are we going after Christmas?" he asked. "District. That shit counts."

James leaned across the desk, sinking into the hood of his over-size sweatshirt and pulling at his fingers. He nodded at what Coach was saying about being part of the rotation and not popping in and out.

"I can't tell people, 'Come to practice, work hard, commit,' and then you go to Atlanta for two weeks and play the same amount of minutes."

James said he'd practice hard in Georgia. Derrick said he wouldn't go against James's family.

"But you're part of the hoop squad now," he said. "And put your hands to the side when you're talking to me, because one day it may not be just talking to Coach Davis. You might be in a financial aid office."

"Yes, sir."

"All right."

The jayvee was waiting in the hall. Derrick dismissed James Marshall: "Send those knuckleheads in."

Thirteen

Those who remembered called him Big Pee Wee. He carried himself like a basketball ghost, all leather-skinned and coiled, stalking the perimeter of the world for an open look, a hood legend from back in the days before "back in the day."

People said he was a stone-cold killer on the court, ambidextrously capable of accurate three-point shooting off the dribble. Some said they'd seen him score more than seventy points in a rec center game with eight-minute quarters. Sometimes he'd vanish, never for long. There were stories of a royal screw job involving the Spurs and other stories that said he'd blown off the tryout. One version of ancient Eastside history told how he'd gone up to New York City on a scholarship to something that might've been called Manhattan University where he couldn't sit still in the classrooms or abide the cold so he'd spent a few months turning spectators' heads and defenders' ankles out at Rucker Park until he got to missing his high school sweetheart and came home.

Closing in on sixty years old, gaunt with a touch of white creeping into his hair, Big Pee Wee would visibly simmer in the bleachers at Reagan High School basketball games, tracking the action with a hardscrabble squint until the inevitable moment when something in him seemed to boil over straight in the direction of the referee: "Call the game right!" At away games in the white strongholds of the exurbs, which he also attended with some frequency, he'd give up on the officials and just yell at JaQuarius: "Don't worry, they gonna call the game their way."

Pee Wee: The nickname stuck to Henry Davis back in the early 1960s, when he was the undersize kid drawn to a year-round sport where, in the words of its poet laureate, Jim Carroll, "you can correct your own mistakes, immediately and beautifully, in midair." He never lived it down, not even when he made the varsity Yellow Jackets squad in tenth grade at L. C. Anderson High School, the original pride of the Eastside.

Founded as Austin City Colored High School, Anderson took its name from the Latin teacher who'd served as principal through the early decades of the twentieth century, a time when Mayor A. P. Wooldridge, credited with organizing the city's first public school system, would speak openly of how the "white man outnumbers you nine to one and is the stronger race. He knows his power and will not hesitate to use it if he must."

By the time Henry Davis enrolled, a decade after *Brown v. Board of Education,* the new school up north in the suburbs was taking black kids from St. John's, but in the city Anderson was still the only real choice. District officials transferred some teachers in from the white schools, but not any white students. They also told black parents their children could start attending white schools in their neighborhoods, though most of the black families lived on the East-side anyway. A defiant strain made itself heard through the refrain of the Anderson High Jackettes:

Hail to the victors valiant
Hail to the conquering heroes
Hail hail to Anderson
Champions of the West

"Champions of the West": The old cheer took a literal turn in 1968, when the authorities finally let the Anderson basketball team start playing the white schools across the highway. The Yellow Jack-ets, decked out in gold uniforms with black stripes, competing in the top division against the biggest schools around, won district right out of the gate. Pee Wee Davis, a junior forward that year, made the all-star team along with three other Yellow Jackets. Se-nior year he scored 27.7 points per game, leading Anderson to an-other district championship. The team won twenty-three games in a row, keeping up the streak even after their MVP center went down with a knee injury, their coach took leave for surgery, and their point guard, Raymond Whitley, was disqualified (for getting married).

"This is the greatest team I've ever had," Coach Lawrence Brit-ton told the Austin *American*. "I've had better individuals in other years, but none of them has ever come through under the circum-stances this team has."

Coach Britton meant the injuries, but those were just the half of it. Federal investigators had been through the school, examining the city's end run around the Civil Rights Act, and the kids could tell what was coming. Their principal, Hobart L. Gaines, talked to the Austin *Citizen* about one student "who walked into class and told the teacher, 'Let's not talk about English today—let's talk about what's going to happen at Anderson.'"

In 1970, when the Department of Justice sued the school district, a judge initially ordered up boundary changes and busing, but the district had a different idea: To comply with the letter of the integration lawsuit, the board of trustees closed L. C. Anderson High. Reform came in a different package back then, but it still meant shutting down the pride of the Eastside. The next year, by the district's count, 121 Anderson students dropped out instead of reporting to their newly assigned schools. Coach Britton, architect of consecutive district championships, couldn't get hired as a coach, so he signed on to teach health class at Reagan High. The Yellow Jackets' trophies were lost, only to turn up some years later in a shed at Mayflower Moving and Storage. The city used the Anderson High building to warehouse plywood for a decade or so until 1984, when it burned to the ground. The old school smoldered for eighteen hours. Arson, said the police. The city finished off the walls with a wrecking ball.

Pee Wee Davis heard the news in San Antonio, where he was playing junior college ball at the top of a 2–3 zone (he'd been a forward at Anderson only because the lineup shifted when the big man hurt his knee). He went on to Jackson State for a semester, until the coach got on him for goldbricking in practice, then came back home to Austin to marry his high school girlfriend. She gave him a son, then a daughter. They stayed married four years.

Pee Wee found a job coaching kids at Rosewood Rec, where the UT players would come to try stuff out in the off-season. He played for a couple of teams sponsored by a service station, the Cougars and the Clippers. He brought his son around, but never let him win at one-on-one. Basketball meant too much.

"I've used it as a tension reliever, body builder—it ain't no one or two categories," Pee Wee would say. "You ain't gonna be the best at it, but you'll be the best you can be. The game is full of adjustments. It's a consistent adjustment, running the floor."

Pee Wee left the family in '76: another adjustment. He missed watching his kids grow up, mostly, but he came back for the basketball part. At the close of the 1980s he started showing up in the bleachers at Reagan High, where his son was stroking outside jumpers for the varsity. The boy's senior year the Raiders went 27–6, the best record in school history. Two of those six losses came against LBJ, but the Raiders came back to win their last meeting of the season decisively, 88–68. Play got rough that winter. One time Pee Wee saw his son throw an elbow. That was when he started his yelling. He couldn't stand by and watch the boy get kicked off the court. People were starting to call Derrick Little Pee Wee.

Una Cena de Navidad
    Gratis
    La Cafetería de Reagan
    El Miércoles Dec. 16
    5:30–8

The Junior ROTC kids lined the sidewalk in their pressed blue uniforms, standing at attention against the early dark, saluting the adults and watching for the superintendent, who was coming to deliver her assessment of the school's progress. Pretty soon the cafeteria was jammed. The old-timers hadn't forgotten the closing of L. C. Anderson High, not after thirty-nine years, not after the building burned to the ground, not after the city smashed its remains, and not even after the district opened a new school called Anderson High over on the west side.

The night of the superintendent's address landed on a festive occasion, the Christmas dinner, and cloths of red and green decorated the folding tables. The agenda included discussing plans for the biggest graduation ceremony in years and raising $24.50 a head for a senior class trip to Fiesta Texas (the discounted price, including food and chaperones), but the signs pointing to the cafeteria took a combative tone, billing the event as a "Stand Up for Reagan Meeting."

As the superintendent made her way to the school, Anabel Garza prepared her own presentation. Her assistant principal, Rick Fowler, had diagrammed the TAKS cells—black, white, and Hispanic; limited English proficiency and economically disadvantaged; freshman, sophomore, junior, and senior—across every permutation. From the data, he said he could spot signs of a learning disability, test anxiety, or tutoring gap.

The JROTC marched into the cafeteria, carrying swords, rifles, and flags, past the game room where volunteers were spooning yellow *queso* over Christmas burritos, past the tables decorated with miniature fir trees, past the teenage girls in their good dresses and the middle-age alums in from all over town. Larry Johnson sang the national anthem, and the crowd rose in a Columbia blue blur. A translator took his place on the stage. The room fell silent. And all eyes followed Superintendent Carstarphen across the stage.

"I believe every district in this country must take responsibility locally for every school in its district," she said. "I can't believe we'd want the state telling us what to do with our schools."

A low murmur circulated. She went on.

"I know this school feels the pressure. I know this community feels the pressure. I feel the pressure."

Heads nodded.

"The team has really been putting forward a lot of effort to make Reagan the school we want it to be."

More nodding.

"There are all sorts of ways that people seem to be able to interpret the law."

Another murmur: Did she know something? Already? Before Christmas?

"I just want to do the very best for this school and its families and let the chips fall where they may," the superintendent said. "We are ahead of the game. The scores are better, the attendance is better, the behavior is better. But it does not mean we're completely out of the woods. It's not even enough to say that no matter what, we've turned the corner. I am certain, at least by what I've seen, that Reagan is on the turnaround. But completely making it 180 degrees: We're not there yet.

"And I'm going to say," she continued, pausing for a deep breath, "there's nothing like planning for a contingency. What happens if? And we need to start having that conversation too."

Five minutes after welcoming her with a round of applause, the audience fell silent. The superintendent had already asked the school board to prepare to carry out an eventual state order to close Reagan. Meetings would begin January 11. A plan would be in place by February. Whispers traveled up and down the cafeteria: Those were specific dates. It was starting to sink in. Even if the school made the numbers, the state could still give the demolition order. So could the district. And the district, it turned out, was already drawing up the protocol.

"I don't want anyone going into the summer not knowing

where their kid is going," the superintendent explained. When there was nothing left to say, she turned the floor over to the principal.

Twin projector screens lit up, flanking Anabel with the school motto in English and Spanish: "Not Without Honor, *No Sin Honor*." She opened with midyear test scores showing a 13.7 percentage-point improvement in science. The state used all kinds of numbers, and she highlighted one called the Texas Projection Measure, which gave schools credit for younger students on track to pass the exit-level TAKS. Using the TPM, Reagan could already report a 56 percent passing rate, good enough to qualify as academically acceptable, by a single point. Nobody could say whether this would count at year's end, but it made the crowd in the cafeteria sit up.

"On this mission, which has been a very tough mission, I have never felt alone," Anabel said, raising her voice. "The teachers here have been working tirelessly. We're tired, sometimes we're snarling at each other, but I've never been on this path alone."

The air in the room seemed to shift.

"It's the holiday season," Anabel said, "and I wake up each and every day thankful that I have y'all with me. Every day, things get better. Every day the scores go up. This is a beautiful story about adults who love children and who want the best for them. And these are the best kids. I've worked everywhere in Austin, and they're the most courteous. They love the adults. Kind of weird, if you ask me. They love you."

While she had their attention, Anabel started to preach: TAKS scores were rising, yes, but more kids were failing their classes. That was bound to happen when the curriculum got tougher. And there was only so much she could do about it on campus.

"I want kids reading at least thirty minutes at home. Get them to a quiet place. Reading is the base for them being able to maneuver through those tests, literacy is the base," she said. She talked about parenthood, saying her Trey had never missed a day of school from pre-K to twelfth grade. "Somehow we need to change the culture of attendance. There's a culture that, 'Ah, we don't have to be here all the time.' If they're not here, we can't teach them. We can't make that data move if they aren't here. There's a rumor going around that your principal will come get you. Horror stories about a van pulling up. They're true. I will come get you."

Then she told about the tutors, not just the paid ones but all the volunteers, the church people, the teachers staying long past dark or bringing kids into their own living rooms.

"We are on our way up," Anabel said. "It's personal for all of us. This is a personal mission of mine, and I know for all of the teachers who have stayed here, it's a decision. I believe in this school, and I know we're going to turn it around."

The only son of Pee Wee Davis took a seat at the front of the bus. It was a regular yellow school bus, painted in grime from the week's service, but on Tuesdays and Fridays he called it the Spirit Bus, conscripted for the night shift to carry his Raider Hoop Squad to away games, some more away than others. The near-winter sunset cast a citric glare through the slatted windows onto his eleven players, who sat sprawled across the bench seats one by one, with their earbuds bleeding enough sound to harness the engine's weary groan to a hip-hop muzzle. Sucking on a candy cane, chasing it with Hawaiian Punch, Coach Derrick Davis made a quick head count, from JaQuarius in the back to George Warren hauling gear.

"Let's be ready to go tonight," he'd just finished saying, and he believed that they were. Over the weekend, they had beaten Woodrow Wilson High by fifteen points at the Chris Bosh Hoopfest tournament up in Dallas. They'd even come within ten points of upsetting Dallas Lincoln, led by LeBryan Nash, a six-seven national recruit described by one scout as perhaps "the most physically gifted player in the 2011 class."

"They got up on us, but we realized, 'Damn, we pretty good too,'" Derrick had said, standing there in his windowless office amid the clutter of aged trophies, waiting for the Spirit Bus. "I know we got fresh legs. I see it. Handle the event. The only time it's gonna get any bigger is maybe in regionals and state. It's our destiny. We're gonna do it. Loud and proud. Hoop Squad on three."

"One, two, three."

"Hoop Squad!"

The bus rolled out past La Palapa and the A+ Teachers' Credit Union, toward the great dividing line of Interstate 35, away from the Mount Carmel Apartments where he used to follow his dad to Rosewood Park. He'd practiced that jump shot on the trash can for hours, the same way every time, just the way his dad showed him, until his dad decided he was old enough to play against the grown men (in fourth grade).

Away from Blessing Street, where his mother raised him and his sister after their dad moved out. He'd talk back when his mother sent him out to buy an onion or something cheaper at the corner store just to get the change from the food stamps, and he'd sass right to her face when she fell for scams like those cellulite-burning creams—"Mama," he'd say, "we're on food stamps. Do you really think you're gonna buy a cream and it's gonna burn fat off your leg? If it does, it probably ain't healthy"—but as he got older he started to understand that the reason she was hard on him probably had to do with how much he looked like his dad, and looked up to his dad, and played ball like his dad, who'd walked out on her and all of them after all.

Away from St. John's, where he'd heard The Talk like most any other black kid growing up, any boy at least: "Here's how you put your hands on the wheel. Stop in a well-lighted place. Be respectful. Keep your wallet on the seat, not in your pocket."

Away from Reagan High, where he'd enrolled even after the Lanier basketball coach promised him playing time alongside a six-ten center. Away from its band hall, where he'd labored under that dwarfing tuba. Away from its fields, where he'd defied a football coach's plans with a tone that felt only a little silly all these years later: "What about basketball? It's my passion."

Away too from its hallways, where he'd paid such little attention to the baton twirler ("Oh, he's so cute," Jennifer would giggle to her friend Tanya) that nobody could have guessed they'd end up married, raising two little twirlers of their own. Mariah was ten, Diva seven, both of them Reagan bound, and far enough apart in age to succeed one another as feature twirler in the band. Jennifer noticed the way Derrick was starting to mention other jobs, other cities, though he'd never even been to New York to see that Rucker Park where his dad was supposed to have laid it down all those years ago (couldn't even tell you what borough it was in). He'd say something nice about Houston, or maybe San Diego, where he remembered visiting cousins once when he was a kid. She didn't make much of it. She didn't expect Derrick to tell her everything he was thinking, of course. That wasn't his way. He could recite the statistics on life expectancy for high school coaches, but instead he'd just declare "family season" every year from the end of baseball until August. He didn't care about baseball, or football either for that matter, but he was a good provider, taking on sideline assistant duties to bring home that $10,789 annual extra-duty stipend for coaching. He had big plans for their family. Teaching, not basketball, was the way up the ladder to administration, so he was trying to put away some money to go back for a PhD. Whenever Jennifer's graphic design commissions slowed down and set them back, he'd get frustrated but rarely mad. She'd repay the courtesy at tax time, when she found out he'd spent about a thousand dollars on the hoop squad, counting the balance on those travel uniforms, the hotel room for the tournament up in Dallas, and the occasional ten bucks so JaQuarius could take his girl, Ashley, out. Derrick said JaQuarius would remember that kind of thing twenty years down the line—"When my momma's car broke down, Coach Davis picked me up for school"—and she figured Derrick had reason to know. Tuesday nights, game nights for the Raiders, Jennifer would watch him come home win or lose no matter how bad to get the trash out for Wednesday morning pickup. Later she'd hear him out in the garage, yelling into the phone about how some kid failed a six weeks and had to drop off the team. She could almost picture him out there, pacing, but that was why she *didn't* worry. She told people her husband was "super-employable: a successful coach and a good teacher."

Derrick worried, though. The superintendent was predicting a $20 million budget shortfall for the district. The board of trustees couldn't raise any more money, because state lawmakers had cut property tax rates in a plan to finance education with business growth and cigarette sales. The state couldn't help, because its own crude oil and sales tax revenues were falling. Even with $79 billion in federal economic stimulus funds designated to carry schools through the recession, districts across the country were laying off teachers, good ones included. Successful coaches were no exception. Maybe in football.

Derrick hadn't told Jennifer about getting his résumé together. He hadn't told her about working his basketball contacts in other cities. He hadn't said the words out loud, not yet: "With a family, you can't live on question marks and promises." Maybe he wouldn't have to. The principal's midyear standardized testing numbers were looking good, and Derrick knew how much it would mean to Jennifer seeing their girls in Columbia blue leotards pulling off lasso straddles and knuckle pops and helicopters while the Soul Raider band kicked those funk grooves they were into now.

Jennifer would follow him anywhere, of course. It all went back to Reagan, where the Latina daughter of a striving middle-class radio technician and a Cap Metro secretary could daydream about dating a black basketball star two years her senior. Jennifer was competitive (she'd picked twirling out of all the styles offered in dance class), but killer instinct wasn't what she'd seen in Derrick. She liked the way he treated sophomores and even freshmen as equals. She liked the way he befriended Charles, the weird German tuba player, and took hell for it from his basketball teammates. She liked the way he stood up to the band director when it came down to a choice between horns and hoops. Those were the things she remembered a couple of years after graduation, when she spotted him at a Christmas party with a bunch of high school friends. Those were the things she remembered a year or so after that, when her little brother said his substitute teacher at Reagan, Mr. Davis, wanted her number. And those were the things she remembered when he called her from a pay phone and they talked for two hours. Those things.

No matter what the chant said, D. Davis never set out to literally save Reagan, or even spend a lifetime there. Gravity, that was. He coasted along at Howard Payne University in Brownwood with a 2.1 GPA, even though his mother called every morning from East Austin to make sure he was going to class. He didn't need to go to class. He was captain of the basketball team (called the Yellow Jackets, of all things), an all-conference player the coaches sent out to meet recruits. It wasn't until senior year, when some realities started to sink in about the NBA and his chances not being much different from his dad's, that he brought his grades up to 3.2 and got serious about a social work major. That degree was his ticket, and his friends back home knew it. That was why they left him behind on weekend nights when he came home to visit his mom. All it took was an arm on his shoulder—"No, D. Davis, you can't come"—and he understood. This too had been covered in The Talk. When Derrick brought his diploma home, he got hired as an assistant jayvee coach at Reagan, assigned work as a permanent sub in math and science classes on the side. Seventeen thousand dollars a year felt like all the money in the world. He called up the twirler girl from his high school band days—she'd grown into her looks—and took her out to Spirits, where the bouncer saw him coming and said, "Hey, D. Davis will save us!" People remembered. Maybe that was what impressed her. Maybe not. People remembered anyway.

Young, in love, and childless wasn't a bad way to be in Austin, Texas, in the late 1990s. Derrick and Jennifer paid $520 a month in rent. Derrick worked as an assistant in the DELTA Lab at Reagan High, helping dropouts recover enough credits to graduate. Pretty soon Jennifer was calling her old high school teachers by their first names. That felt grown up. Grounded too. Part of something, even if the Reagan they'd known as students had new kinds of problems. Derrick would come home from work talking about kids with third jobs, kids deported over Christmas break. To the extent he could understand their troubles, the way the Rio Grande loomed over everything, it was because of Jennifer, who understood about JaQuarius and the other boys and Interstate 35 through the frame of Derrick's family.

Derrick didn't drop hints about leaving, not back then. Reagan was comfortable, or at least familiar. They wanted a family, though, so he started angling for a promotion inside the school. When the man who'd been his own basketball coach, Gail Simpson, retired after twenty-one years with more than five hundred victories, the varsity job went to his assistant, Brad Oestreich. Derrick moved up to head coach of the jayvee. He was a step away, or so he thought. "Being an alum of Reagan High School," Derrick wrote on a job application in 1998, the year he married Jennifer, "I have had the pleasure and misfortune of seeing a community at its best and worst."

Around the time Mariah came along, Derrick finally landed a full-time teaching position, $31,888 a year. The athletic director called the next day to offer coaching duties, worth an $8,337 stipend, but it all came with a catch. Two, actually. The job was at A. S. Johnston High, which was in worse shape than Reagan. Derrick walked into the basketball office and found six uniforms on the floor. This was summertime, months after the end of the season. He gauged expectations for the team accordingly. When he brought Jennifer in to take a look, she told him: "We're not at Reagan anymore." He coached the team to a 7–19 record, counting on the job to lead to a head coaching position someplace better. The only way Jennifer knew how to describe watching her husband coach against Reagan was to tell you to clasp your hands like for praying, thumb over thumb, then switch the thumbs: "It just doesn't feel natural, does it?"

The other catch was that full-time teaching called for certification. "If you are not accepted into the program, you will need to resign your position effective May 26, 2001," an HR coordinator told Derrick in a letter. The state rejected his application; his GPA from Howard Payne U fell short of the standards for the Social Studies Composite certification program at the University of Texas. The letters started to strike a more dire tone. When his emergency permit expired in 2001, the district applied for a hardship extension, citing a shortage of qualified teachers. In a letter to the state, a certification analyst pleaded: "He is doing an exceptional job at Johnston High School." Turned down again, Derrick agreed to serve as an intern to a mentor teacher. He also had to take history classes at ACC. If the implication that his degree from a fully accredited historically black university wasn't good enough gave him any pause, he didn't let on. As he agreed to the terms of the state's "Deficiency Plan," Derrick kept his next job application upbeat:

"I have always had an interest in others, since high school," he wrote, concluding, "My future plans include more professional development in the areas of classroom management and Internet technologies/capabilities, to improve my overall teacher performance!"

Derrick got his certificate. A. S. Johnston High, a few years away from the state closure order that would turn it into an unrecognizable tech academy, hired him as a history teacher. He did not stay long. After the 2003 season, when Ortralla Mosley was stabbed to death in the hall at Reagan, Coach Oestreich decamped for the exurbs of Pflugerville, leaving the Raiders varsity coaching job open again. Derrick called in every favor he could think of. To Jennifer, "it seemed preordained, it was so easy, almost like he didn't have to interview." Publicly, the athletic director said he had received seven applications, but Derrick didn't tell Jennifer what he'd heard: There were two candidates. He was the runner-up. The first guy passed on the job, "and they call that fate."

Either way, Jennifer was thrilled. She volunteered to wash the team uniforms. She took their girls to the games. The Raider band didn't have a twirler anymore, but that didn't mean it couldn't again. The '04 squad went 14–14, no small achievement for a new coach at a school shaken by violent tragedy. The next year Derrick took the Raiders to the playoffs.

A year later, the state found the school academically unacceptable, the Vincent brothers bolted, and the Raiders won only seven games. In '07 they won ten. "That's a losing season," Derrick said. "I've been a winner all my life." It took four years to rebuild the program under the state's label, a full graduation cycle, but he did it. In '09, he took the team three rounds into the playoffs, losing to LBJ. Now, with JaQuarius and Brandon back as juniors, leading the 2009–10 team to impressive preseason victories, people were starting to fill the bleachers again. Derrick could emphasize his role in the classroom all he wanted—"It ain't what you can teach the kids, as a teacher, it's about what you can make them want to know," he'd say, "and it's hard as hell to make them want to know about Martin Luther and his ninety-five theses"—but the people starting to fill the bleachers were some of the same people starting to fill the cafeteria for PTSA meetings. It was only basketball, until it wasn't. Maybe this was a coincidence: His father, who seemed to know and be known by everybody on the Eastside, started finding it a worthwhile use of his time to drop by his son's house on weekends to do yard work.

Nobody was expecting the hoop squad to win tonight. Nobody said so, at least. Westlake High served West Lake Hills, gateway to the Hill Country, a rarified enclave billing itself as "perfectly situated to take advantage of everything that Austin offers." In particular, where it was situated was just outside the reach of the city school district, operating its own separate district with a feeder system of six elementary and two middle schools, all of which were rated exemplary by the state. Though their schools were technically public, the people of West Lake Hills provided additional money through a foundation devoted to "funding the gap between adequate and excellent." Every year they held a gala at the Renaissance Hotel, and their tax-deductible gifts provided nearly a million dollars to pay for more than a dozen extra teachers. Their teachers stayed for fourteen years on average. Their sons and daughters scored an average of 1,774 on the SAT. Eighty-five percent went on to four-year colleges. Only one-tenth of 1 percent dropped out. Westlake High dominated the field in golf, tennis, soccer, cross-country, and wrestling. Its football team, which had won a state championship in 1996 with the future Super Bowl quarterback Drew Brees, was set to play for another Division 5-A state championship this very weekend. And the basketball team, drawn from a student body of more than twenty-four hundred, starred Cody Doolin, a six-two guard on his way to setting a new team scoring record. Though some recruiters said Doolin would need to put on weight, he already had serious interest from the University of San Francisco. One scout wrote that he "has deceptive quickness and speed and he is quite good in the open court. His wiry frame and polished handle allow him to weave his way through traffic and he can deliver the assist as well. He has a high basketball IQ and he rarely makes mistakes."

In spite of all that, Reagan's performance at the tournament up in Dallas had given Derrick some hope, which he'd tried to convey to the team. After arriving late to the last practice for the Westlake game, delayed by a test monitoring assignment in the library, he'd found the boys dressed to scrimmage in shirts and skins, with the smallest one sitting under the hoop to provide an obstacle for an alley-oop contest (though only JaQuarius could get up high enough to dunk).

"Everybody off the court," Coach Davis had yelled, "except the varsity."

As the boys stretched, he'd promised to take the two with the highest grade-point averages out to dinner.

"I want to start rewarding y'all," he'd said. "Hey, your GPA is like a batting average. It's hard to raise up, but it's easy to go down."

When they finished stretching, he'd promised a ride home to anybody who needed one.

"Hey, man, this is deadly serious, where we're at," he'd said, looking around at the seniors, Josh, Corn, Jerold, and Willie. "We can't afford to lose a game. You know I get emotional about y'all. After these games, we're not going to have these guys with us any-more. We won't have these guys, and these are the memories you'll have when you get to be my age. More than anything, the winning and the losing, this time with these cats is what you'll remember."

He'd called the boys in to a huddle, told them, "Watch your-selves, your skirts, your GPAs, everything," asked if there were any questions, then dismissed them with another "Loud and proud, on three."

And now there was nothing more he could tell them. As the Spirit Bus climbed an overpass skyward across Interstate 35 into the first shadows of Friday night, the boys nodded their heads to the beats in their earbuds. Derrick eased his nerves with small talk. His assistant coach, Thurman Lewis, said they might get a strong turnout tonight, for an away game at least. That science teacher, Ms. Kaiser, would probably bring a bunch of kids. She hadn't missed a game.

"She hasn't missed a scrimmage," Derrick said. "She's looking to latch on to something positive. We're the most positive thing around."

Derrick took a bite of his candy cane. Coach Lewis left him to his thoughts. The bus lurched through the rush-hour traffic.

"I was just thinking," Derrick spoke up again, "we may be walking into a hornet's nest tonight. They've got their football championship tomorrow. They had their pep rally yesterday, and if you're just looking for something to do, you might be like, 'Oh, there's a game tonight. We good in basketball too.' They'll go to the Web site and be like, 'Reagan? Look who's getting off the bus.'"

The streetlights were coming on. The Spirit Bus rolled down Mopac, the western highway separating the wealthy central city from its even wealthier outskirts. Derrick glanced to the back of the bus. He kept his voice low, even though the boys were all wearing earbuds.

"Back in town, now, I know we got to play the game with all the calls and stuff, just the general attitude about the school," he muttered.

At the West Lake Hills exit, the Spirit Bus curved up a road winding past Christmas displays, Baptist churches, and office parks set among open forest.

"It's like a whole different city, ain't it, Coach?" Derrick said.

"Uh-huh," Coach Lewis affirmed.

The bus driver turned on the light and fumbled for a map.

"You wanna come help me?" she asked. "I ain't been out here in a while."

Derrick squinted at the map. He looked back out the window: a sushi restaurant. A bank called Prosperity. Down a slope, the lights of Westlake High came into view. Coach Lewis let out a small gasp.

"They got a field hockey field," he said.

"Yeah," said Derrick, "they probably play, um . . ."

He thought for a few seconds, and the name of the sport came to him: "Lacrosse."

Under the curvilinear awning of Westlake High, the Raiders filed into the atrium, past a concession stand sponsored by Chick-fil-A. At separate entrances marked Lecture Hall and Competition Gym, they chose the latter. Inside, balloons floated over a sign that said Welcome Alumni. Risers flanked the parquet floor on either side. Some in the crowd wore ties, more wore gold watches. Banners acknowledged the sponsorship of Bishop London & Dodds, P.C., Capitol Courier, Ramsey Chiropractic, and more. The boys kept their earbuds in, blocking out the sound of an announcer calling raffle winners. On their coach's signal, they headed down a hallway where glossy signs touted their opponent's "core principles."

"I'm gonna need to give them a good talk," Coach Davis told his assistant, "let them know what we're up against."

The boys changed into their uniforms.

"Hey, we ready?" Coach Davis asked, and he suggested they were. The Westlake Chaparrals' zone defense would be predictable enough: "1-2-2 all game, half, full."

Then he walked out and closed the door to let the boys pray. He passed the time marveling at the plastic antifungal drainage material on the locker room floor. He heard a chorus of "Amen," then "One, two, three: Hoop Squad," and then his players came out. He huddled the boys and said to watch No. 45, the Doolin kid.

"High screen and roll, running and passing, that's the Westlake offense. They have great fundamentals, good shooting, copy a lot of UT's playing style," Derrick said in the huddle. "For me, tonight, it's a mental thing to see how we are in terms of maturity. We've played fourteen good teams, but if we get up by twelve, they gonna do what they do. Let's come out early, let's be ready to play. One, two, three."

"Hoop Squad!"

When they emerged from the locker room, the boys heard a whoop from the far side of the gym, where dozens of their teachers, parents, and classmates were waving Columbia blue Hoop Squad signs.

The bleachers on the Westlake side were full of parents in sport jackets, teenage boys with beach bum haircuts, and teenage girls in fluffy boots. The Westlake players took the court in mop-top haircuts and bright red soccer-style warm-up jackets. On the sidelines, four little boys took their places in shirts that said Ball Boy in the Westlake colors. Before the game began, the crowd viewed a performance by the PiPs, a group of elementary school children dressed in a modified version of the high school uniforms, who danced and dribbled white basketballs across the floor. This was high school recruiting, West Lake Hills style.

Coach Davis shook hands with the Westlake coach. The announcer called out the Reagan starting five—JaQuarius and Brandon, the seniors Josh and Corn, plus Alex Parish, the five-eight son of the middle school coach who'd brought the team together—and then introduced Coach Davis as "Derrick Lewis."

The Raiders scrambled for the tip, brought the ball downcourt, and scored first, on a free throw by Corn (it turned out the refs, two of whom were black, weren't afraid to call a foul on Westlake), but then Cody Doolin started shooting from outside the arc. Pretty soon the Chaps were up 10–1, running their zone as a full-court press. The little boys in their PiP uniforms leaned against the sideline barricades, jumping up and down. Again and again the Raiders turned over the ball under pressure. Down 22–7, Coach Davis called timeout, but when play resumed the Chaps returned only more dominant. They swarmed the lane. Their versatile guard, so recently deemed undersize by the college scouts, came up with several rebounds and did not hesitate to drive the length of the court. The gap widened. Brandon, the Raiders' best shooter, who'd turned in a fine tournament performance up in Dallas, went cold. His outside shots, usually dependable for at least ten points to keep the Raiders competitive in tough games, kept clanking off the rim. Cody Doolin's did not. Down more than twenty points, Coach Davis called another timeout. The announcer took the opportunity to acknowledge the ball boys: "Thanks, guys," he said, "for helping out the Runnin' Chaparrals."

After the timeout, little Alex Parish sank a three-pointer. The Reagan cheering section applauded wildly, though the basket had narrowed the score only to 51–23. By the third quarter, the Reagan fans were getting restless, watching Brandon find his rhythm only to keep the margin within twenty-five points.

"Come on," Candice Kaiser yelled from the bleachers, then scolded herself: "I'm bitter. I need to pray on it."

Up by more than thirty points, the Westlake boys showed no signs of letting up, or even switching to two-point shots. When it was all done, 87–53, the Raiders filed back onto the Spirit Bus, idling in a parking lot jammed with late-model Hummers and SUVs. Coach Davis skipped up the stairs, resigned to accept a shellacking at the hands of a big, rich 5-A school in pursuit of a 4-A playoff run against schools the same size as Reagan.

"Let's get out of here," he told the driver. A certain kind of laughter, the sound of teenage boys at the start of the weekend, filled the bus. Coach Davis jumped out of his seat.

"Hey, hey!" he yelled, turning to face his team. "We did get beat by thirty. Not too much celebrating! We didn't lose tonight. We got humbled."

Then he sank down low and rode the Spirit Bus back across the interstate to the Eastside, past the pawnshops, the taquerías, and the Marine Corps recruiting billboards, all the old landmarks. Outside the parking lot, he fell back into conversation with his assistant coach. He talked about that science teacher at the game, Ms. Kaiser, the one who was always bringing kids out to cheer. She'd asked him to help her with something big. She was taking some students to Africa and needed another chaperone, one the boys looked up to.

"What'd you tell her?" the assistant coach asked.

Derrick Lamont Davis—Little Pee Wee to an earlier generation, D-Davis to his own, and Coach to the next—kept his seat, waited for the driver of his Spirit Bus to cut the motor, and watched the boys of his Raider Hoop Squad file out under the blue glow of the big *R* in the high school parking lot.

"No thanks," he said. "I know where I'm from."

Fourteen

The girl in the red hoodie, lost in a cell phone reverie, struggled to her feet last in the class, revealing a belly not quite as wide as she was tall. She'd need to leave for occasional counseling and less occasional bathroom breaks, but her science teacher would hear no excuses during the Pledge of Allegiance.

"You don't have to say it," Candice Kaiser told the class, "but you have to stand. Out of respect."

So the pregnant girl stood, like everybody else, *one nation, under God, indivisible, with liberty and justice for all.* Welcome back, Raiders: The spring semester promised the start of district play for the basketball team, an MLK Day Battle of the Bands in Houston for the Soul Raiders, and tests tests tests tests tests. Out in the courtyard, new signs proclaimed "It's time to get down to brass TAKS." The library's front window appealed to the most popular source of hallway chatter with biographies of Kobe Bryant, Shaquille O'Neal, Latrell Sprewell, Jason Kidd, and Allen Iverson, no matter that the library was closed for standardized testing sessions. And in the back corner of her chemistry classroom, Candice still displayed the four-month-old Post-it Notes she'd collected from her students on the first day of school.

We are truly lucky to live here

Be thankful for what you got

A lot of other people in the world don't have schools like we do

Her students sat back down. Candice patrolled the room for the Electronic Scourge. She confiscated Corn's cell phone right away. She tried to ignore the furious-fingered exertions of the pregnant girl; then she couldn't anymore. She whispered the girl's name and mimed putting something in her pocket.

"During the break," she announced, "I made folders with all your TAKS data in them. I know that doesn't seem like a big deal. I think it's really important that you know your TAKS data and how it's set up and what you need to study strategically, because you don't have much time."

The exit-level science tests were scheduled for the end of April, less than four months away. Candice had already tried tailoring in-dividual study assignments to TAKS results. For the final stretch, with the fate of the school on the line, she was ready to let the kids confront their own score breakdowns. Maybe if they marinated long enough in the data and methodology, they'd develop some exper-tise in this modern American survival skill, making the numbers.

Candice called the kids up one by one. Not the pregnant girl. The other kids passed her folder down, and she pursed her lips and examined her test results, but when her cell phone signaled an incoming text message she scanned the screen, whispered something to her deskmate, then returned her attention to the problem of TAKS. Pretty soon she got up and left, taking the permanent hall pass that was her belly.

Candice didn't have to ask where she was going. The pregnancy counselor was one of her roommates at the house on Carver Avenue. Instead she turned to the marker board.

"How many questions on the TAKS test?"

"Fifty-five!" came the chorus.

"And how many do you have to get right?"

"Thirty-two!"

"Thirty-one!"

Actually, Candice tried to explain, the passing score did change from year to year. A score of thirty-five, or 64 percent, would probably count as passing in any year, so thirty-five would be a good goal. She charted the objectives on the board, added the formula for gauging percentage scores, and turned back to face the class.

"Do y'all kind of understand how it's broken down now?"

"Mmm-hmmm," somebody mumbled. Most of the kids just stared at their folders. The lesson was getting complex, though it had little to do with chemistry. Practical math, this was. Candice passed around highlighters and told the kids to illuminate each objective where they'd scored below 60 percent. She lit up the projector screen with her lesson plan for the semester. In double-size bold print, she'd underscored a section called TAKS:

You have 4 options to prepare/prove TAKS skills

Pass 2 mock TAKS tests by Jan. 13 and I will basically set you FREE

She explained this option aloud: "I will set you free to go back to work on other things. I'm not trying to cause you extra suffering."

It was also true that Candice had little time to spare for kids who could get over on the TAKS. As the testing calendar moved into the thick of the season, the principal was shifting additional juniors into her classroom to cram for the exit-level assessment. It was a vote of confidence, recognizing the scores she'd produced in '09, but it was also a lot of pressure.

The remaining three options, Candice told her class, mostly involved tutoring. She'd seen it work.

"Last year, when I developed this method, I had a seventy-five percent passing rate, and that is not usual around here," she said. "Well, it is for social studies, but not for science. And that doesn't mean I'm superawesome; it means this is a method that works."

She gave the example of the basketball players getting weekly tutoring from an engineer. Every Wednesday, a practice day, the usual mix of ball handling and rebounding drills came with math and science drills too. Everybody wanted to be like the basketball team, right?

"They're going to pass," she said. "I don't want you to feel like tutoring happens to you; I want you to feel like it happens for you."

Candice checked the clock. Forty-five minutes gone. Three-quarters of an hour into the first class period of the spring semester, she hadn't said a thing about chemistry. And wasn't even about to. She asked the kids to highlight the days when the group tutoring labs would focus on the objectives they needed to master. She told them how Mr. Fowler, the assistant principal, had authorized double attendance credit for tutoring sessions. She collected cell phone numbers, sorting them by TAKS objective so she could send reminders via text message. Her prescription called for eight hours of tutoring per missed objective.

"You have until April 29," she said, "so if you get started now it should be no problem."

Then she collected the folders. Some kids were getting restless, some were drifting off. It had been a long time since breakfast for anybody who'd eaten one.

"All right," Candice announced in her best bright loud voice. "Can we move on to what we're really going to go into in chemistry now? I see some heads dropping in the back of the room. No! Shay! Don't go!"

Cuing up her Africa video one more time, she said she'd been thinking over Christmas about things that get taken for granted. Maybe tutoring was one of them.

"I saw them," she said. "I looked into their faces. I looked into their eyes, and they wish they could come to America because of education. To remember where you sit and remember what you have, I think it's worth the four minutes to watch it again. Most countries are not like us. Most countries do not have what we have. Just remember that."

Again the Kenyan faces lit up the screen, again the titles flashed the comparison to the Reagan science wing, and again Candice's far-away voice could be heard asking: "And what do you want to tell kids in high school in America?"

Again the Reagan kids watched, spellbound, chins to palms, not a cell phone in sight.

"Remember," Candice said, flipping on the lights, "when you're upset about having to go to tutoring, how privileged you are, because there are real people who would probably really like the opportunity."

An hour and a quarter had passed since the opening bell.

"Okay, we're going to move on to conservation of matter and balancing equations. Which . . . is . . . on . . . the TAKS test!"

Handing out worksheets marked "Cost: fifty cents if lost," she assigned partners to compare observations of a graphic displaying molecules in various states. Rico, the JROTC kid, wrote down "two elements bonding" to describe a covalent pair of hydrogen and oxygen molecules, but when he tried to share his observations with his partner, who'd spent the allotted time scrolling on his iPod, little was accomplished.

"Rico," Candice asked. "What did your partner write?"

"Two elements bonding," Rico averred.

At the stroke of noon, the pregnant girl returned to class, shuffled to her chair, squeezed her belly in behind the attached desktop, and started flipping through the worksheets she'd missed.

Candice called for volunteers. She lined up Jesse, Rico, Jasmine, Shay, and Veronica. She told them to make like molecules and lock arms. She put a diagram up on the board.

"Which are the reactants, products, coefficients, and subscripts, how many molecules are in the equation, and how many hydrogen?" she asked the class, trying to get it all in before the bell. Some kids called out answers; most stuffed their backpacks. Lunchtime: Everybody made for the door, except the pregnant girl, who was still packing up. She hoisted herself from the chair, hitched up her jeans, and listened as her deskmate explained what she'd missed in class: the TAKS prep options, the weekend tutoring schedule.

"¿Sábado?" she asked, pulling on her hoodie.

The survey results from the last PTSA meeting still grappled with big abstract problems: attendance, parent participation, teen pregnancy, and "students are supporting families, can't make it to school." None of that stuff was going away, not in the real world. The Reagan High School PTSA might as well have decided to address the wealth gap, say, or global warming, or mean people, or the tides. But when they were asked "what positive things have occurred at Reagan High School," the parents got more specific:

A principal who cares and holds students accountable

Student leadership

Volunteers

Dedicated teachers going the extra mile

Band

And:

Boys basketball program

A day after the survey results made the rounds, the Spirit Bus pulled into the brightly lit parking lot of the Delco Center, a six-thousand-seat athletic facility across from the XTC Cabaret. Officially named for the lone black voice on the school board during the shutdown of Anderson High, the Delco Center was technically neutral turf, not attached to any one school, but LBJ coach Freddie Roland's nephew Sterling had rechristened it shortly after the ribbon-cutting by going on a fifteen-point third-quarter scoring spree against the Raiders to clinch the district title. That night, February 7, 2003, loomed large in Reagan history. In hindsight, it was the last good time. The Raiders had gained an eight-point lead on the Jaguars, district champions five years running. They'd nearly pulled off an upset. A month after their fortunes turned, Tralla Mosley was stabbed to death. Two months later, the basketball coach quit. And three years later, Reagan High was labeled academically unacceptable. None of that happened because of a basketball score, but it happened, and people could make of it what they wished.

Since that night, the police turned out in force whenever the two schools played for Eastside bragging rights. The ticket seller worked behind thick glass, collecting two dollars for students and three for everyone else. An armed guard stood by the ticket taker. The floor-level bleachers were closed. Arrows pointed to separate entrances for Raiders fans and Jaguars fans, and the separate entrances led to separate staircases, which led to separate bleachers elevated twenty feet above the court and cordoned off by a rail.

The streets were cold and never far. The cheerleaders wore black tights under their skirts. The hoop squad wore blue jerseys. They'd meet LBJ again here as the home team before the season was out, but tonight they were away. Anabel Garza took a position courtside. She wore her blue polo with the school logo. She held her coat. Up in the Reagan bleachers she could see women in pressed blouses and men in long-sleeved blue T-shirts and teenage boys in wide-brimmed caps and saggy jeans and some with tattooed necks. Candice Kaiser maneuvered through the gathering crowd with a dozen students in tow. A young woman sang "The Star-Spangled Banner," persevering through the mangling effects of a damaged amp (the sound system was the reason nobody wanted to have graduation here), and then the players were introduced.

"Last but not least," the announcer called, "the junior, Number 33, J . . . Q . . . Daniels!"

The cheerleaders called:

We ... are ... the Raiders
We are the Raid-ers!

JaQuarius scored first, a free throw. The cheerleaders cheered. When the action resumed they kept on cheering. They were supposed to wait until something good happened again but instead they cheered nonstop. Both teams ran the floor, a furious exchange of fast breaks. The crowd cheered too and directed much unsolicited advice toward JaQuarius from twenty feet up. When the Raiders took a four-point lead, Coach Davis slowed the offense, though he personally kept on running up and down the sidelines at breakneck speed. LBJ started a full-court press before the first quarter was done.

Get up on your feet
The Fighting Reagan Raiders
Can't be beat

In the second quarter, Coach Davis rested JaQuarius. Corn was the only one who could match him for height and strength but Corn didn't step up. He'd taken a hard charge in the first and looked rattled.

"Corn, why ain't you shoot it?" Corn's mother yelled from the bleachers.

"Sometimes you gotta be selfish!" a man's voice yelled.

"You gonna let 'em catch up," his mother added. She stood up in her seat. "That's all right, Raiders, that's all right."

LBJ cut the lead to five with JaQuarius riding the bench.

Coach Davis called timeout. The LBJ dance team watched the Reagan cheerleaders for an opening, but the Reagan girls kept cheering.

> *Go Big Blue*
> *Go Big Blue*

Still on the bench, JaQuarius watched Jordan miss an easy layup. The Jaguars went on a fast break.

> *Pull it down*
> *Pull it down*
> *Raiders get*
> *That rebound*

The halftime buzzer sounded. In the bleachers somebody yelled: "Y'all can't get upset; y'all just gotta play ball."

The half-broken speakers played R&B. Boys chatted up the cheerleaders and parents kept their seats and Anabel stood courtside in her blue polo. When the game resumed, Corn took another hard charge.

"Get in the game, Corn," his mother advised from the bleachers.

JaQuarius, back on the floor, restored the Raiders' lead with a sneaky putback, but then an LBJ forward made a thunderous dunk. It was the kind of thing sportscasters in the NBA would call a momentum changer. It was the kind of thing cops in the Delco Center would call a provocation. The Jaguar faithful went wild. The Reagan fans appealed to their star.

"Come on, JQ, let's get it baby," somebody called. "Take over the game."

He prowled beneath the basket, the unyielding JaQuarius, pulling down rebounds and forcing mistakes. He neither closed LBJ's lead nor let it extend. As the quarter neared its end, the ball came loose. He pushed it downcourt alone, executed a dizzying stutter step, and scored.

Come on Reagan

"Bust him up, JQ!" called a voice in the stands.

JaQuarius scored again and reduced the lead to one. He stole the inbounds pass and was tripped and the referee called a technical foul. Coach Davis assigned the free-throw duties to his best shooter, Brandon, who made them both. Reagan was winning again. When the fourth quarter began, the Raiders shot three-pointers over the LBJ press and JaQuarius kept pulling down rebounds.

"Get tough, Corn," his mother yelled. "Take yours!"

The score was tied. JaQuarius, fouled, approached the free-throw line. He knew everybody was watching him: Coach Davis, Ms. Garza, Ashley, everybody.

He missed.

"Come on, JQ, take your time!"

He made the second. Again he was fouled. This time he made them both.

"Come on, Q!"

Tie game. JaQuarius swatted the ball from a guard's hands but couldn't score. The Jaguars came racing back and went up by two. A cacophony of contradictory advice rose from the Reagan bleachers. Coach Davis fell into a dispute with the referee. Frantically the cheerleaders cheered. 1:47 to play. LBJ inbounded the ball and killed forty seconds of clock but did not score. JaQuarius made the rebound but then lost control. The ball rolled out of bounds. Corn was just standing there watching.

"Ya gotta help him out! Help him out!"

We . . . are . . . the Raiders
We are the Raid-ers!

LBJ inbounded again. Loose ball, and the boys collapsed in a scrum. They rose in fighting stances, pulling each other back. Coach Davis gathered his players and yelled at them. He benched Corn. He sent JaQuarius back into the game. If he could put the ball into Brandon's hands outside the arc then maybe . . .

"One, two, three: Hoop Squad!"

But when he returned to the court, JaQuarius fouled out. LBJ went up by six. A celebration began on that side. The Reagan fans made for the door. LBJ scored again. Anabel Garza folded her arms and stood her ground courtside. There were forty-three seconds left on the clock, star player or no. Time did expire, but not before an LBJ forward could extend the lead to ten with yet another dunk. That did it. The players pushed and shoved and some raised fists. Young men started dropping out of the bleachers like paratroopers into the fray. Some stripped off Reagan blue and LBJ purple for gang shades of bright red and blue. The fight spilled into the frigid night. JaQuarius Daniels jumped off the bench with his fists raised but somebody held him back. It doesn't matter who; somebody was there and did.

. . .

The girl in the red hoodie was not in class the next day; her baby had arrived a month early. That was not the big news on campus.

That same day, Governor Rick Perry announced plans to boycott the Race to the Top. The amount Texas stood to gain—$700 million—meant little in the scope of its $26.1 billion education system. Still, forty other states were in the game, scrambling to win Education Secretary Arne Duncan's favor with new laws promoting charter schools, ranking teachers by test scores, and moving even more aggressively to close "low-performing" public schools. But Governor Perry, whose unspoken presidential ambitions loomed over every pronouncement, cited neither the paltriness of the sum nor any substantive objection to the education reform policy prescriptions required to win. Instead, he delivered his decision with an antigovernment zinger. The way he put it was: "If Washington were truly concerned about funding education with solutions that match local challenges, they would make the money available to states with no strings attached."

That was not the big news on campus either.

"Man, those referees were tripping," a girl with a Hello Kitty backpack called to Coach Derrick Davis, who was standing in front of the gym, hands deep in the pockets of his tracksuit, shuffling his feet against the cold that blew in from the open double doors. This was the big news on campus, the officiating at the LBJ game. Derrick had been hearing it all day. He'd heard it from the assistant principal, Rick Fowler, and he'd tried to change the subject.

"That's a big thing in this neighborhood, responsibility," Derrick had said. "'Cause they're going home and their parents are telling them, 'Oh, you got cheated.' I want to focus on what else we could have done."

Fowler had nodded in agreement, and they'd hurried some kids off to class. Derrick had looked around the courtyard and said: "I'm starting to get a sense of what we mean on campus, man. Just the mood here. It's somber. Like, people feel like we lost something."

Now his star athlete was coming through the gym door, dressed in a sleeveless uniform shirt despite the weather and carrying a big drink from Sonic. Derrick led the team into his office, past a sign that said "Letter jacket ordering has been rescheduled."

Derrick cued up video from the night before, shot from a single camera in the crowd, Zapruder quality.

"The pressure forced us to do some things we don't do," he said. "I.e., body language. Walking off the court. We got to handle that. Because games like this, these are the kind of games we're going to face in the playoffs. I thought I could have done some things different throughout the game. We stopped doing what we do at the end of the game. One thing I want to address: Corn, I pulled you out because you stopped playing with us. With a minute and seven seconds, you had your hands on your hips like the game was over, and you forced me to pull you out."

He cut the lights. He started the video. He called the boys out for their inadequacies as they flashed across the screen: JaQuarius for not running fast enough. Corn for watching the ball instead of his man. Everybody for not getting back on defense. Again and again he made his assistant coach rewind.

"These are little basic things we need to be doing," he said.

The images flashed across the bare wall. JaQuarius leaned forward.

"Right here, JQ—Everybody knows we in Kansas but you," an assistant coach said, using the name of the formation.

"Yeah," JaQuarius said. "I was supposed to post."

"Think what could have happened if you'd been doing what you were supposed to do from the start," the assistant coach said.

"Little things," Derrick said, shaking his head. "I'm going to start getting on y'all about the little stuff. When we're in the zone and I tell you to put your hands up, it don't mean put your hands up if you feel like it. It means put your hands up."

JaQuarius slurped the last soda from his Styrofoam cup. The assistant coach said the players were making mistakes against LBJ because it was LBJ. Derrick said the team was leaning on JaQuarius and Corn too much, causing foul trouble.

"When we get into these situations, we as a group got to grow up," he said. "We got to play, and do what we ask you to do."

On-screen the Raiders were standing around while the LBJ players crashed the boards. In the office Derrick stood still, arms at his sides, nodding in agreement with himself.

"They were tougher than us when it came to that! They didn't go to the gimmick stuff! They went *mano a mano*! And we didn't handle it. We got to let that girl stuff go. You just got to let that shit go. We got to play!"

JaQuarius leaned in toward the screen. His soda cup was empty.

Fifteen

nabel Garza sprayed sanitizer across the conference table, wiped down the surface, pried open the window, and then closed it back again, halfway. They'd be here any minute.

"The ladies get cold," she mumbled, picking through her candy drawer. Fresh out, but she found some packaged crackers. Her trainer would be pleased if he knew. She wasn't totally sold on the boot camp deal—fitness buffs can and do drop dead jogging—but she knew something had to change. She could still hustle across the courtyard to enthuse her way through a big rally speech, but the sitting did her in. Sitting and listening, sitting in meetings, sitting and crunching the numbers. Even with Gloria taking a first rake through the e-mail, still, the sitting. Candy was the wrong way to get the energy back, she knew that, but the gym was torture if you weren't the athletic type, and Anabel wasn't. The trainer had her partnered up with this twenty-eight-year-old guy: Hold a push-up position while he runs four hundred meters, then switch, that kind of thing. She stuck it out, but the energy wasn't the real question anyway. You can't just take the kids home forever, you can't adopt them all, you can't really save anybody. That's a fake answer, and two decades into her accidental career she was starting to accept an answer that seemed real, or at least more real: "We're supposed to teach math and science and social studies," she told people, "but you have to teach the kids how to be resilient. It's very hard to teach how to come back from a defeat, but that's become our responsibility."

Anabel dumped the crackers into a ceramic bowl and turned to the shelves. There was always a little candy hidden, somewhere, from herself. Hidden too well this time. Instead she set out heart-shaped bookmarks with slogans proclaiming the value of a good education. She was still rummaging around when an assistant principal brought in a transfer application from an LBJ basketball player. Anabel pulled up the particulars on her computer screen.

"He doesn't live in our area," she said. "And he's not a TAKS passer. He's going to be that one African American kid that kills us."

"Tell him to go back to LBJ?"

"If he's registered somewhere else, he belongs to someone else. If he comes back to us, we're going to take the hit for his not passing."

How long had JaQuarius been standing in the doorway? The AP left. Anabel motioned toward the conference table, but JaQuarius already had a packet of crackers open and another in his hand. Dressed in his basketball sweats for tonight's game, he sat at the head of the table. Even sitting he seemed to tower over her. In her heart she saw a fearless leader. In her head she saw a big puppy. She had such grand ambitions for him and so little time to affect his course. Maybe it was too much to ask anyway. He was still a kid and not necessarily ready to lead others just because he happened to be tall and popular and good at sports at a school that happened to be in trouble.

Half a dozen more kids filed in. Anabel riddled her talk with standardized testing jargon, like the acronym for the middle-of-year exams and other terms the kids heard every day.

"You all are already expert at this," Anabel began, "because yesterday you took the MOY, and some schools can afford to blow it off but we're fighting for our lives . . ."

She trailed off, turning to the door. The AP was back, poking his head in and mouthing something about the transfer applicant.

"He lives in our area?" Anabel said. "No! Is he an M?"

The kids got to work on the crackers. The AP nodded that yes, the LBJ boy qualified for an alternate TAKS exam.

"It's still no good," Anabel mumbled. She looked around the table and picked up where she'd left off: Saving the school was complicated business and would take everybody's efforts and she needed to figure out how to fire up the whole student body for the home stretch and that's why she'd called them to the office—

And then she was interrupted again, this time by the voice of Lil Wayne erupting from somebody's pocket to signal an incoming call.

"Really?" Anabel said. "Really?"

The kid cringed, apologized, and shut down his phone. Anabel started again, drilling down into the latest on the TAKS cells.

"Every student carries a different weight to get us across the line. Right now, the heaviest cell is the African American male," she said. "That's how important every single person is. That's why everybody needs to be here every day. I've gone to people's houses and gotten them out of bed. People get up and want to punch me.

I'm like, 'Bring it down.' But I can't do that nine hundred times a day. I need to build in you, every day, a purpose to get up and get here. Next time, when we have the next LBJ game and the stands are crawling with people, we're going to have this talk again: 'How can you be here, but you're not in school? How come you went out and bought a new dress? How did you know there was a game to-night, and how did you know how our basketball team was doing?'"

"Text message," one of the kids said.

"Well, text them about being in school," Anabel snapped. Next she asked the kids to name some teachers who'd inspired them. They went around the table. Somebody reached back to junior high, somebody named a coach, somebody said Ms. Kaiser. James Marshall from the basketball team said "you." Anabel saw her opening.

"If the school closes down, I'm out of a job, but I'm here," she said. "You've got to start believing. When I got here, people were like, 'Aw, this is Reagan.' What do you mean, 'This is Reagan'? We've got twelve kids this week trying to transfer in here, and they're not good enough to attend our fine institution. Once we start saying it and believing it, people will start to see us differently."

JaQuarius's turn: "I would say my seventh-grade teacher, Mr. Cunningham. Before I met him I was doing crazy stuff, and he told me, 'Just because you're a black athlete doesn't mean anybody's going to give you anything. You're just like everybody else, and you got to work for it.'"

Wait a minute: crazy stuff? What about at the Delco Center the other night? Anabel pressed him on it.

"I had just said about you that you would never hurt a flea, un-less," she said. "And you held it and held it and held it, and then we held you. We have to make up for a big bad reputation. We don't fight around here. I have a philosophy that if you have to use your fists to talk, you're ignorant. If you have to fight to communicate, you don't know the words, you didn't learn the words, because you weren't in school."

The kids laughed: Leave it to Ms. Garza to bring any topic back around to her attendance spiel.

"Anyway," Anabel said, "I'm proud of you."

So, she asked, moving on: What about this seventh-grade teacher? What was so inspiring? What worked?

"He told me I wasn't going to be nothing," JaQuarius said, "and I was going to end up in jail like everyone else, and that motivated me to prove it to him."

"So it was negative?"

"No, he was challenging you, putting it like it is—"

James interrupted: "He told me, 'I'll take you there my damn self.'"

Enough about jail already. Anabel checked the time, and the cracker bowl, then moved the conversation along to the place every conversation was ultimately headed: TAKS.

"When you get kids who aren't passing," she said, "they're embarrassed, and they act up and cause trouble."

"If they fail them twice," James said, "that means they don't want to be here."

"What if their lightbulb doesn't go on until they're seventeen?" Anabel said. "Who are we to give up on people?"

"Well," James said, "do you think the people who are failing would be, you know what I'm saying, embarrassed if we tried to help them?"

But Anabel wasn't talking about that kind of help. She couldn't keep doing remedial tutoring year after year. That wasn't nourishing. That wasn't sustainable. That wasn't a school. There was a reason she was making the classes harder, even as she pushed for all the after-school fun. There was a reason she had these kids in her office. She was starting to think there was something more a school needed to provide—or maybe just stand for—in a working-class neighborhood in twenty-first-century America, but she couldn't figure out how to say it yet. Instead she pointed across the table at her star athlete and talked about resilience.

"You set a race between me and JQ, with JQ's legs against my legs," she said. "I could work twenty-five years and never be as fast as him, but I'm going to try. I'm going to try to beat him because that's what's burning inside of me, and that's what I need burning inside of you. You need to be ready to say, 'You're going to have to burn my skin off before I say ouch.'"

Somebody had to tell the parents. Somebody had to tell the teachers too. The superintendent sent her assistant, the onetime principal of Reagan High, Glenn Nolly.

Dr. Nolly took his seat in the cafeteria, which had been decorated early with Valentine hearts, and waited his turn. He waited while pizzas and soda were served. He waited while Deborah Warren reported an increase in PTSA membership to 123, while she distributed new applications in both English and Spanish, and while she told of a dance to benefit the scholarship fund. The parents heard an appeal for more volunteer tutors. Anabel described the results of her classroom "interventions," pulling kids out for instruction specialized by objective. A woman complained in Spanish about the attendance campaign, which was costing her five hundred dollars in truancy fines, and Anabel told the woman tough luck. Dr. Nolly waited through all this, then he stood up and said: "Now, what I'm here to talk about is not something anybody wants to talk about. Everybody knows we are in danger of the school being closed."

Anabel translated. He went on: "Option one, our students make the gains, the school is academically acceptable, and we're done.

"Option two, Reagan does not meet the standard and a contingency plan is adopted for the school to be closed and for our kids to go to various schools in the district.

"Option three, the commissioner of education could say, 'Close the school, repurpose it,' much like what happened with Johnston."

He concluded: "Option four, the commissioner of education closes the school completely and brings in an outside agency to run the school. That means the district would have no hand at all in operating the school."

Anabel translated all the options, but they didn't sound any better in Spanish: Options two through four were pretty much the same. The PTSA president was the first to put her hand up.

"So," Jacqueline asked, "the charter agency would bring in a new administration?"

Dr. Nolly nodded.

"What about the teachers?"

"The charter school would choose the teachers too."

"So . . . everybody?"

Dr. Nolly nodded.

"You're not helping the kids," somebody yelled. "You're just making yourselves look better."

Dr. Nolly made no argument.

"When they're really going to suffer," Jacqueline said, "is when they go to other schools and kids say, 'Oh, you came from Reagan, that's the school that got shut down.'"

Anabel spoke up for her boss: "That decision is something

that's coming from above us. It's coming from the commissioner. And we're fighting that." Then she translated what she'd just said into Spanish. The politics were getting tricky. She worked at the pleasure of the district superintendent, who had publicly disclosed making contingency plans for a closure order from the state commissioner. At the same time, she needed the trust of the parents, the teachers, and the kids. She'd worked to gain acceptance here, with her light brown skin, her South Austin address, and her border town upbringing, and moments like these could bring all the suspicions cascading back: Who exactly did she mean by "we"?

Dr. Nolly said they'd hear from the state by May.

"I do not want to leave us with a sense of gloom and doom," he said. "We already know we're going to make the completion rate. Our expectation is that our principal, our teachers, our other staff, and our students are going to make the grade."

Two days later, Dr. Nolly stood in the same cafeteria again, tailoring his message to a different audience—dozens of the young and idealistic and the not-so-young or idealistic anymore—the teachers.

"This is not the fate you want for Reagan," he said. "And the work that you're doing will ensure that doesn't happen to Reagan. You're doing everything you possibly can to meet the needs of your kids."

Then he got to option four, the one where the charter company would fire everybody. He offered a voluntary transfer list, open to any teacher who didn't want to stick around and see how things played out. Official district policy, distributed on leaflets at the meeting, said those left behind when the charter company arrived could try their luck at the district job fair, where they'd be given preference over outside applicants. Of course, there would be no job fair this year, what with the economy and all, but they could meet the principals from other schools at an "Internal Transfer Fair." Some might become "contingency teachers," on probation at schools where they wouldn't count against the principal's budget so as to stave off resentment. They'd need to find new permanent assignments within two years or else their contracts would be voided. The questions started coming.

"What if you're on the transfer list and the transfer goes through and Reagan stays open," somebody wanted to know. "Do you have to accept the transfer or can you stay at Reagan?"

"If, God forbid, this becomes a charter school," the librarian asked next, "would you be an employee of the district or the charter school?"

"Should Reagan close," another teacher said. "And we will not, isn't that right, Reagan?"

"Yeah!" the teachers yelled.

Then Anabel took the mike.

"I've never seen people work so hard for kids," she said. "And you all do. Day and night you talk about kids. Sometimes you yell at me about kids. I love being here. They'll have to drag me away if they make some crazy decision. In order to make great things, you have to take great risks. And we are risking our professional reputations to be here for the kids. The greatest things that have ever been done have not been done by people who played it safe. I love this place and I love these kids. Here we go. We're in the stretch. You're teaching, and the kids are learning. They're tired, and you're tired, and you've lived, and we're still going at it. Good luck to us all. I'm glad I'm with you."

Between all those meetings, on a Tuesday night, there was a basketball game. There was a crowd, some dads and more moms, some teachers and tutors and church people and people from the neighborhood. There was the hoop squad, dressed in home whites to play the Rebels of William B. Travis High School, going up strong, getting back on defense, and chasing down every loose ball. There was Coach Davis, bent on one knee, fist to chin. There was Corn Cammock, pulling the Raiders ahead from the free-throw line in the last minutes. There were the cheerleaders, stomping and shouting and dancing in cramped confines. And as the last shot went up to close the score at 66–59, a much-needed victory in district competition, there was the ball, in the hands of the only player who could leap high enough to dunk it home, the junior forward, No. 33, the reluctant face of Reagan High, known across the Eastside by his initials alone.

In February, the district solicited proposals from independent contractors to manage Reagan High. Superintendent Carstarphen cast the idea as a last chance to maintain local control: Declare victory and get out before the state could issue a closure order. She called her plan the Turnaround Initiative. She called for "proposals nationwide to build a robust portfolio of innovative and proven programs and practices to accelerate student achievement."

Anabel decided to write a proposal of her own. At the next Friday morning meeting, she invited only boys. She wanted straight talk, and teenage boys don't talk straight around teenage girls. She wanted to explore the limits of what the school could provide.

JaQuarius arrived in his basketball sweats. His algebra book was covered with a wrapper that said Big Daddy.

Anabel, dressed in a gray jacket with a brooch spelling out the name of the school, said, "I need ideas. I just had a kid that wants to transfer to our school from McCallum. Unheard of. Usually everybody wants to go somewhere else. He's made it to nationals in track.

He's scored a twenty-four hundred in math. I said, 'I'll think about it, because you can't just get into this fine institution without stress, pressure.'"

The boys gave up a small laugh. Sometimes it was hard to tell when Anabel was kidding. She asked what they thought about flex schedules, year-round schooling, block schedules, extra tutoring. "We don't have the money to serve everybody," she said, "so who do we serve?"

"I'd say freshmen and sophomores," JaQuarius ventured, "because they're the most behind."

When the boys had warmed to the conversation, Anabel turned to more delicate matters.

"We do have 110 parenting teens," she said.

"Damn," JaQuarius whispered.

"So, say you're a teen mom. You have to get the stroller, get the baby, get your science book, get it all on the bus, the book falls on you, you drop the baby off at the day care, see if they'll take the car seat. And that's just getting here in the morning. So how are we going to stop them from having babies?"

"Maybe you got to talk to people who are having babies about what it costs, what you got to go through," JaQuarius said.

"Where along the way did you decide not to make those poor choices?" Anabel asked. "What, even now, is keeping you from doing that? It's an embarrassing conversation, but all of us have been there. Maybe as a man, you would be like, 'Come on, baby.' But what made that thing in your mind say, 'Not me'?"

JaQuarius shrugged: "I don't plan on having kids yet."

"This is something that will keep you up all night, that you can't just say, 'Ah, I want to go to the prom, you take care of the baby.'"

JaQuarius was staring at the table.

"I got pregnant in high school, and it was a terrible, ugly story,"

Anabel said. "My parents were wonderful people, but they didn't show you they loved you at home. Nobody hugged you. Nobody told you they loved you. We had food to eat. We were well taken care of. I know they'd die for me, but there was no, 'Oh, I love you so much.'"

Now one of the boys spoke up: "Sometimes when you don't get that, you go looking for love in other places."

"And you don't even know that person," JaQuarius said.

Anabel said, "I might think, 'Oh, oh, JQ knows I love him, every morning I'm cooking his breakfast.' But it's not me telling him, 'I love you,' and instead some bum, a boyfriend or girlfriend . . ."

She started over: "So just talking, do you feel like you can just talk at home? Do you get that kind of stuff at home, the affection?"

The boys studied the table.

"And how can a school be affectionate?" Anabel asked. "Can you feel affection at school?"

"It depends on the kid," JaQuarius said. "Because if your teacher knows you're a troublemaker and you're always skipping, they're going to treat you different."

"So the equation is, if you come out of home acting the fool, you're not going to get it at school either because you're acting that way?" Anabel asked, thinking out loud. "So they're coming in already wounded. The parents of these kids have those dark moments, they don't have the money to pay the rent; they work two jobs or three jobs. So what kind of affection can we provide at school for those kids who don't have it at home?"

"What if you start showing them affection," JaQuarius countered, "and they start using you and taking it for granted?"

He rubbed the rim of his empty plastic water cup and watched her think about that.

"Can you have serious conversations with kids where you're

listening to them, and does that satisfy the need for affection?" Anabel asked. "You all go with Ms. Kaiser, right? I don't know what you talk about, but I can guess what you do, because I was like Ms. Kaiser when I was a teacher. I'm sure all that stuff is good. I'm sure it trickles down to the school."

She went on: "Can you make a relationship happen like this in a school like this, where you're buds and I'm not going to let you fall and you're not going to let me fall? Is that way out there?"

"The question is: Are they going to want to be around all those people showing them affection?" JaQuarius said, lodging it comfortably in the third person. "Are they going to want to let people know what's going on in their lives?"

Anabel likened the problem of building a school to compiling a winning record in football. That got JaQuarius talking.

"It's about dedication," he said. "At the beginning of the season, everybody is all fired up, but then you lose everyone and somebody stops playing hard. Then somebody else says, 'Yeah, he's right, we suck.' And then it all starts to fall out. We got a whole bunch of people playing for themselves and not the team."

Anabel dismissed the boys: Good luck against LBJ tonight. "It's the confidence," she said. "You all have got to be you."

She watched JaQuarius slip on his earbuds and disappear into the music.

"Yeah," she muttered, "this boy always leaves a mark."

Sixteen

Ashley Brown leans in for a kiss. Her boyfriend is sitting on the platform at the side of the gym, across from the faded Coca-Cola scoreboard, swinging his legs over the edge. He's watching his teammates, who are supposed to be practicing their free throws, goof off. They're teenagers. They tried bouncing the ball over the backboard and bored of it; they're moving on to half-court peg shots. From his high vantage, JaQuarius Daniels assumes the posture of a man among boys, but Ashley knows better. She adjusts her tight pink T-shirt and gives his basketball shorts a playful tug and gazes up into his dark brown eyes. JaQuarius and Ashley just finished their own game of one-on-one, a low-scoring contest given to giggling flirtation, and now she wants to talk. This isn't new. For a year or so she's been trying to get him to really talk. It's not like she blames him—she's never been much of a talker either—but she knows time is running out. She missed the

UT–Austin deadline, so she's leaning toward Prairie View A&M, especially if a full track-and-field scholarship comes through. That's two hours away speeding, more than halfway to Houston, not that either one of them has a car. She's got to go, though. It's the right thing. PV has a good premed program and a better relay team. It's a historically black college, so there's that. JaQuarius tells people he isn't worried—says things like: "She's still gonna be the same her. She was with me when I was doing wrong, she was with me when I was at the top, and she was with me when I was at the middle"—but there's no pretending he'll follow her to PV next year. It's not like following her from Pearce to Reagan, where he could pin it on his crazy plan to get noticed as the conspicuous standout on an otherwise miserable football team, which actually seems to be working so well that he's thinking about UT or OSU or maybe even Notre Dame. It's hard to know what's realistic. The future is still a big place.

The future isn't what Ashley wants to talk about; the past is. Ever since she got into the biggest fight ever with her mom, the one where her mom finally said she couldn't take the attitude anymore and maybe Ashley just needed to go talk to her dad, Ashley has been convinced that what JaQuarius needs is to forgive his dad too. She's been trying to tell him about how it helped her, but it's hard to explain. All the stuff with Ms. Kaiser and the church people and Africa. College. Leaving home. The world, the Two-Three. It was all mixed up together, but what she knew was that she was changing and she wanted him to change with her. Needed him to, and knew he needed to too. Maybe he didn't lash out at people the way she did. Maybe he didn't have an "attitude." Maybe he could just plug in his earbuds and float around like he wasn't even here, but Ashley knew better. She knew better, but that didn't make it any easier, talking. It used to be they just talked about sports. For five years.

She'd tell him what he did wrong on the field in the latest game and then she'd nag him about grades a little and then she'd let him do some of what he wanted to do.

JaQuarius kisses Ashley back and pulls her up into his lap. She holds him like a carnival prize and somebody says get a room.

"JQ, come on man," one of the players calls, but JaQuarius leans back on his palms. Sits and watches. Half-court peg shots: That's high percentage. Maybe they're just blowing off steam. People have been talking up this game against LBJ for months. Even Coach Ivany from the D-1 Ambassadors, the biggest name in feeder league basketball statewide, has tonight flagged in his newsletter.

"I'm going out on a limb here and will predict that Austin LBJ's streak of 10 outright or shared District titles is about to end," Ivany wrote all the way back in December, before LBJ beat the Raiders in that first game. "This Austin Reagan group is for real. They've got skill, size, shooters, and are not INTIMIDATED by LBJ like past teams have been. Don't get me wrong, LBJ is no pussycat and Coach Freddie Roland will not let them go down easily. Get your seat at the Delco Center."

Or maybe the boys aren't just blowing off steam. When you're sixteen, it's hard not to imagine every big game ending with a buzzer-beater from half-court and the fans bum-rushing the floor and coach cutting down the net and your dad smiling in the bleachers and somebody from the Lakers seeing the video on YouTube and the cheerleaders lining up in a pretty little row. Why not practice those desperation heaves?

Finally, when the catcalls die down and it doesn't look like he's answering to anybody, JaQuarius slides away from Ashley and stretches and walks out under the basket at the pace of a man taking out the trash. His oversize shirt is untucked and flowing; a

Soul Raiders headband covers his brow. Right there on the court he kneels and carefully ties one shoe and then the next as the balls rocket past his skull and make their pinging racket and ricochet off rims and walls. His preparations are timed precisely to the arrival of his coach, who is dressed in a pin-striped suit and turning out the lights and ending the silliness in the gym and leading his charges down the hall to an office where empty pizza boxes remain in stacks.

"At some point tonight," Derrick Davis tells the boys, "you guys are going to have to decide to fight. And I don't mean physical fight. It's gonna be a possession of ours, or a turnover, or a possession of theirs, but it's gonna get past basketball at some point, and we're gonna have to fight. It can't just be our front three. Role players got to step up. They've got what we want. It's not rocket science, gentlemen. We got to take it. They've got the championship. If we want it, we got to go take it. I've been thinking about this all day. They're not going to give it to us because we're Reagan High School. We got to take it. Understand?"

"Yes, sir!"

"Alright, Hoop Squad on three."

The boys circle and join hands.

"One, two, three."

"Hoop Squad!"

And then they're off to board the Spirit Bus for the short ride to the Delco Center and a rivalry game as old as their schools. The coaches hang back for a minute, talking about their jobs and their boss and the numbers.

"It's like basketball," the assistant coach says. "You can't get on the court and play for them. She can't get in and take the test for them."

"It's about processes," Derrick says. "Anything you do. Processes, baby."

There was no pep rally. Anabel Garza figured tensions were running high enough already, and besides, she didn't have time to plan any pep rally. She'd finally ended up in the cardiac ward, just as predicted, when her blood pressure hit 167 over 110. In the relative calm of the hospital, her blood pressure had stabilized, and she was back at school in time for the LBJ game, wearing her Columbia blue polo. The players were in uniform, the band was in uniform, and the cheerleaders were in uniform, so she was in uniform too. In her office she was putting up a clip from the sports section, an article about a girl on the basketball team at some school down in the suburbs, because she thought the headline was funny: "Garza's Game Cooks When Pressure's On," it said. Sure enough, her day began with three freshmen and a sophomore, the school cop's main suspects in a vandalism case, discovered in the gym. A light cover had been broken, an Exit sign dented, and some ceiling tiles smashed. When her little criminal inquiry was done, she moved on to graduation planning.

She joined two dozen seniors in the big conference room, debating the usual concerns: the holding of applause, proper lighting and attire, the acoustics of the Delco Center.

"I know this sounds stupid," said Princess Ohiagu, "but I want confetti coming down."

"And streamers and balloons," somebody suggested.

"And water," somebody else said.

"Do you know what those *chicas* have spent on their hair and heels this high?" Anabel asked. "Water is not going to work."

Another girl asked: "Can we get Obama?"

"Or at least his wife?"

They negotiated down to Beyoncé, then on down to the assistant principal's daughter (she was just a little kid, but she'd been on that show K-Ville).

"What if we collectively wrote a letter to Obama?" said the assistant principal, Rick Fowler. "Shoot for the moon, at least if we miss we'll be among the stars. Who wants to be on an Obama letter-writing committee?"

All hands went up.

"If he knew," Anabel said, "he wouldn't be too busy for you guys."

Inside the Spirit Bus, Valentine hearts hang from the ceiling. Derrick Davis climbs the steps, pulls on his cap, and takes a seat. The boys are silent; their earbuds are not.

"Mind-set, gentlemen, mind-set," Derrick calls. "It ain't a video game tonight. We need to be able to accept stuff and get back in and fight."

His voice drops when he turns to his assistant coach: "We got to be willing to eat niggas up."

The driver pulls out onto Highway 290. She points the bus toward the Delco Center.

"These are good kids," Derrick tells Coach Lewis. "So I want them to do well. Last year's knuckleheads I kept on a tight-ass rope."

"You got to have a little swagger. It's okay to be a little greedy."

"Greed and selfishness are cousins, but they're definitely different."

The lights of the Delco Center come into view. The bus smells like gas and old rubber. Its engine talks back to the cold.

"Hey, Coach," Derrick says, addressing his assistant by the only name either of them ever uses for the other. "Since what happened at the end of the game last time, they're gonna be calling it tight. Should we run some Texas and Syracuse early?"

The driver shifts into park. The coaches count police uniforms out the window.

"Man, they deep tonight," Derrick says. He taps his players on the back, one by one, as they shuffle past, blue hoods up against the February wind, drumbeats in their ears. The boys get a look at their opponents. They watch the jayvee play. A laundry smell succumbs to a perfume smell and now the teenage athletes have an audience. Cheerleaders, musicians and photographers, parents, teachers, and missionaries, representatives of every social clique from Math Club to the Crips, all have come down tonight, middle-aged black couples and older white ones who lived this rivalry in its various and connected incarnations and who live it still. Some have brought balloons.

The jayvee squads finish up and shake hands. Out come the Soul Raider tubas and trumpets and trombones and drums and the Soul Strutters in their silver short shorts and the cheerleaders in their blue skirts, all hip-shaking to the triumphalist sound of rising major scales. The varsity players take their real warm-up, not like all that hotdogging in their home gym. The guards keep looking over their shoulders at the LBJ boys. JaQuarius dunks a ball and the horns kick in. This game has played out across four decades. Tonight could be the last time, the numbers say.

"You got to fight, gentlemen," Derrick says. The boys encircle him, arms locked. "We know basketball. It came down to execution last time. This is a playoff-type atmosphere. We got to fight."

Then the boys take the court and there's nothing left anybody can do for them. Their parents sit twenty feet up in the bleachers, behind a rail. Candice Kaiser is sequestered up there too. Anabel

Garza stands behind the baseline, trying to see over the cheerleaders. Even Derrick Davis has to watch from the bench, where he rocks back and forth and rubs his thumbnails together and gets up and paces but cannot go take the ball in his hands and let the leather roll off his fingertips nice and easy and save them. This is their time, the 2010 hoop squad, these boys in the uniforms many other boys have worn. Somebody should get a panoramic shot of the whole spectacle, the boys and girls in blue on the court, the generations in the bleachers. The yearbook industry exists to remind us that we ever felt so unified and conflicted, so throbbingly alive, when we're older and compromised and need convincing.

LBJ grabs the jump ball but can't score. The Raiders go up by three, taking their time. The Jaguars step up the pace. Another three, a fast-break layup, and Reagan is winning 10–2 when timeout is called. Coach Davis turns to the bleachers and pumps his fists in the air and beckons applause for these fine young gentlemen. They are fine ones, yes, and seasoned by now: Tonight they play with poise, they force mistakes. Over on the LBJ bench, Coach Roland, scowling and arms crossed, looks ready to bust out of his purple suit. The Reagan cheerleaders are performing jumping jacks.

On the court JaQuarius shows no such emotion. He is methodical and composed except when diving for a loose ball, and even then he seems to approach his task stoically. Subbed out for a rest on the sidelines, where his ability to affect the outcome is temporarily withdrawn, he turns indignant at the sight of a hard foul. He stands and yells. The assistant coach steps in front of him and starts to say, "Hey, if something goes down, you stay here," but now Coach Davis is in his star player's face and the admonishments come loud and harsh, blustery and profane. This thing JaQuarius has in mind, Derrick makes clear, is not what he meant by "fight."

In the second quarter, with Reagan leading by nine points,

Derrick sends JaQuarius back into the game. Right away he takes a full-court pass from Corn and dunks the ball, light as air, having regained his composure only by rejoining the flow. His teammates, though, are falling apart. They give up a thunderous dunk. Corn travels. The momentum turns.

Bringing the ball downcourt, JaQuarius dribbles off an opposing player's heel. He's big and fast and nimble but no ball handler. All season, Coach Davis has been trying to play him on the perimeter, where colleges might take a kid who was big only by high school standards at six five. Some scouts have come down from places like Tarleton State, though it's no secret JaQuarius is more of a football prospect by his own inclination. Placing him with an NCAA tournament contender, even a Division II school, could do a lot for recruiting at Reagan, but tonight Derrick has to think about this team, this year, this game, which the Raiders are still winning at the half, by three points.

Derrick leads his squad into the locker room, where blue sweats and bags cover the tile.

"The one thing that's kind of different tonight, and everybody who's looking at us can see it, is it's a team effort," Derrick says. He keeps his voice low and even. "On the floor, on the bench, it's a team effort. Now, we got in some foul trouble, so I want you to keep your aggressiveness within three fouls."

Derrick picks up a red marker and hopes it can transmit something about basketball and rivalry and loyalty and life across a generation. He draws a play on the whiteboard, raising his tone: "At some point in the game we got to take our matchups personally."

He pounds the whiteboard.

"You got to take this shit personally," he says, "in your individual matchups."

An assistant coach tells the boys to calm down and take

advantage of their size; JaQuarius and Corn and Jordan are the three biggest players in the game.

"We know what we can do," Coach Davis says. "We got to go out and execute. Pressure will put you back in your habits, and our habit is good basketball."

His voice rises again: "Regardless of what you think about them or feel about them, they got what we want. We got to go in there as a family and take it. I'm going to stop talking X's and O's with this group, 'cause this group got to dog. What's down the road, we can't see it, but it's called faith, gentlemen. Somewhere in that dark room is that district championship we want. And you got to reach into that dark room and take it."

He says: "Okay?"

He says, "Hoop Squad on three."

He says, "One, two, three."

"Hoop Squad!"

And he's still clutching the red marker when he leads the boys back out under the bright lights of the Dr. Exalton and Wilhelmina Delco Activity Center where the flags are flying and the Reagan band is serenading the crowd and a yearbook photographer does walk the floor.

In the second half LBJ takes the lead and Derrick throws up his arms and addresses no one in particular: "We got to decide if we're going to match their intensity."

JaQuarius hits a jump shot and the cheerleaders take their cue: "We . . . are . . . the Raiders!" Corn keeps drawing fouls—that's how you take advantage of size—and the lead seesaws within a point. Derrick never sits down. Soon every basket for either side draws deafening applause. The LBJ coach expels a stream of spit. His players go on an unanswered run and take a seven-point lead and jump up to bump chests. Coach Davis calls the Raiders to regroup, but when play resumes JaQuarius is double-teamed under the basket. He can't score. LBJ picks up the pace and extends the lead to ten. From the bench, Corn calls, "Hey, we going down."

What happens next matters not because it was foretold in the coach's office but because it concerns inspiration and fellowship and what used to be called grit. What happens is that the role players step up: Brandon Golden with his sweet outside shot and Alex Parish and Willie Powell driving the lane so that when the third quarter expires, the score is tied again and Derrick is on the court hugging the boys because there's only so much he can convey with a red marker.

"It ain't just planning," he tells them in the huddle. "You got to want to do it. I want to see you down on the ground for loose balls."

An assistant coach smacks the back of a chair and says: "Hey, if a man is fucking hot, feed him the goddam ball!"

Back and forth the lead changes hands through the fourth quarter. Tied at 66. LBJ gets a steal, Reagan gets a steal. JaQuarius travels in the lane. Derrick calls the boys to the bench with no specific instruction to give. He brings out the whiteboard and just bangs on it.

"Hey, raise your hand if you're in the game," he says. "Hey, defense, defense, defense. Let's go!"

LBJ dunks the ball on a fast break for a four-point lead. LBJ sinks a three-pointer with four minutes left on the clock: 73–66. Again the Raiders fight back. A jump shot, a turnover, a fast break, and Derrick is removing his jacket and flailing his arms at the bleachers where people are already standing and stomping and shouting as loud as can be to answer the cheerleaders, who are chanting, "Everybody say, R-H-S!"

Corn gets called for traveling in the lane and breaks his coach's heart. The Raiders are losing by one. A minute and five seconds left to play.

"Fuck, Corn!"

Reagan inbounds the ball. JaQuarius breaks free of the double-teaming defenders in the lane, catches a long pass, makes the layup grinning and gets knocked down for it. And one. If you could hear the crowd. Derrick physically pushes his players into their seats for the timeout.

"I need the board, I need the board!" he says, and someone hands it over and he scribbles in red marker.

"This is the point we talked about," he says, "where we got to take it. We got ourselves into this position, now we got to take it."

Back on the court, JaQuarius makes his free throw. Reagan by two. LBJ ties the score again at 78 and adds a free throw. LBJ by one, with forty-six seconds to play. Again JaQuarius is fouled, but this time on the free throw line his shot misses.

With fifteen seconds left to play, the Raiders turn over the ball. They'll have to foul. They take another ten seconds to do it. LBJ's shooter clangs the ball off the rim, and Reagan comes up with the rebound. Timeout. The crowd is at the rail. The cheerleading squads are directing their chants at one another.

Derrick Davis figures he has four dribbles to get the ball down-court, one for each second on the clock, with one second left over to shoot. He draws up a play for that second, the leftover one. He calls it "Last Second."

"Hoop Squad on three," JaQuarius says. He walks out to mid-court and takes his place. The inbound pass goes to Willie Powell. Willie Powell, who has been playing with these same boys since junior high. Willie Powell, whose penetration of the lane has kept the Raiders in this game. Little Willie, the senior, the role player, the kid who stopped growing at five foot eight, the big talker who always says he wants the ball in his hands for the last shot but never takes it.

Willie Powell catches the inbound pass and dribbles. That's one.

Willie Powell dribbles behind his back and evades a defender. That's two.

Halfway to midcourt, Willie puts the ball up in the air. It's too soon, way too soon. He hasn't used the clock to close the distance. He studied the marker board, the red X's and O's, the detailed plans of credentialed experts, but out on the floor something changed. Something intervened. Something didn't respond as predicted in the modeling. This is the desperation heave, the teenage fantasy, the dream that never comes true. The ball ascends toward the glaring white lights, hovers at the eye level of the bleachers, quiet now, and succumbs to the earthbound pull at work always on all things. It descends several feet shy of the basket, into the outstretched arms of No. 33, the junior, JaQuarius Daniels, who catches it and stumbles into the lane in that last unspoken-for second and tosses up an off-balance prayer that kisses the board.

A year from now—when the standardized test scores have been tallied and the school has been deemed academically acceptable and the seniors have graduated and some have gone on to college and others have fared less well and the teachers who had the guts to keep their names off the transfer list are still teaching at Reagan and Anabel Garza has asserted herself in full—there will come a time when a player named Jordan Giddings will announce his intention to quit the basketball team. Every day, on the way home from school in Derrick Davis's car, JaQuarius Daniels, a senior bound for Iowa State on a football scholarship, will listen to one side of the telephone conversation between his coach and his longtime teammate. There will be talk of paperwork, there will be talk of commitment, there will be talk of everything in between. JaQuarius will sit and listen. Finally, one day, in the gym, in front of everybody, Coach Davis will ask, "JQ, you been real quiet, what do you think about this?" JaQuarius will catch the ball he's been bouncing between his palms with a great staccato smack. The room will fall silent. Jordan will brace for a punch. Derrick will sense his muscles tensing to break up a fight. But JaQuarius will just gaze across at Jordan and say, "Really? You gonna leave us?" Jordan will hold back a tear. Coach Davis will cast his memory back to the end of this LBJ game. He will think maybe, in this moment, JaQuarius became a true leader of young men. He will also remember something his grandmother told him a long time ago. She said: "You can't make nobody do nothing, baby."

But now, as the ball comes falling through the net and the buzzer sounds and the scoreboard clicks up to read "Reagan 80, LBJ 79," Derrick Davis, jubilant, triumphant, and overwhelmed, leaps onto a chair with a werewolf look in his eye. Jennifer Davis rushes their girls down. Anabel Garza comes staggering along the sideline tear-streaked and hugging. The players swarm JaQuarius Daniels. The celebration spills into the locker room, where Derrick plays the reasonable adult: "Everything's still the same," he says. "You got your tutoring for the TAKS tomorrow."

But tonight it seems as if all the Two-Three is waiting in the parking lot. JaQuarius Daniels poses for photos with his teammates, with underclassmen, with middle school kids, and people from the neighborhood, two fingers raised in the salute somebody devised and everybody agreed upon all those decades back to stand for Reagan High.

Seventeen

The living room of the Carver house, decorated in the style of postcollegiate scavenging, featured an eight-by-ten photo of Candice Kaiser circa 1994, hair poofed in creepy-sexy child model fashion, the work of some shopping mall Glamour Shots. Irony was intended in its framed display, that and a small lesson on vanity. The latter-day Candice wore neither makeup nor jewelry, and her hair was lucky to get pulled back in a band. When the kids showed up for the next fund-raising meeting, she was already in the thick of a "roommate meeting," the kind that becomes necessary when four or five passionate young people with lofty ambitions move into close quarters. So Ashley and Briana and George and Princess and Kay Kay and Nijalon and Devyne and the others let themselves in, taking places around a big yellow sheet marked Prayer Requests.

Candice knew the Africa trip was crazy. She wasn't naive to the obstacles bound to arise before the joint efforts of well-meaning if perhaps overzealous white people and desperately hopeful black kids reared on an academically unacceptable education. They had maybe a month left to finish their sponsorship letters. Two kids had dropped out in the past week alone. The initial romantic notion remained—returning the love expressed by the Kenyan children in the video—but the trip was starting to take on a significance of its own: a chance to become worldly. A chance to be givers of charity, not recipients. One day the trip seemed like that rare something kids who'd heard "no" all their lives could actually do; the next it seemed safely impossible, a dreamy fiction to pass the time. Then there was the part nobody wanted to say out loud: For all the talk of pride and loyalty and saving the school, all the posters and marches and meetings, all the continuity and tradition restored to lift the next generation, the class of 2010 still needed to get out of the Two-Three.

Candice tried not to see the cell phones during the opening prayer. Facebook during the reading from Ephesians proved too much.

"I'm serious about this," she said. "If we have to go to Africa with just five, God is good, and I'm excited about that."

Then she asked the meaning of the Bible verse.

"Unity?" said Ebony.

"Nailed it," said Candice.

The girls had some questions about unity. The adults had strikingly different answers. One of the prayer leaders said unity didn't mean being phony. Another talked about being a peacemaker. Candice's roommate, Lindsey, talked about her mission trip to Haiti. Said she'd seen poor people reach for Jesus. That brought Candice to tears.

"We reach for all kinds of other things in this world," Candice said. "The first thing they reach out to is Jesus. I deal with that every day. I come home upset with students or upset with teachers, and Jesus is not the first thing I reach for. I confess, I reach for other things. And I went to Africa and I saw how they don't have any food, and still Jesus is the first thing they reach for. And I wish I could do that."

Candice trailed off. The sophomore class clown, Nijalon Dunn, took over the unity discussion: "How many people here want to go to Africa?"

Sixteen hands.

"We aren't just one group," Nijalon said. "There are groups inside this group. And when we go to Africa, we all have to be one group with one purpose. Seriously. So let's help each other out."

"But it's natural for us to have people we talk to more," said Devyne Byrd, a cheerleader who wanted to be a writer. "Would you ask somebody for help if you knew they were talking about you behind your back?"

Candice regained her composure: "Is there anybody you need to reconcile with in this room? Because it's now. If you need to go upstairs and talk to that person . . ."

Her voice was commanding, like it sounded in the classroom. Three of the girls went upstairs. Six more followed, then four others, some to argue, some to eavesdrop, some with more than one agenda. They were teenagers. Candice closed the meeting with a prayer. She set out a casserole with green beans and brownies and soda for when the kids came back downstairs.

L*ittle Shop of Horrors* was opening. Payments for Valentine arrangements were due. Students had raised $210 for Red Cross relief efforts in Haiti. After school there would be tutoring for science objective two, with complimentary chili served and double credit hours to earn. All of this at Reagan High, that scary place on the Eastside. The morning announcements said so.

Inside her chemistry classroom, Candice was giving a lesson on solubility. She assigned a "buddy quiz."

"Meaning what?" somebody asked.

"Meaning you can work with your neighbors," Candice said. "In America we like to think it's all about us, but really it's about each other. So if you know something, man, help each other out."

The kids talked it out: the effect of rising temperatures, the formation of potassium chlorate. Candice made her rounds.

"Do you know about TAKS tutoring after school today?"

"Yeah, but I work today."

When the kids were done, Candice lit up the projector screen with a review of TAKS objective 3.7(b): the theory of biological evolution. It wasn't chemistry, but this was crunch time, so every minute of every teacher's day was spoken for. The idea was to maximize the data from the assistant principal's master spreadsheet. Candice told the kids who'd already passed the exit-level exam to find some homework for another class. Then she taught the theory of biological evolution.

After running through some multiple-choice questions, Candice put on another video from Africa. This one showed birds and hippos: communalism versus mutualism. The biology lesson seemed to stick. Candice turned off the video. For an instant, her screen saver appeared on the projector screen, displaying a shot from the Delco Center last Friday night, the pandemonium right after JaQuarius's layup fell. The kids stared until the image faded, then looked back down at their test prep folders.

Candice taught science. That was her job. She was good at it. Her students scored well on the TAKS. Her bosses gave her more responsibilities. The job was like any other job, but also it wasn't. One of the people she worked with at her job was Khari-yyah Johnson, a seventeen-year-old student in her chemistry class. Everybody called Khariyyah Kay Kay. Sometimes Kay Kay called Candice Mom.

Kay Kay danced with the Soul Strutters, gossiped with the other girls, and wore shoulder-length extensions, but she never really fit in. Her mother had been in and out of prison on drug charges since Kay Kay was ten, and Kay Kay lived with her dad. Everything's relative, especially when you're a teenager, and having a dad but no mom made Kay Kay the opposite of all her friends. So she called Candice Mom, starting when Candice took Kay Kay to a doctor's appointment. Not all public-school teachers take their students to doctor's appointments, but more do than you might think.

Sometimes Candice took Kay Kay and a couple of the other kids to places like La Tazza Fresca, a coffee shop across the highway on the college drag. Candice usually brought Ryan, the young man she'd met through the church. They were together all the time now, plus Ryan could drive the boys.

La Tazza Fresca served hummus and rented hookahs and had a stage for singer-songwriters. It was something different. It was the Not-Two-Three. One night in the middle of February, Candice, Ryan, Kay Kay, and Nijalon chose a wooden booth near a statue of a rooster. Ryan ordered smoothies. Nijalon talked about his chances of making the varsity hoop squad next year. Candice ordered a comically large bowl of coffee. She gave Kay Kay her leather-bound Key Word Study Bible and opened a pocket-size one for herself. They read for a while, and then Kay Kay pulled out a letter she was writing to her dad.

"I don't think he knows how I really, really feel about him," Kay Kay said. She was trying to decide whether to give her dad the letter. One of her aunts had told her that she needed to respect her mom because her mom had carried her for nine months. Kay Kay wasn't so sure. "That don't make her a mother," she said, "because she gave birth to me. That don't make her a mother."

Her letter began:

Dear Daddy,

It's hard to talk to you about what I go through with boys, school, friends, even my mom. I feel like you're not going to understand.

Kay Kay told Candice about her mom showing up to ask for money and selling food stamps for drugs. Candice advised her to pray.

"It ain't gonna help, in my situation," Kay Kay said. "When I was little I used to pray for her to come back all the time, and she didn't. I'm done praying."

"Sometimes it helps to pray," Candice said. "It's okay to tell God you're angry."

"Sometimes I feel like God's not listening. I know He is, but I feel like: 'What's the point?'"

"No, I know what you're talking about. I've been there. I don't go to Him first. It's like an underlying anger, or apathy."

"Sometimes I wonder what would happen if I end up like her."

"How?"

"Like my mom. What if I end up leaving my kids?"

"Would you do that?"

"I don't know."

"It's possible. We're all capable of those kinds of things."

Candice raised her precarious coffee bowl. Jazz was playing

over the speakers. Ryan and Nijalon were staring into Bibles. She leaned in toward Kay Kay.

"Do you get frustrated with yourself?" Candice asked.

"Sometimes I just give up. Like in English, if we have to write an essay or read a book, I'm like, 'I can't do it, and I'm gonna be a senior next year already.'"

"You can read, though. I've seen you. I know you can."

"I want to go to college, I want to be a doctor, but you have to be good in science and math and all those things and I'm not good at all that."

"I don't think it's that you can't do it. I think you hit a wall, and it's like, 'I can't' comes into your head. 'I can't.' I don't get it. What other thoughts come into your head? 'I hate this'?"

"Yeah."

"All those thoughts can come in and screw up any chance you have."

"When I take tests, like the TAKS test, I'll just sit up there and look at it and I'll just go to sleep."

"Because you're frustrated?" Candice asked, opening a notebook to record methods for the disposal of negative thoughts. "When a teacher hands you a test, what do you want to happen?"

"That I know this stuff."

"It's not that you can't or you don't or you hate. You don't have to think this way. We all know that if you just put your head down, it's your choice to fail."

Kay Kay's cell phone rang. It was her dad. She took the call. When she came back, Nijalon was talking about finding his motivation on the basketball court. He was going to make the varsity, he said.

"At least you get motivation," Kay Kay said.

"Girl, I motivate you every day," Candice said.

"But you didn't give birth to me. You weren't there from the beginning."

"But you've got people here now."

"Yeah, but it's like it's at the last minute. Like it's too late."

"You've got to know that's not true. It's okay sometimes to feel it, but you've got to know it's not true. You've got to center your thoughts on, 'God, I feel like I can't do this. I need your strength.' He wants you to go to Him."

Raising sixty thousand dollars for the Africa trip was never really a problem. People in the Stone Church had money. Look what they were building, right across the highway. This was the real problem: None of the kids had ever traveled farther than Atlanta. DeVonte used to live in California, but that wasn't traveling, and it wasn't Nairobi. Hearing about world travel from White Candice of the Suburbs didn't exactly fill in the blanks.

So on a Monday night near the end of February, when they got to the house on Carver Avenue, the kids found an extraordinarily tall black man with a trim beard and a crisply ironed Oxford sitting in the corner, talking in low tones with Chase. They didn't seem to notice him at first. He was so big he couldn't be real. The kids chattered on about the playoff game and the track meet on Saturday and how to get the girls together for a group photo to go on the fund-raising blog while Candice set out tortilla soup and mentioned the ice cream sandwiches in the freezer and took her roommates upstairs to get out of the way. The kids squeezed onto the lumpy sofas, pushing aside Bibles and DVDs of that show *Friends*. Nijalon showed up late, in a T-shirt that said Every Day I'm Hustlin'.

The man stood. Chase introduced him as Torey C. Owens, who had seen the world. The kids froze. They stopped messing with their cell phones. When the girls heard Owens was a military contractor on leave from Afghanistan, they lost their bashfulness and jumped up and asked to stand next to him for pictures, which he allowed.

"Let's get the obvious out of the way," Owens said. "I'm six nine. I don't play basketball. People say I should."

The talk he gave started with a lesson about other people trying to put something on you that doesn't fit. He borrowed Kay Kay's jacket to make his point. He told about growing up in Oak Cliff. He talked about avoiding temptation and getting a straight job and losing a lot of the money to taxes. Some of the kids already knew what FICA was, so he figured his message was getting through.

"If you've never been outside of America," Owens said, trying to transition into the foreign travel part, "it's easy to buy into that message of 'I hate America.'"

Owens said he'd been to Lagos.

"That was the best trip, yet it was a culture shock. You get off the plane, and you're greeted by four guys holding AK-47s. There's a heat that's followed by a stench, and there's people all around you. Everybody's standing in line, so you stand in line."

Owens told of the questions he'd been asked in Africa: "'How did America get to be so united, as in United States?' 'Why did all the blacks in the U.S. want to rap or play ball?' I was stunned, but I had no response. I said maybe it was because we just don't know the opportunity we have."

He talked about people living in ruins and mothers washing babies in dirty rainwater.

"I told them, 'In some ways you're better off here, because you see reality. There's this age in America where everything seems fine, but behind the scenes it's a wreck.'"

Returning home, Owens said, he'd turned on the tap, flushed the toilet, and thanked God. Besides Africa and of course Afghanistan, he'd also been to Scotland. In conclusion, he said, each trip had broadened his views. Then he took questions.

One girl raised her hand and said she'd seen a movie where there were child bombers in Iraq and she wondered if he'd seen any of those. Owens said he'd seen an adult suicide bomber. Somebody wanted to know how you could tell when you were ready to travel overseas.

"I always had a hunger for that," Owens said. "You guys, traveling with people you trust, people you have faith in, you're going to help each other."

One girl said she was going to catch a fit if she ordered a burger with ranch in Africa and got mayonnaise instead. Devyne said she was still stuck on the lesson about taking things for granted. Why shouldn't she take her cell phone for granted? Everybody had one. Owens said the trip would change her view.

"I came back from Africa thinking people in the ghetto are blessed," he said. "You're really going to begin to see what it is to serve. To have a service heart. They think we have money trees; we're living on golden streets. You're going to go back to your warm house, plus feel good about yourself—"

Ebony cut in: "So what is Africa about?" she asked. "I feel like it's selfish of me to go and see other people's poverty just to make myself feel different."

"They need physical things," Owens said. "We need spiritual things."

"The impression I'm getting is that Americans are spoiled, stupid," Devyne said. "I don't think we're stupid. I like to have an iPod and listen to music all day."

"Be grateful for it," Nijalon yelled. "Be grateful for what you got. Be grateful for your cell phone."

"I think Reagan is like, the Africa of here," Devyne said. "When we all come together and do something good, it's like, 'Aw, we made Reagan look good today.' Like, they don't have to do that at Westlake."

"I don't want you to walk away thinking it's bad to have things," Owens told her. "It's not. But you have to know who you are and what you're made of. In America we sometimes think things make us. Things won't make you on this trip."

Besides, he said, they'd have to live without their cell phones for a couple of weeks in Africa. It wouldn't be so hard. Think back, he said: What else did previous generations live without?

"Did they have weed?" Nijalon asked.

Chase closed the session with a reading from Proverbs. Nijalon adjusted his ball cap. Owens urged the kids to keep journals.

"I admire y'all for even being here and thinking about going," he said.

Candice and her roommates came downstairs for prayers. Somebody offered a prayer for Chase. One of his brothers, Dalton, was in intensive care at a hospital in Florida.

"We're basically saying nothing is too hard for God, but things might not go the way we want them to go," Chase said. "So I'm leaving tomorrow. Indefinitely."

The room fell silent. Candice spoke first.

"What does indefinitely mean?" she asked.

Chase said not to expect him back before the end of the school year. He said his brother, the one in the hospital, had once told him: "Wisdom is like college. It's good for your education, but it costs too much."

Somebody wanted to know how they'd pass the math TAKS without his tutoring. Chase said: "Don't take this as an opportunity to not study hard. I think y'all are gonna blow this test out of the water, but you've got to hold up your end of the bargain. Now is the time for you to do what God's given you to do. Not tomorrow."

Then Chase sat on a chair in the center of the room and Candice and her roommates and the kids and Torey Owens all laid hands on him. They pressed together, heads bowed, solemn and reverent under the puttering ceiling fan.

"Yes, Jesus," Candice murmured. Somebody said the Lord can do all things. Somebody said death is not the end. Somebody said there is a better world beyond this one.

"Dear Father in Heaven," Nijalon prayed. "We come to You in our prayers. You are the almighty doctor, there is no doctor better than You, You are the doctor within doctors. We just ask You to watch over us in the hard times we going through and tough times right now. In Jesus' name we pray."

"Yes, Jesus," Candice answered, leaning in over the kneeling students to reach the suffering math tutor. "Yes, Jesus."

Eighteen

On spring break, Anabel Garza went home to Brownsville. There was someone she needed to see. For years she'd been writing letters, but she'd never heard back. At last she stood on the porch. She knocked. The woman who answered sized her up.

"Are you one of his students?" she asked.

"I was," Anabel said. "Thirty years ago."

And then she stood before him, Mr. Ericson, thin but still muscular in his early seventies, a pipe smoker with gray hair, blue eyes, and a mustache. Anabel hugged him. He agreed to meet for lunch the next day.

The following afternoon, Anabel watched Mr. Ericson's truck pull up to a restaurant decorated with pictures of dead movie stars. The menu had avocado burgers and veggie burgers and bacon burgers and fried chicken burgers and more, but Mr. Ericson ordered a plain cheeseburger. When the girl at the counter recognized him, Anabel said, "He's mine right now." She wasn't about to share this time. She'd told her husband she would rather eat lunch with Mr. Ericson than even President Obama. She'd picked the right place. The menu said, "If you don't get your food in 15 minutes, relax, you'll get it in 30 minutes."

So it was here, a month away from the most daunting test of her career as an educator, at a place called Spanky's, that Anabel finally got to tell Mr. Ericson: "I live with you every single day. Sometimes I look at a painting and think, 'What would he be thinking?' It's almost embarrassing how much you've impacted my life."

The words kept tumbling out. She'd been shaped by his gift for teaching art and literature, but she was here now because of the extra step he'd taken after class that day, all those years ago, when she still thought she could curl up and vanish. Someone else could have confronted her in time. But it was her English teacher who did.

"I just had to tell you," Anabel said. "I work with teachers every day and they say, 'I've been teaching five years.' Sometimes the reward doesn't come until many years later."

When she had finished, the old teacher spoke softly. Anabel leaned in to hear. She would remember these words for a long time.

"Aw, girl," Mr. Ericson said. "That's just what I did."

For a company with replicable models capable of filling orders on a bulk scale, there was real money to be made in a troubled high school. The Austin Independent School District's request for proposals drew thirty-five submissions from all over the country, mostly from big education-services companies with names like Mosaica and Sylvan. America's Choice filed hundreds of pages of boilerplate material describing branded programs called Literacy

Navigator, Mathematics Navigator, and the like, with documented success raising scores in Georgia, Arkansas, and Rochester, New York. The company promised "ongoing mechanisms for parent and community engagement," "enrichment activities for students," "professional learning communities (PLCs) as the primary vehicle for job-embedded professional development," and "personalization and strong teacher-student relationships." It gave a phone number in Washington, D.C. It wanted $180,000 to implement "Year One."

Anabel finished her own proposal in a thirty-hour session at the end of spring break, with help from the PTSA president, a community organizer, and the president of the teachers' union. They called their group the Reagan Community School Alliance. Their submission ran just thirty-seven pages long, with cover photos depicting the school's tree-lined courtyard in rain and in shine.

"Under our plan, the campus will have control over academic programming, including staff development, hiring, training, support, evaluation, and recommendation for dismissal of all staff members," Anabel wrote. "The reform strategies adopted and implemented to date have fallen short, and progress is inadequate. The time has come for the administration and union to forge responsibility to stop the reform churn, establish a strong and stable school environment, and give educators the resources and tools to transform this school so that, once and for all, students receive a genuine opportunity to obtain a quality education."

In a section headed "Community Involvement," she set out her vision. Of the sixteen hundred teenagers living in the neighborhoods around Reagan High, she wrote, about seven hundred had transferred out to other public schools. Some had joined a magnet program attached to LBJ High. Some had just gone to Lanier and McCallum, the nearest available alternatives. Some had traveled as far as Austin High, downtown across the highway, to get away. To draw those middle-class kids back, she wrote, Reagan needed to offer relevant education programs, but it also needed to show some signs of addressing the poverty and pregnancy and language problems. In her view, the work was already under way: Most of the teachers had stayed put this year, risking their careers under the specter of a potential closure order from the state. The community organizers behind the Stand Up for Reagan movement had recruited six hundred volunteers. The PTSA president, who worked three jobs, campaigned "tirelessly" for the school. And there was solid support from the churches, not just the booming Austin Stone but also the immigrant congregations of Iglesia Familiar Ebenezer and Iglesia El Shaddai.

"Reagan has long had a strong presence in northeast Austin," Anabel wrote. "And is much loved."

Candice Kaiser was serving lasagna with salad, bread, and lemonade. The mood was celebratory. Some of the kids were still waiting for their passports in the mail, but they'd raised the whole sixty thousand dollars. It said so right there on the living room wall, under the names DeVonte, Devyne, George, Kay Kay, Princess, Nijalon, and the rest. On this Monday night in early April, the kids gathered on the sofa watching Chase, who was back from Florida (his brother had died, but he didn't bring it up at the meeting). Nijalon, the sophomore on the jayvee team, sat a little close to Ashley Brown.

"Is JQ outside?" Ashley asked loudly. JaQuarius came in and sat between her and Nijalon. Kay Kay squeezed in next to Ashley. The girls shared a blanket. JaQuarius flipped through a Bible, then tossed it back onto the ottoman. Ashley knew his patience wouldn't last all night.

"Ain't we supposed to be out of here by nine?" she asked.

"Hello, hello, hello," Chase began. "For the last couple weeks we've been talking about Kenya, Kenya, Kenya. And we ain't been talking about Reagan, Reagan, Reagan. But we're here right now. I know how easy it can be, at the end of the year, to coast. But we got to try not to do that."

Chase suggested a scripture reading. JaQuarius rubbed his water bottle.

"All right," Chase said, "let's do a show of hands. How many people think reading the Bible is boring?"

Nijalon's hand was the first up, but not the only one. Chase started reading anyway, from the book of Matthew. Candice held her Bible four inches from her face, with a highlighter poised at the ready. Ashley leaned on JaQuarius's shoulder. The passage, a parable, concerned talents.

"Is anybody here afraid to use what God has given you?" Chase asked. A few hands. He went on: "I'm with y'all every day at Reagan. I see students with gifts they aren't using."

Somebody asked whether the meeting was supposed to be about Reagan or the Africa trip. Chase said both. He spoke of hard work to be done and strange people to meet and bad smells, none of it worthwhile unless the lessons came home to the Two-Three and the school. Again he asked the kids to describe their talents. Nijalon made a joke. Briana said she didn't see what volleyball had to do with going to Africa. Chase pressed on.

"This trip isn't about whether we get the praise or 'Look at how poor these people are in Africa,'" he said. "As long as God gets the glory, it's okay."

JaQuarius was tracing a pattern on his knee. Ashley, still on his shoulder, closed her eyes. Briana was fiddling with Princess's hair and Princess was batting her away.

"One day all of you guys are going to be where we are," Chase said. "And you're going to have another set of young people. And you're going to know that what you're trying to offer these kids is maybe not *the* best thing, but one of the best things a person can receive. And they're going to be looking at you like, 'What?' And you're going to have to recognize you have these gifts, and hope they're ready to receive it."

Nijalon started freestyling on the Bible verse:

Since I'm kind of scared
I'm kind of nervous
I'm gonna go to the Word with a shovel
And I'll be digging it, see
If you were paying attention you'd get it
And I'm gonna take that man's talent—

Finally somebody cut him off.

"In short," Chase said, "we all have the ability, whether it's the talent we're afraid to use, we all have the ability. It all goes back to increasing our faith. People celebrate us because we're going to Kenya, but God's like, 'I'm working on them. They're my people, they're special, but I'm working on them.' I know that God's word meets each and every one of you where you are right now. Some of you are saying you've got no talent, some of you are saying you've got one talent, some of you are saying you've got two. I can't afford to stand by and let Nijalon not use his talent."

Briana asked: "So what you're saying is He got mad because that one servant didn't use his talent?"

Nijalon asked: "Did He tell them what to do with their talent?"

Chase said God did not.

"I don't want to put JaQuarius on the spot," Chase said, "but I'm gonna put JaQuarius on the spot."

JaQuarius squirmed.

"Everybody knows JaQuarius. He's the quarterback, he's the tallest guy in the school. I know you've been on teams that feel like they don't have any talent, and you've got talent. You don't sit there and let them fail. You push them, right?"

JaQuarius allowed an affirmative nod.

"The onus that's on us is the same onus that's on JaQuarius," Chase said. "He can't be walking around campus before the season watching people say, 'I don't want to lift weights; I don't want to try.'"

A girl named Loren rescued JaQuarius from the spotlight. While she talked about learning to use her dancing talent, he gave her a grateful look, rubbed his ear with the water bottle, and went back to playing footsie with Ashley. Candice asked the kids to write down on note cards the talents they could use and the talents they were still too scared to use.

"But I'm not scared of anything," said Briana.

"I don't have a talent," said Kay Kay.

"Don't be silly," said Candice. "Everybody has a talent."

Candice made a round of the room, addressing the kids one by one in a stage whisper:

"You're gentle."

"A good listener."

She kept it up until she had note cards from everyone. It was almost nine o'clock. Chase called for prayer requests.

"That everybody finds their talent," said Nijalon.

"College, you know, and what I'm gonna do," said Princess.

"My nephew," said DeVonte. "Pray for my nephew."

Somebody mentioned the dwindling school year.

"We take these prayer requests," Chase said. "Let's just not forget each other when we go to our separate homes."

The kids stood up, bound for Africa with twenty-six hundred dollars apiece in Christian sponsorship money, to pray for guidance.

JaQuarius, whose own summer plans centered on basketball camps and August football practice, joined the circle. His parents' cars were sitting immobile in the driveway, his little sister's emotional outbursts weren't getting any better with pregnancy, and his girlfriend's scholarship to Prairie View A&M looked like the end of a five-year relationship, but he made no prayer requests. He just held Ashley's hand while Chase prayed:

"Heavenly Father, we want to thank You for allowing us to assemble here tonight."

Chase told God about DeVonte's prematurely born nephew and Princess's college decision, about various ailments and senioritis. He said: "We just want to thank you for being faithful in spite of our faithlessness."

Nijalon picked up the prayer: "I want to thank You for my brothers and sisters. I love them a lot. Help us be able to use our talents. Let me be a young man of God, and not a young man of the streets."

"Amen."

"Amen."

"Amen."

"Amen."

"Amen."

Three days later, in a concrete-walled conference room at the Wilhelmina Delco Center, Superintendent Meria Carstarphen sat across from half a dozen preachers, as many community organizers, and the grand dame of Eastside politics herself, Wilhelmina Delco.

Carstarphen made no secret of her frustration. Promised a big cash bonus for raising test scores, she'd arrived only to find a state order to close Pearce Middle, a federal rebuke to the entire district, and a $15 million budget shortfall. The turmoil made for a tough hand, complicated by racial politics. Across the district in the last decade, white enrollment had fallen by 5,182 students, black enrollment had fallen by 3,348, and Latino enrollment had grown by 14,320. There were 11,000 more kids studying English as a second language and 17,000 more qualifying for free school lunches. The Eastside was the center of all the upheaval, and Reagan was the center of the Eastside.

She'd come to the Delco Center, bringing the school board president along, to make the case for drastic action. The board was reviewing dozens of proposals from national education services firms ready to take over Reagan. But handing over control of a storied Eastside high school came with its own set of problems. And the voices of those problems were sitting here waiting for her to start the meeting. Everybody in the room knew the kids hadn't even gotten their chance to try to pass the tests yet this year, so Carstarphen opened her pitch in a deferential tone.

"No one could disagree that the school culture, the parent involvement, the leadership of the principal is night and day from what it was ten years ago," she said. But "if Reagan doesn't make it this year, we can pretty much expect the commissioner to intervene."

Waving a copy of the district's strategic plan in the air, she went on: "Should our school not make it and we get state intervention, what is going to happen to our kids? Usually, they get spread all over the district."

She acknowledged the district's failings, reading the unfulfilled promises aloud.

"'Item 1.22: Develop a plan to effectively serve East Austin schools and their communities,'" she said. "You can see it just sitting there in an ocean of action items."

She called out a variety of rumors, including one about combining Reagan and LBJ.

"It's about impossible for me to have a conversation with people because I get crushed with conspiracy theories: 'Oh, I know what y'all are going to do, because of what's been done in the past.'"

The preachers made her point for her. They all wanted to talk about communication problems and who was to blame. Rev. Freddie Dixon, dressed in a Longhorns jacket, asked whether all the trustees were singing from the same hymnbook.

"Am I making sense here, folks?" he said. For the next several minutes that question was argued. The board president, Mark Williams, spoke at length about policy making and budget setting and fact finding. When somebody asked whether he was "a partner in this initiative," his answer was that he supported the superintendent.

Finally, Wilhelmina Delco silenced the table. In the same voice she had used to win a seat on the school board back in the 1960s, when the district's desegregation lagged behind New Orleans and Atlanta, she began:

"The elephant in the room is race, and we have to put it on the table and discuss it. We have not made education affordable, and we have not made it a priority. Most of the people in this area have abandoned the concept. They go until they can leave without the truant officers chasing them, and then they leave."

Another preacher spoke up: "These are the only schools we have east of I-35. You can't fix something when it's almost all the way broke. You've got too many schools over on the other side performing well, and we're not performing well. If it's a race issue, let's call it what it is."

Carstarphen started making notes on a poster board.

Larry Johnson, the Reagan High worker assigned the title parent support specialist, disclosed this piece of information: The Soul Raider Band, despite all its laurels and acclaim, still depended on Henna Chevrolet's charity and his own private insurance policy to get to competitions.

"Whenever you can't handle something that simple for fourteen people that would kill an institution for that school," Johnson said, "you know there isn't any communication in anything big."

Another preacher addressed the board president directly: "Mr. Williams, I don't think it would be out of order for you to exert your leadership here. Too often as minority groups we end up fighting among ourselves over resources. I don't want to get into it with the Latin American community. They're not my enemy. But I don't believe Larry Johnson ought to have to fund the band at Reagan for them to have a band, because I don't think that happens other places."

Williams acknowledged the changing demographics, the fight for resources around the city, the bad economy.

"It's not perfect," he said. "It's democracy in action."

"How long does this disenfranchised part of the city need to suffer?" Reverend Dixon asked. "We didn't make any moves on it when we did have some money."

Larry Johnson said maybe they should reach out to the former mayor, Gustavo García, to put up a united front: "The things that we're asking for aren't bad for the Hispanic children. All things are political, and if you don't recognize that, you won't get anything done."

Now Carstarphen was yelling: "Maybe I'm going to sound melodramatic. I get emotional about this stuff. But I'm going to say it: You will end up with no secondary schools in East Austin. That is where we are, because of the way the decision making is going. He's looking at the past. He's looking at ten years ago. If we don't do it right for Reagan, Pearce or LBJ is vulnerable. We need to clean this mess up. I'm sorry, I know some of y'all are ministers, but it's a hot-ass mess."

She praised other districts for the courage to preemptively shut down schools.

"I get my butt kicked from the boardroom to the boiler room. I get a lot of pressure to hold on to the status quo," she said. "We have no real Hispanic leadership or parents in meetings like this. That's missing. And we have a separate community, the Mueller community, that's moving into East Austin. What we're not doing is meeting together. And the future is in that."

"I'm out of time," she said. "I'm coming up on May results. The commissioner is saying he's going to make decisions early. I will deal with whatever comes down from the commissioner, but we can't keep getting knocked down and dusting ourselves off and dragging along."

A week later, Anabel Garza was summoned downtown. Superintendent Carstarphen, the district headquarters staff, and the board of trustees wanted to hear more about her proposal for Reagan High.

Nineteen

Finally, in the middle of April, long after the end of football and even basketball season, Anabel Garza scheduled a pep rally at Reagan High. As the big week of exit-level TAKS testing drew near, she marched up and down the halls, poking her head into classroom doors.

"How many of you are testing next week?" she asked a social studies class.

"All of us," a girl called.

"I'm here to give you some information about yourselves you don't know," Anabel said, but then the bell rang and everybody scattered. In the courtyard she came across two boys in oversize green T-shirts. An alternate color of the Folk Nation, an alliance of street gangs: One more would confirm her suspicion. As if on cue, a football player in an identical shirt turned the corner. "Lost

Boys," these kids were calling themselves, wannabe Crips playing a dangerous game. Anabel had no time for it. Not the week before TAKS.

"To my office, all of you in green," she called. *"¡Andale!"*

The boys obeyed, but they didn't exactly *andale.* Anabel shooed them along.

"You're not stopping! You're not standing around! This is not Highland Mall!"

Pausing to interrupt a make-out session—"Don't make her late. Real love doesn't make people late"—Anabel collected the green T-shirts. She gave the two smaller boys white Standing Up for Reagan T-shirts. She sent an assistant to find a bigger shirt for the football player. While they were waiting, she told him: "You are a great person and a good athlete. And you will blow it if you keep sniffing around where you're sniffing around."

One of the smaller boys said he wasn't really in a gang.

"That's even worse," Anabel told him in Spanish. "You're putting yourself in danger. Like walking into Jurassic Park with all the dinosaurs."

Then she resumed her rounds.

"We are a school that was in trouble at one time," she told a geography class. "Now we're up-and-coming, but this is it. This is going to be the week that'll make or break it for us. Next week is going to be a hard week for you. You're exhausted. Your teachers are exhausted. You are all way smart. You all can do it. I expect a lot from you. I'm going to expect you to be here, to work hard. I have no mercy for absent and no mercy for tardy. You need to be at tutorials this week. We have tutorials Saturday. Be here. I know some of you have other things to do. Cancel them."

She went on:

"Next year I expect you to be here each and every day. I will push you, because inside all of your brains is a universe of information. It's our job to bring it out, so you understand. But I need you to work hard. I can't do it for you. You need to make smart choices. I know all of you are on Facebook and Myspace and Myface. Go to bed early. Make good choices."

Then she turned and asked the geography teacher: "Do you have anybody in here who can't do it?"

"I think all my students are capable," the teacher said.

"I believe the same," Anabel said. "And I don't think there's another school in this city that will love you as much as we love you. You are somebody's baby, and I can imagine how much love there was the first time they saw you, and I think it's my responsibility to love you just as much."

The kids stared at Anabel. Anabel told them only teachers who loved them were allowed to work at Reagan High.

"Maybe you don't have anyone to say that to you at home, so I'll say it here. We don't want to have the school fail so you don't have anywhere to go."

She turned for the door: "Good luck. Try your very best. Go to tutorials. Eat right. What else? Did I miss anything? You are loved. I think you feel that every day."

Next she came to Mr. Grady's government class.

"Do you feel loved in this room?" Anabel asked.

Shrugs came back. Anabel told the kids she loved them.

"Has anyone told you that before?" Mr. Grady asked the class.

Two girls shook their heads no.

"And do you believe her?"

The girls nodded yes.

Anabel looked up at the ceiling, holding back tears.

"Don't you get emotional on me," said Mr. Grady. Anabel had known him for twenty-two years, but now she couldn't look at him. She moved on down the hall, yelling at kids to get to class, until she got to the social studies classroom of Coach Derrick Davis.

Anabel knocked. Derrick waved her in. She stood near a mobile depicting the great thinkers of the Enlightenment.

"We're on a mission, and the mission is next week," Anabel said. "You are at a pivotal point in your life. How you do next week will determine the future of an entire school. How much more power do you want? We have a chance to show the state how smart we are and get them off our backs for good. We won't have to be hassled anymore. I know you can do it. I've never been around smarter kids, and I've worked all over Austin. And talk about good-looking . . ."

That got a laugh. Anabel went on: "Part of my job is to make sure the people who are here care about you and love you. Do you think it's for my benefit? Maybe in the long run: Maybe I'll fall down as an old lady, and you'll be my doctor."

Derrick thumbed his textbook. Anabel said: "We have a task that no other teenagers in this town have. You started it with me, and we finish it next week."

"We just talked about this, right, y'all?" Derrick asked.

The kids nodded, and Anabel said: "You are that strong. You are that powerful. I believe in you. And I love you dearly. I know you don't understand how I can love all of you, so many faces. I only imagine the love your mom had the first time she saw you . . ."

Anabel trailed off, choking back tears.

From her desk, Devyne Byrd—who'd seen the basketball season up close in her cheerleading uniform, who'd raised the money to visit a school in Africa with her classmates, and who wanted one day to be a writer "to express my ideas and opinions"—spoke up before Anabel could get to the door.

She said: "We love you too."

Downstairs in her chemistry classroom, standing next to a plastic container full of donated school supplies ("Kibera's Box"), Candice Kaiser was running out of time.

"Work the teachers," she said. "You can go to the bathroom. But when you break the seal on the science test, what's the first thing you do?"

Without waiting for an answer, she put the kids to work on a practice quiz: ionic bonds, covalent bonds, the sharing of electrons. She moved from desk to desk, floral skirt sweeping the tile, Soul Raiders lariat dangling from her neck. Metalloids and noble gases, transition metals and alkaline earth metals: exit-level science was coming up next Thursday. Half the trick was controlling the room—"Stephanie, leave her alone, she's got to memorize this!"—while framing the interaction of subatomic particles for a teenage audience.

"Lose, donate, transfer, gain, receive, accept: Memorize it now, because I'm about to put another one in front of you."

Candice raced through the conduction of electricity, a mnemonic for the types of elements and more. This was supposed to be review, all material she'd taught in December, but every once in a while came a jolting reminder that the people she was working with, poised on the verge of adulthood, still had one foot in the dependent world of childhood.

"Ms. Kaiser," asked a kid in a JROTC uniform. "Do you have any paper towels?"

"Why?"

"I'm all sweaty."

"Did you have to do a fitness test this morning?"

Candice got the kid a paper towel, then started another quiz. Right away a hand went up.

"I can't tell you anything," Candice said. "Just put what you would answer if you saw this question. If it's wrong, that's not a big deal. If you don't have anything written down, that's a big deal. I want you to try."

When the quiz was done, she demonstrated the method for determining mass, proton counts, and group numbers. Would sulfur become an ion or a cation?

"A cation!"

"See," Candice said, "I'm so proud of you."

She let Kay Kay out to take a call from her dad, then started yet another quiz.

"Did I show y'all the alkali metals?" she asked.

"I'm tired," a girl called. "When can we get out of here, Miss?"

"Eleven minutes. Did I work y'all to death?"

And when the bell rang, Candice was still rattling off reminders: "Did they get more or less reactive?"—"More."—"As you go down the what?"—"Periodic table."—"If they are in the same what, they act alike?"

But the kids were already out the door.

"Family!" Candice yelled, leaning her head out into the hall. "In the same family!"

Anabel missed the pep rally; a death in the family called her home to Brownsville. But what she'd started went on. At three o'clock in the afternoon on Friday, April 23, the Soul Raider band marched into the Reagan High gym, past tables draped with bunting, volunteers in blue T-shirts, a JROTC color guard, hundreds of students, and nearly as many signs: Hammer Out the TAKS, Get a Grip on TAKS, and Put Your Future in Good Hands—Your Own—Stand Up for Reagan High School.

The kids pledged allegiance to the flags. An administrator with a microphone said the coming week would be the most important in the history of the school. Devyne Byrd led the cheerleaders in a dance routine: "P-A-S-S—Pass the TAKS!"

JaQuarius Daniels sat at a table in the center of the gym, the pride of the school, on display, laughing with the teachers. Nijalon Dunn got the crowd up and chanting:

"Can I get a yeah?"
"Yeah!"

"It's time to take the TAKS test."
"It's time to take the TAKS test."

"And I got to score real high."
"And I got to score real high."

"Oh let's take it."
"Oh let's take it."

"We gonna make it."
"We gonna make it."

"'Cause we Reagan."
"'Cause we Reagan."

Kay Kay led the Soul Strutters in a hip shake. A raffle was held. T-shirts were thrown. Teachers danced to "Super Freak." Jesse

Martinez danced on his hands. Candice Kaiser turned a quadruple cartwheel. A dozen kids charged the floor to turn cartwheels. JaQuarius got up from his seat and turned cartwheels. In the bleachers kids took pictures with their cell phones. They wore Raiders Basketball T-shirts, Raiders Baseball and Soccer T-shirts, Lady Raiders Track T-shirts, and Reagan PTSA T-shirts with slogans that said: It's About Us.

Again the Soul Raider cymbals crashed. A lone snare struck up a rhythm, hips swayed, and kids did The Wave. Under a banner displaying the lyrics to the old school song, "Not Without Honor," the kids of Reagan High stood with their teachers and sang along to a different old song:

What you want
Baby I got it
What you need
You know I got it
All I'm asking . . .

Twenty

Along the front walk at Reagan High School, impatiens
bloomed, a splash of bright color against the old brick
facade. Anabel Garza, twenty-five days into her no-
sweets diet, hurried past in dark slacks, tasseled loafers, and a blue
polo with the school insignia, dressed to look vaguely official for her
self-appointed rounds. Her first stop was the auditorium, where the
freshmen would watch a movie while the upperclassmen bent over
the decisive standardized tests.

Commissioner Scott and federal officials had agreed to judge
the state's troubled schools by a formula called the Texas Projection
Measure, which counted as passing any student who could demonstrate sufficient progress toward that goal on the standardized tests.
Designed as a counterweight to the automatic yearly increases built
into the standards of the original legislation, the TPM seemed temporary and somewhat arbitrary, but no more so than any other aspect of the testing system. In Texas, the whole structure would be

replaced within a year, when a set of tests called STAAR (State of Texas Assessments of Academic Readiness) would replace TAKS (Texas Assessment of Knowledge and Skills), which in 2002 had replaced TAAS (Texas Assessment of Academic Skills), which in 1990 had replaced TEAMS (Texas Educational Assessment of Minimum Skills), which in 1986 had replaced TABS (Texas Assessment of Basic Skills).

The clock struck 9:30. Across the state, kids were breaking the seals on testing booklets. Elaborate rules governed nearly every aspect of the process. The education agency provided a voluminous FAQ. It read like a book of riddles:

> If a student is marked absent at 10 a.m. and arrives at school later, should she be allowed to take the test even though she has been marked absent?
>
> A student who started testing on the regular testing day became ill and was not able to complete testing. Can this student take a makeup for the test he was unable to finish?
>
> What should a test administrator do if a student asks for a translation of a word that the test administrator does not know?
>
> If a student refuses to take the test or is obviously recording answers randomly, how should I mark his scorable document?

By the projection standard, the kids at Reagan High were agonizingly close to passing. Last year, they missed the TPM by less than a percentage point, in the category "African American math." As of Christmas, their numbers were on target this year.

The movie was *Avatar*. The honor student checking IDs had seen it before. "He becomes human," she said, "so he can walk around, find love."

Onstage, Anabel took the microphone.

"We have confidence in you," she said, by way of explaining the temporary reprieve from pretest drilling. "This is our school. It's more your school than my school. We're going to leave this place clean, because we're coming back tomorrow. We are in a very serious situation this week. We are testing for our lives, almost. Remember last year, we had it except for one percent of one person in one subject? That's how important you are. Everybody matters. We love you. We want you to be here for the next four years. Have a great day, and enjoy the movie."

As Anabel made her way back to the office, stopping to pick up litter, a sophomore boy pulled her aside. In whispered Spanish, he said he needed to withdraw from school, effective immediately. Anabel heard him out. On this Tuesday in late April, sophomores were the key demographic. Of the 163 enrolled, 155 needed to take the tests for the school to qualify by measure of participation.

From their classrooms, teachers were dispatching back-of-the-envelope attendance reports to the main office. Administrators were comparing the names against enrollment lists. The plan was to make sure the best 155 sophomore test takers were in the building. Anabel asked an assistant principal, Jennifer Mendez, to deal with the kid who wanted to withdraw.

"He's probably going to Mexico for a week," Anabel said. "Got a family emergency, he's got to find a job."

Mendez double-checked: The kid was a sophomore, after several years as a freshman. Not a prime candidate to raise test scores. Still, Mendez argued, there were the participation numbers to consider.

"Well, he's not enrolled as of today," Anabel said.

"Does he count?"

"Not if he's gone today."

Mendez gave her a look.

"He goes out, somebody comes in," Anabel said. "Don't you worry."

Anabel had backup plans for her backup plans. She'd already sent a school employee named Daniel to rent a minivan. Out in the hall, Rick Fowler tallied the sophomore attendance: 155, just enough to make the participation numbers. From the full enrollment list, he picked three absent sophomores who'd scored well on the midyear benchmark tests. He slid the addresses into a manila folder. Mendez took the folder to Anabel. It was time to go.

"But he's still your dad," Anabel was in the middle of telling a girl when Mendez got her attention. The minivan was ready. Anabel cracked a bottle of water for the road. Daniel started plugging addresses into a GPS device.

The minivan pulled up to a redbrick duplex. Anabel knocked loudly, three times, looking for a kid named Antonio.

"Antonio, the whole school came to get you," she called. After more knocking, a woman in a red tank top opened the door.

"Soy de escuela," Anabel said. "Necesito Antonio."

"No está."

"Oh, qué malo. ¿Sabes sus amigos?"

The woman said she did not know Antonio's friends. Perhaps, she suggested, Antonio was in the auto body shop at school. She asked whether he could make up the test. Anabel said she'd look into it.

The minivan drove north up Cameron Road, past any number of places to obtain hair extensions or a payday loan. The GPS screen announced its status: "Waiting for Accuracy." Anabel turned on the radio.

"Let's use everything this van has got," she said. "Does it have a massager? We have to sing while we search."

A girl named Leticia was supposed to live at the next apartment complex. Anabel knew Leticia. She was smart, bored in class, a good test taker. Anabel knocked.

"Leticia! It's Ms. Garza from Reagan."

In a whisper, she added: "Don't be scared."

Knock, knock, knock. No answer. Daniel, on his cell phone, got the dad's voice mail.

Knock, knock, knock. No answer. Anabel, on her cell phone, tried a different number for the dad.

"Hello, Mr. Culpepper, this is Ms. Garza from Reagan High School, and I think I'm standing outside your door. We need Leticia for testing. Do you think if you call her, she'll wake up?"

Following the dad's directions, Anabel found Leticia's window. It rattled under her knock.

"Leticia, it's Ms. Garza from Reagan High School! Wake up! Come answer the door."

She went back to the door.

"Leticia, don't make me call your dad to come home!"

Back to the window.

"Leticia, we're going to get the police to come because you might have fainted. Can you give me a sign that you're okay and alive? I'm worrying your dad."

Back to the door, cackling a little. It opened halfway, and here was Leticia, sleepyheaded, hair up, dressed in her pajama pants.

"Slap some water on your face," Anabel instructed. "You need to be testing. We're going to take you to school."

Leticia did not take the news well. Anabel tried a different tack.

"You want me to make you some tea or something?"

Leticia said she was sick.

"Were you throwing up all night?" Anabel said, leaning on the doorjamb beside a gray, unadorned wall. The apartment smelled like an ashtray.

"I just can't do it right now," Leticia said. "I'll do it on a makeup test. My grandmother has cancer, and I haven't slept all week. I can do it for you tomorrow."

"All right," Anabel said. "I'll be back for you tomorrow. Call me if you need anything."

Back in the car, Anabel asked Leticia's classification. The girl looked white. The twenty-two white kids at Reagan, 2.5 percent of the student body, had 99 percent passing rates in science. Even their worst subject, math, measured well above the state standard. Daniel flipped through Leticia's paperwork: Hispanic.

"Hispanic?" Anabel said. "Oh, girl, we need you."

Her cell rang, somebody from the office: The third kid on Fowler's list had shown up. The minivan started back down Cameron Road. The sophomores had made their participation numbers, but the scores were a different matter. The week was just getting started.

"Ay-yi-yi," Anabel said as the school pulled into view. "Antonio, where are you?"

The Turnaround Initiative ended with a whimper. The district never officially selected Anabel Garza's Community School Alliance proposal, but it didn't bring in any of the big education services firms or charter companies either. At the next school board meeting, on a Monday in the middle of May, while the state education agency was still crunching the standardized test scores, Superintendent Meria Carstarphen deferred to the board on her proposal to preemptively close Reagan High and Pearce Middle. Mark

Williams, the board president, who'd accompanied Carstarphen to hear out the preachers at the Delco Center, made a persuasive argument.

"When you close a school, there is an adverse impact on students," Williams said. "If they make it this year, then they're entitled to stay at the school."

The numbers came in at 3 p.m. on Friday, May 21. At Reagan High, an orderly plan was in place, but the plan fell apart when Anabel started running in circles around her office. She forgot her e-mail password. Her secretary, Gloria, ever the cool head, summoned the APs. Word spread quickly. Pretty soon a crowd of teachers had gathered outside, trying to peek through the blinds. Fowler realized he'd forgotten his cell phone.

"You can't go get it," Anabel told him. "You'll be mobbed."

Category by category, Anabel and her assistants scanned the new numbers. In social studies, 94 percent of the kids passed, a twelve-point increase over last year. English showed an eight-point increase, to 80 percent. Science scores rose twenty-six points to 68 percent. In each of those categories, the scores surpassed the state standard by a comfortable margin. The small group of white kids scored the highest. The black kids, a much bigger group, scored second-highest. Their science scores more than doubled to 73 percent. The Latino kids brought up the rear, but they showed double-digit gains in every category.

In the last category, math, the black kids scored only 56 percent, four points short of the standard. The scores for the whites (63 percent) and Latinos (62 percent) looked high enough to raise the campus-wide math score to 61 percent, beating the state standard by a single point, but the "African American math" category still counted separately. For that last number, it came down to the projection measure. Including students who improved their scores significantly over the prior year, the administrators calculated, the black kids scored 67 percent in math, good enough to qualify Reagan High School for the label "academically acceptable."

Anabel's cell rang. The caller identified herself as Meria. Still flustered, Anabel had trouble placing the name.

"Meria?" she said. Then: "Oh . . . Meria!"

They agreed to keep the scores quiet over the weekend. Other schools were not getting such good news. After a state closure order, $6.5 million in renovations, and a housecleaning that had cast off more than half its teachers, the former A. S. Johnston High, newly rechristened as Eastside Memorial Green Tech High School, missed the state standards in "African American math" by sixteen percentage points and science by five, even using the projection measure.

On Monday night, at the next school board meeting, Superintendent Carstarphen announced the preliminary scores. Reagan High, she said, would remain open. Shedding the stigma of the state's label, the school would once again serve all the kids of the Two-Three, the northern section of the Eastside, St. John's, and University Hills. The school would recruit staff members qualified to teach college-level courses, allowing students who might otherwise have transferred away to start earning advanced placement credit or even associate's degrees. It would strengthen its ties to Pearce Middle School, where prep classes for the college-level coursework would begin in the fall.

Anabel did not get much time to celebrate. The next Friday, May 28, she opened her door to a seventeen-year-old girl who had given birth at twenty-six weeks. The baby didn't make it. The girl was alone.

"Been there, done that," Anabel told her. "You just have to make a decision. You're a kind person, and I want to see that person back.

There are some who grieve with you, but you attract others who create more drama. They're trying to draw you into, 'Now you have an excuse to make bad decisions.' You already know in your heart what you're working for, all those successes that seem so far away right now. I know you have the resiliency to maybe even take my job one day."

The big puffy sofas were gone. The walls were bare, stripped of the fund-raising charts and prayer boards and even the Glamour Shot of teenage Candice Kaiser. She was planning to couch-surf until the Africa trip, then find a place for July, but Ryan ended up proposing to her at 3 a.m. the day before the flight. They'd been up all night at Kinko's, making journals for the kids with inspirational passages from scripture, converting the hard copies to PDFs, printing out thick paper, and fixing the bindings. In the parking lot at the Star Cafe, Ryan told her: "I want you to be my wife. I want God to lead both of us. Will you come with me? Will you follow me?"

Ryan gave Candice a ring with an inscription from the book of Ruth. The proposal was not a big surprise, to her or anybody else. Their courtship had started back when she asked for help driving some kids from Reagan High to a basketball game. They sat together in the bleachers at just about every game, talking about their hard partying days and about how they'd each found the church reluctantly and about Jesus working in their lives, a conversation interrupted whenever Candice felt the need to scream at the refs. Their wedding would have to wait until after the Africa trip, but when the time came they picked musicians from the Soul Raider band. Ryan's folks offered to supplement their rent across the highway, but they said no thanks. They found a place off Martin Luther King Jr. Boulevard, a little farther southeast. Ryan got a job teaching chemistry at LBJ High.

On this Friday at the end of May, the empty house on Carver Avenue served as a staging ground. Twelve kids were going to Africa—DeVonte dropped out at the last minute, leaving Chase to return the money to his sponsors—and they needed shots. Half a dozen girls crowded into a church volunteer's SUV. Devyne was singing "Girls Just Want to Have Fun," a song she'd learned from a teacher. She was pretty sure it was by Madonna.

When they got to the clinic, in a sprawling medical center on the northwest side of the city, Nijalon was standing in the parking lot, doing the Rocky pose, chanting, "We goin' to Af-ri-ca!" Inside, a white girl and her mom decided to wait for the next elevator. All twelve Reagan kids squeezed in, rode upstairs, and spilled out onto the polished hardwood floors.

"I'm scared," Ebony said. "I don't like shots."

"What does typhoid fever do?" Devyne asked. "Are they going to put it in me?"

"You're making it worse than it already is for those who don't like shots," Ebony said.

They passed the time with idle talk: Who's going out for track next year? What will happen after graduation? What's New York City like? Who's getting the first shot? A nurse came out. She was a Christian. She told the kids: "I want y'all to know that y'all are pretty much heroes for what you're doing, and I'm glad to be part of it."

The nurse explained the shots. Somebody asked if the side effects would linger through prom tomorrow.

"No, darling."

One by one, the kids went back for their shots. Devyne, dressed in tight shorts and a T-shirt with her hair in a bun, cradled her cell phone, clutched the arm of her chair, and started breathing hard.

"It's like getting your ears pierced," somebody told her.

"I was a child," Devyne said. She kept giving up her place in line. She watched the other girls rub their arms.

"Okay, okay," Devyne said. "All right, I'm ready."

But then the sound of Ebony howling in pain carried out to the waiting room. When Ebony emerged her eyes were filled with tears, but she was laughing.

"All right," Devyne said. "Rainbows and happiness."

She tiptoed into the exam room. She stood under a map of the whole wide world and a portrait of Jesus, next to a biohazardous materials receptacle. She rolled up her sleeve and then pulled back.

"Okay, wait, wait."

The church volunteer put an arm around her. Devyne started breathing even harder. She held out her arm to the nurse, then jumped back.

"Okay, wait, wait."

Twice more this happened, then the nurse stuck her with the needle. Devyne yelped. When the nurse had finished her work, Chase asked: "Did anybody cry?"

A techno beat thumped across the ballroom of the Norris Conference Center, where blue balloons in the shape of stars decorated the banquet tables, kids clung to the walls, and a singer's recorded voice chanted, "Baila! Baila!" Anabel Garza shimmied across the empty dance floor, showing off the effect of no sweets in a sleeveless black dress, clapping her hands and shaking her hips.

JaQuarius Daniels and Ashley Brown stood around a table

with his basketball teammates, impossibly young and handsome, watching a conga line gather a quorum from the incentive of Red Bull mocktails. JaQuarius took off his jacket to eat a paper tray of ballpark nachos. His Columbia blue vest matched Ashley's dress. When the nachos were gone, he found a place in the middle of the dance line, stepping in formation with his classmates and their teachers and the school administrators, all together for a night of celebration with pretty pink gowns and black tuxedos and a class clown in oversize shades and shy girls leaning together at big round tables and a sign that spelled out: Congratulations! John H. Reagan High School.

Anabel stood by a water cooler and folded her arms and smiled a nervous smile as the royal nominees took the stage. Princess Ohiagu was named the prom queen, and a boy named Pedro her king. They turned across the floor. Anabel snuck up behind JaQuarius, whispered in his ear, pantomimed a dance move, and pointed at Ashley. JaQuarius took Ashley's hand. He led her onto the floor. Anabel walked off, singing along under her breath:

> *Forever young*
> *I want to be*
> *Forever young*

Then she laughed her big head-back laugh and stuck out her tongue and said: "No!"

Expeditions, F-150s, and Town & Countrys filled the lot at the Delco Activity Center, big parent machines with windows marked in shoe polish to celebrate the seniors, "Class of 2010." They shined fresh from the morning car wash put on by the Reagan

High class of 2011, a fund-raiser for a prom and senior trip still to come.

Inside the hall, the acoustically imperfect scene of the hoop squad's defiant triumph over the Jaguars of LBJ, spectators by the hundreds gathered under clusters of balloons. The Soul Raider band was tuning up. Two hundred and seven graduating seniors in mortarboards and black gowns with Columbia blue trim walked in procession to 207 metallic folding chairs. Ariana Buenrostro, Carmen Becerril-Rodriguez, Leticia Casiano, Kanisha Grant, Eduardo Lopez, Janet Maldonado, Princess Ohiagu, and Alex Ortiz wore the gold stoles of the National Honor Society. The program listed college scholarships for twenty-one students, including nine scholarships raised by the Reagan Parent-Teacher-Student Association. The band played "Pomp and Circumstance."

There was Ashley Brown, who would soon travel to Africa, start her freshman year on a track scholarship at Prairie View A&M, and temporarily drop out in the first semester, pregnant. The baby's father, JaQuarius Daniels, had another year left in high school. He would go to Iowa State on a football scholarship.

There was Jesse Martinez, who had a job lined up at Home Depot. There was Chriss Conway. There was the pregnant girl from chemistry class. There were Willie Powell and Cornelius Cammock from the basketball team. There was George Warren, vice president of the senior class, athletic equipment manager, member of the prom court, soon-to-be world traveler, leading the Pledge of Allegiance. All eyes turned to center stage.

"Good evening. I am Anabel Garza, the principal of John H. Reagan High School."

Anabel did not keep to the standard graduation platitudes for long.

"This is the senior class of John H. Reagan High School, who decided their school would not be closed," she said. Then she addressed the seniors directly: "I'm here to tell you this evening that you can do anything you want to do. You've already proven that."

She told them the future was scary but full of promise.

"Know without a doubt that we love you and are cheering for you," she said, stopped for a moment by tears. "Everywhere you go, you will always be a Reagan Raider."

She passed the microphone to Dr. Carstarphen.

"You have no idea how much stress I have been under with Reagan High School and all this drama going on in this state over that TAKS test," Carstarphen said.

The stress wasn't just from the state. During a visit to Reagan, Carstarphen had given Ebony her cell number, and Ebony had bombarded her ever since with text messages concerning every aspect of TAKS accountability.

"It said to me that you care about your school, and not just for yourselves but for the babies that are coming up behind you," Carstarphen said.

Anabel sat at the back of the stage, hands clasped, legs crossed at the knee, gazing around the glorified gymnasium as her boss acknowledged the $650,000 in scholarships, the thousand volunteer hours of tutoring in science alone, the group going to Africa, the victories at the MLK Battle of the Bands, and the playoff appearance by the varsity basketball team.

"This woman, your principal, Anabel Garza, has done an extraordinary job of exercising grace under pressure," Carstarphen said, drawing a standing ovation. She called for quiet, to little effect. Anabel pumped her fist. The choir sang "Like an Eagle," voices carrying to the rafters, harmonies fit to succeed the storied Reagan Madrigal Singers of the 1960s. In her valedictory address, Sofia Vasquez invoked her brothers and sisters.

"I want Reagan to stay open so that they'll follow in my footsteps and graduate from there as well," she said, repeating her remarks in Spanish, dabbing at her eyes and finishing with a vow to study education. "I want to come back one day and say, 'I will be a Reagan Raider and a Soul Raider forever.'"

Anabel introduced the graduates, their honors and awards. She asked the class "to stand with honor and dignity, as you are certified as a high school graduate."

One by one the kids made the long walk to joyous applause, shrieks, and air horns. Anabel let a trustee hand out the diplomas. She waited at the center of the stage, offering each of her new graduates an enveloping bear hug. From Juan Aguirre to Vanessa Zavala Zuniga, not one turned her down.

"To our class of 2010," Anabel said, resuming the lectern. "I expect you to make us forever proud."

Told they could sit, the people chose to stand, teenagers and their parents and brothers and sisters, teachers and coaches and janitors, right hands aloft, fingers crossed in the old school sign, swaying to the old school song, singing, "Live with honor, Reagan High." When the band hit the big drum build, caps flew high. Then the kids turned out onto the asphalt under the daunting sun, tethered only by diplomas and memories, on the way to hugs and photographs and summer and whatever may come.

Notes & Acknowledgments

This is a true story. I witnessed nearly all of these events. I heard the dialogue as it was spoken. For the scenes prior to 2009 and a few others, I based my reconstructions on interviews with the participants and other observers, government documents, school documents, church documents, video recordings, personnel files, private diaries, news reports, scouting reports, and other sources. At a few moments in the narrative, I've quoted or described what certain people were thinking. I did not make this choice lightly. Human memory is notoriously fallible, self-serving, and unverifiable. In the imperfect journalistic bargain, my subjects gave me the honor and burden of their trust. Through their candor, sincerity, and constancy, they earned mine. Anabel Garza, Derrick Davis, Candice Kaiser, JaQuarius Daniels, Ashley Brown, and all the others who let me into their lives have my eternal gratitude and respect.

The fact that this story got told at all is a credit first and foremost to its subjects. I'd also like to thank Elyse Cheney, whose vision shaped the narrative, Virginia Smith, whose steady hand refined the prose, and Kurt Eichenwald, whose wise lessons inform every interview I conduct. In the years I spent working on the book, my storytelling skills got some indispensable jolts from Thomas Lake, Ben Montgomery, and the crowd from the Auburn Chautauqua in Ludowici, Georgia. Good writers and confidants in Texas—including Thomas Huang, Steve Scheibal, Kathy Blackwell, and Maya Perez—provided necessary support and encouragement. Peter Weber, Jen Furl, and Mary Keith Trawick generously offered up quiet rooms for writing. The staff of the Austin History Center, particularly Mike Miller, answered my abundant queries with patience and professionalism. The photographers Ben Sklar and Chris Reichman shared their estimable talents. My research assistant, Lena Price, who got the lousy job by being the first of nearly a dozen *Daily Texan* staffers to jump at the opportunity, chased down and conducted smart follow-up interviews. Don't let anybody tell you the J-school kids are afraid of a little hard work.

Most of all I'd like to thank my parents, who read to me every day; my brother, Jeff, who picked me up every time I fell; and my own teachers, particularly Ms. Reese and Ms. Chiever at R. L. Turner High School in Farmers Branch, Texas, and Ms. Christie at St. Thomas Aquinas School in Woodbridge, Virginia. This book is dedicated with love to my wife, Stacy, without whose faith, encouragement, and insight I don't know what, and to my beautiful children, Celia, John-Henry, and Sadie.